"This proposal represents a ground-breaking addition to the field of applied sport psychology. Its unique blend of theoretical depth, practical guidance, and real-world insights makes it an excellent resource for both students and supervisors. This book has the potential to redefine the landscape of supervision in sport psychology, providing a comprehensive and accessible guide for students and supervisors alike."

Dr Robert Morris, *Associate Professor in Sport Psychology at the University of Stirling and Senior Sport Psychologist at the UK Sports Institute, UK*

Practical Supervision in Applied Sport Psychology

Practical Supervision in Applied Sport Psychology delivers a 'how-to' guide in the supervision of sport psychology trainees and qualified practitioners. It serves as a resource for the supervisee and the supervisor, supporting scholarship in applied sport psychology at the postgraduate level, especially for those training to become sport psychology practitioners.

This new book offers a compact and comprehensive manual on supervision that meets the needs of supervisees and supervisors by educating and supporting them within applied sport psychology to deal competently with the challenges of supervision and the supervisory process. With practical examples and scenarios throughout, the text helps supervisees become better informed about the supervisory process, its challenges, and its drawbacks. *Practical Supervision in Applied Sport Psychology* also enables supervisors to get to grips with beginning supervising trainees, while holding a resource that is accessible and informative for lifelong learning in supervision.

Emerging from decades of experience in both supervising and being supervised in applied sport psychology, this new book is vital reading for scholars, teachers, researchers, and those practising supervising and receiving supervision within the field of applied sport psychology.

Paul McCarthy, PhD, leads the taught doctorate in Sport and Exercise Psychology at Glasgow Caledonian University, Scotland, UK. Paul is a BPS-chartered psychologist, HCPC-registered sport and exercise psychologist, and Senior Teaching Fellow. In 2017, he developed the first taught doctorate in sport and exercise psychology in Scotland and the UK. Supervision accounts for a significant proportion of his current role on the taught doctorate programme and private practice. His research explores the practice of applied sport psychology and elements of emotion, attention, and motivation amongst sport performers. He served as editor of *Sport and Exercise Psychology Review* from 2013 to 2017. He has run his own private practice for the past 20 years, splitting his work time between academic teaching, supervising, researching, writing, and supporting clients from amateur to professional levels, especially in golf, football, rugby, gymnastics, and athletics.

Zoe Moffat, PhD, is a practitioner psychologist working for an international professional sports organisation. She is a chartered sport and exercise psychologist with the British Psychological Society and a practitioner psychologist with the Health and Care Professions Council. Zoe has published several peer-reviewed papers in sport and exercise psychology. She works with Paralympians, Olympians, and professional athletes in several sports (e.g., rugby, golf, netball, tennis).

Lindsey Burns, PhD, is a Senior Lecturer in Health Psychology at Glasgow Caledonian University, Scotland, UK. She is a BPS Chartered Psychologist, an HCPC-registered Practitioner Health Psychologist, and a Senior Fellow with AdvanceHE. Her research focuses on interprofessional working and collaboration, alongside interests in performance and wellbeing. Lindsey's professional role spans academia and private practice, where she provides supervision to trainee and qualified psychologists, supporting reflective, ethical, and evidence-based practice across diverse settings.

Practical Supervision in Applied Sport Psychology

Paul McCarthy, Zoe Moffat, and Lindsey Burns

Routledge
Taylor & Francis Group
NEW YORK AND LONDON

Designed cover image: Getty Images

First published 2027
by Routledge
605 Third Avenue, New York, NY 10158

and by Routledge
4 Park Square, Milton Park, Abingdon, Oxon, OX14 4RN

Routledge is an imprint of the Taylor & Francis Group, an informa business

ISBN: 978-1-032-77976-8 (hbk)
ISBN: 978-1-032-77974-4 (pbk)
ISBN: 978-1-003-48566-7 (ebk)

DOI: 10.4324/9781003485667

Typeset in Sabon
by Deanta Global Publishing Services, Chennai, India

To Lesley, Liam, Euan, and Niamh, for all time.

For Michael, Delia, and Phoebe whose love and presence shape every good thing I do. – Lindsey Burns

Contents

Tables

Preface

Several researchers, practitioners, and educators have written extensively about supervision and its importance in our field of professional practice (Andersen 2000, 2021; Poczwardowski et al., 2023). Despite their encouragement for supervision in applied sport psychology practice, it remains on the periphery. Our goal in writing this book is to offer trainees, supervisees, supervisors, practitioners, and training directors a resource to refer to in their roles. To meet their requirements, we aimed for a practical lens over a purely theoretical supervision text. We leaned towards an applied, sport-specific nuance and integrated theory and research where necessary, while keeping a keen eye on the practicalities of supervision. In short, this book intends to provide a practical and relational guide to supervision for supervisees and supervisors in applied sport psychology.

For some of you reading this preface, you are transforming from a student of psychology to a practitioner of psychology (Falender & Shafranske, 2012). It is a daunting transformation for anyone. In practical terms, the change might mean moving from reading a case study about treating a football player presenting with low mood following an injury to leading this work with a football player at their training ground. Occasionally, some trainees embark on this applied journey with little support or guidance, which places the trainees and their clients' welfare under great strain. Every trainee deserves education, training, and supervision to develop the knowledge, skills, and attitudes to work competently with clients, and although the focus within this book is on supervision, supervision works best alongside appropriate education (e.g., learning about CBT) and training (e.g., working in triads to develop Socratic methods). After all, supervision is psychologists' third most frequent professional activity (after psychotherapy and assessment – diagnosis), though diminishing time is devoted to it (Falender, 2018; Norcross & Rogan, 2013).

Supervisees need to know what supervision entails, how to use it, and how to thrive within it. A good-enough supervisor will help you marshal the knowledge, skills, and attitudes you need to be a good-enough supervisee.

Supervision is a blend of art and science. Yet, this blend creates a tension between art and science: Should I lean more towards art or science? In the workplace of sport, we see athletes, athletic backroom teams, coaches, and fans who crave data, reason, and explanation, and yet they also revel in the artistry and insouciance of casting off convention and doing it differently. Perhaps supervision also gets tossed from art to science and back again, but for trainees and practitioners, it remains a staple to maintain good health within our therapeutic relationships and our lives outside the office (Adams, 2024; Norcross & Guy, 2007).

Supervision, therefore, represents our ballast. It offers us a base of professional support and guidance, a soft place to land when things fall apart, and the encouragement we need to stretch ourselves when we wish to avoid and escape. Imagine client sessions not going so well on a practicum placement at a professional rugby academy. The feedback from the staff feels overwhelming, and the shame insurmountable. It is within this crisis of confidence that supervision offers a way forward. Supervision sessions, whether with a supervisor or in a group, offer an opportunity to manage shame and progress with the work.

Good practice in applied sport psychology relies heavily on the supervisory relationship. Often, supervision is an ethical requirement, especially in training. We wrote this book for the supervisor and supervisee, not as a binding set of standards, but as a guide from which each can take what they need. What matters most is that the supervisor and supervisee can recognise the parameters of their roles and responsibilities in a supervisory relationship. Depending on one's experience and developmental path, we encourage you all to give and receive the support, validation, and challenge that fits. The book's distinctiveness comes from its focus on applied sport psychology, its integration of ethics, professional standards, and relational practice, its emphasis on practical application, and its consideration of the immense value of effective supervision. We wish you all the best on your journey.

How Is This Book Organised?

When we started writing this book, we felt it might be endless, considering the extensive range of principles, processes, and practices in supervising applied sport psychology. To explore these concepts, procedures, and methods, we divided the content into three sections: getting started in supervision, managing the supervisory process, and supervising in diverse contexts and challenges. Beyond this structure, our intention was twofold. First, to help those being supervised to appreciate the scope of the supervisory process and, second, to help supervisors recognise the strengths of their practice and consider how to fill any gaps. Some chapters will appeal more to supervisees than to supervisors and vice versa; however, we feel that cultivating an appreciation of each other's roles will bring empathy and compassion to the supervisory process. We also intended to lean towards the practical rather than the theoretical or research landscape, though we blend theory and research as necessary in different chapters. Several themes recur across chapters (e.g., relationship quality, developmental stages, power dynamics); however, we feel this is appropriate for an introductory text on supervision. Although there is a scarcity of books specifically on supervision in applied sport psychology on the shelves, related fields offer excellent supervision titles, along with book chapters and research articles in applied sport psychology for reference. This book is not about competing with existing works. Instead, we want to provide a short, comprehensive, and helpful starting point for new supervisors and those being supervised in the applied sport psychology field (Henderson, Millar, & Holloway, 2014).

Choosing the Right Supervisor

Choosing the right supervisor will bring various criteria into view. As a supervisee, you may seek to meet essential criteria like a supervisor who is knowledgeable, approachable, and warm, with experience supervising CBT. Or perhaps she has worked in a particular sports setting that matches your practicum placement. We encourage you throughout this book to consider which supervisor fits you and your process best. One's process means an ongoing personal journey of self-understanding, growth, and change; it occurs for those working in applied sport psychology and often begins in supervision and coincides with personal therapy for those who choose it. Supervision provides another perspective, another space for thinking (Mollon, 1997), and in this space, an opportunity to visit unconsidered viewpoints, theories, elements of transference and countertransference, what has been created and what has been lost. The endless list of challenging countertransference issues (e.g., anger, erotic attraction, frustration, missed appointments, needing control, over self-disclosure, wanting to be liked, rescuing) means we need someone to help us explore our responses towards our clients, what these responses mean, and work out a way to understanding them rather than to act upon them (Adams 2024).

Through your education or training, you might be familiar with scenarios where sport psychology practitioners leverage their role to exert control, as opposed to fostering empowerment and self-governance. And because it is so familiar, you might not consider it to be unhelpful to your needs. Sometimes we cannot find a supervisor who feels right for us. One reason for this circumstance might be what we are seeking or, more precisely, avoiding. Adams (2024) suggested we might seek collusion, soothing, and complacency to avoid challenge, exploration, and insight. A supervisor might collude to keep a firm grip on their grandiose position or to avoid the work of delving into the cluttered corners of supervisees' working lives. But we spend our time in the internal world of our clients. We work with clients to understand, manage, and support them to change their internal world. If we are to help them, we need to look within to understand ourselves and ourselves in relation to our clients.

Our motivations for becoming psychology practitioners are many and varied. Our pure motivations for becoming psychology practitioners seem clear (e.g., to make a positive difference, help others feel better; other people believe we are good with people) and yet our shadow or unconscious motivations (e.g., drive for power, meeting our own needs, need to be liked) trip us up and thwart the good work we can do with our clients. After we understand these hidden intentions, we can collaborate with our clients instead of taking advantage of them, unknowingly using them for our own purposes, or projecting aspects of ourselves onto them. Supervision offers us an opportunity to see both sides of our motivation. It is not the rightness or wrongness of our motives, but the opportunity to see all of them as they appear and not deny their existence. We, as health professionals, are bound to uphold our ethical and professional standards, prioritise personal growth, and address our internal challenges. The privilege of working with clients brings with it a deep responsibility to understand ourselves as much as we want to understand those we serve.

At the outset of supervision, we might work at cross-purposes because what the supervisee needs might be at odds with what the supervisor needs. The supervisor's zeal to impart bundles of knowledge in a few sessions might inadvertently mean that establishing a positive supervisory alliance is relegated to a position further down the list. The supervisee's need to feel safe and develop a sense of trust does not receive the time, space, and openness it deserves. Or, for some trainees who have completed a master's degree and are eager to begin practicum placement, the grandiose professional self acts as a defence against their feelings of helplessness and lack of knowledge at the beginning of their professional training (Teitelbaum, 1990).

Depending on the stage of your journey (early, middle, or late career), we present these challenges as points for reflection. At each stage, your needs will change; finding the right fit for your needs seems wise.

1 What Is Supervision?

In this chapter, we shall summarise what supervision is (and is not), as well as its key definitions and core concepts. Next, we shall present the essentials of supervisory practice within theoretical models and frameworks, and some functions and purposes of supervision. Then, we shall explore the historical development of supervision in applied sport psychology. Finally, we conclude with a brief discussion of the evidence base and current trends for effective supervision.

1.1 Defining Supervision

Supervision in applied sport psychology refers to the collaborative relationship between a more experienced practitioner (supervisor) and a less experienced one (supervisee), designed to enhance professional competence, monitor the standards of service delivery, and ensure ethical practice in applied sport psychology contexts. Unlike traditional clinical supervision, supervision in applied sport psychology encompasses unique dimensions related to performance enhancement, team dynamics, and the high-pressure competitive environments in which practitioners typically operate. Some of the core concepts we explore in this book encompass reflective practice (i.e., systematic examination of one's professional experiences to improve future practice), professional development (i.e., continuous growth in knowledge, skills, and competencies), ethical decision-making (i.e., applying ethical frameworks to complex applied sport psychology scenarios), competency assurance (i.e., ensuring practitioners meet and maintain professional standards) and knowledge transfer (i.e., transmitting explicit and tacit knowledge from experienced practitioners to developing ones).

Applied sport psychology is typically theoretically guided, empirically grounded, and practically meaningful. One aspect of the field of applied sport psychology is supervision. Supervision facilitates personal and professional development, promotes practitioner competencies, and supports

DOI: 10.4324/9781003485667-1

accountable service delivery. Defining supervision, however, like supervision itself, is a complex task because there are roles and responsibilities for at least three stakeholders: the supervisee, the supervisor, and the client. To help these parties develop a scaffold for their work in the supervisory relationship, we draw upon the definition presented by Hawkins and McMahon (2020) and define supervision as a supervisor and supervisee working together to attend to the supervisee's clients, client-practitioner relationships, and the wider contexts of their work. This joint endeavour improves the quality of their work because it transforms client relationships and continuously develops the practitioner, their practice, and the profession.

Within this definition lie at least three meaningful strands. First, supervision is collaborative. It means the supervisee and the supervisor work together to address the tasks, goals, and bond of their working relationship to support the work of the supervisee with their current and future clients. Second, supervision is client-focused. The core purpose of supervision is to examine the supervisee's client work. The client might be an individual, a client group, or an organisational client. It is likely that the wider context of the supervisee's work includes organisational and professional contexts with their unique social, cultural, and political leanings. An applied sport psychology practitioner working in a professional organisation (e.g., rugby, basketball) works within its systemic and ecological context. Working with a youth athlete within this organisation might also involve the family and social context of the client and their ecological contexts. Finally, supervision focuses on learning. Though supervision may appear to attend to what happened (i.e., a reflective process), it does so to help the supervisee learn and raise the quality of their work with current clients, future clients, their organisation, and the profession. This focus on education and training means activities such as observation, feedback, and evaluation fit alongside modelling, instruction, and problem-solving.

1.2 Why Is Supervision Necessary?

In short, this endeavour by the supervisee and supervisor aims towards setting standards for supervision to ensure that practitioners are professional, competent, ethically secure, and innovative scientist-practitioners fully suited to service delivery in sport. The specific functions of supervision might be developmental, resourcing, and qualitative (Hawkins & Smith, 2013), formative, restorative, and normative (Proctor, 1988) or educative, supportive, and managerial (Kadushin, 1976).

For this chapter, we focus on Hawkins and Smith's (2013) work. The developmental function focuses on developing the capacities, understanding, and skills of the supervisee through the supervisee's work with their clients. Supervisees hold various levels of experience as trainees or professionals; yet time spent in one's profession does not always mean personal and professional development matures. It is the evidence of the work with clients that helps the supervisor understand where on this developmental trajectory the supervisee stands. Reflecting, exploring, and learning are key functions of development, but without cases to reflect on and explore, it seems unlikely that each step of service delivery: assessment, formulation, intervention, evaluation, and communication unfold at the leading edge of learning and current practice. Observations, audio and video recordings, and process reports allow the supervisor to 'be in the room' with the supervisee and the client. These examples allow the supervisor to witness assessments unfolding, to hear the dynamics of interactions between the supervisee and their clients, to see the threads of formulations and interventions weave together, and to see the consequences of the decisions and actions of the supervisee. A supervisor might compare an example with one client (e.g., a child athlete) with examples from other clients (e.g., a master's athlete) and their unique systemic and ecological contexts.

The resourcing function reflects the resilience required to work in a helping profession. Distress, pain, loss, disorientation, uncertainty, success, and a host of other universal life themes affect each practitioner differently, but the challenges of working with others mean practitioners need to reflect upon how this emotional labour affects them. Compassion fatigue influences the practitioner and their work with clients. Practitioners might, for instance, over-identify with their clients or protect themselves against being further affected by their clients (Hawkins & McMahon, 2020).

The qualitative function of supervision reflects the parameters required to work safely with people. This quality assessment forms a safeguard against those things that are seen (e.g., lack of experience) and unseen (e.g., blind spots). When all stakeholders, such as the supervisor, supervisee, and organisation, recognise their responsibility for client welfare, the ethical and professional standards steer them along suitably.

At each stage of one's supervision, one's developmental, resourcing, and qualitative functions are at play. As novice practitioners, much of our supervision was formative because we sought knowledge, but as we gained competence, our growing experience developed into consultative supervision, encompassing the breadth and depth of our work. At one moment, a supervisee might need to develop a specific skill for their client work (e.g., developmental) and at another receive support to handle delicate ethical challenges (e.g., resourcing) while learning to be positive in their work with a client and ensure a quality of work (e.g., qualitative). For experienced practitioners as supervisees, they will need feedback on content and process in client sessions (e.g., developmental), need validation as a person and a professional (e.g., resourcing) and to continue to use their professional resources better (e.g., qualitative). Some supervisors might supervise yet be in a developmental phase in their supervisory experience as they gain knowledge, clinical wisdom, and organisational experience in the field (Creaner, 2014).

1.3 Functions of Supervision

Proctor's (1987) clinical supervision model outlines three functions of supervision: formative, normative, and restorative.

The formative function reflects the fostering of trainee development. Next, the normative aspect involves protecting clients' interests and performing gatekeeping tasks. Finally, the restorative function provided by supervisors to supervisees is to help them share their needs and address them, preventing burnout (Bernard & Goodyear, 2018). By exploring the formative function of supervision in applied sport psychology, we can see its central role in enhancing knowledge and abilities. A key part of education, training, and supervision is teaching those supervised the theories and practices of applied sport psychology. The supervisee will then focus on honing their abilities in assessment, formulation, intervention, evaluation, and the communication of their understanding. With the supervisee's progression, they can combine research with their practice and undertake research activities, which will contribute to their professional growth and help them as sport psychologists in training.

The normative function checks quality and upholds ethical standards. Supervisors encourage and engage with supervisees from the beginning to foster professional standards and ethical guidelines in practice. This initial step guarantees quality service by consistently reviewing contracts, boundaries, and conducting check-ins with everyone involved, including athletes, coaches, teams, and organisations. Whether you are a trainee or a qualified professional, providing a service to clients requires evaluating risks and following organisational and legal rules. Recording cases and maintaining records is a crucial process that benefits clients and supervisees, involving the supervisor and supervisee.

The restorative function focuses on the supervisee's emotional and psychological health. One of the primary goals of this support is to prevent burnout, including compassion fatigue, in environments with high emotional demands. Some applied sport psychologists often work unpredictable hours, travel frequently, and handle many cases, all of which must be carefully managed to ensure the practitioner's health. In performance-driven environments, the emphasis is primarily on results and achievements, and such settings are also challenging for the practitioner. Practitioners' hidden biases and emotional reactions, stemming from the environment, subtly influence their interactions with those with whom they work in high-pressure sports, making countertransference probable.

1.4 Theoretical Models and Frameworks of Supervision

Supervision models and frameworks represent an organised way in which supervisors apply supervision. With different models or frameworks, we witness different aspects of supervision being applied, and a choice remaining with the supervisor and supervisee about how they wish to work together. One challenge for a neophyte supervisee in applied sport psychology is to first understand a therapeutic modality (e.g., person-centred therapy or cognitive behaviour therapy) and apply it in a sport setting. Next, they must negotiate supervision with a supervisor, often without learning or being taught about the process of supervision, supervision models, and ways of working together. The first step on this journey is to understand a sample of supervision models and frameworks, which helps neophyte supervisees to negotiate and use supervision. It is possible to organise three broad categories of supervision models: models grounded in psychotherapy theory (e.g., cognitive behavioural, psychodynamic), developmental models (IDM Stoltenberg and McNeill; reflective developmental models), and process models (e.g., discrimination model by Bernard or Hawkins and Shohet seven-eyed model). Supervisors use various approaches, blending elements from each of the three model categories (Bernard and Goodyear, 2018). It is beyond the scope of this book to offer detailed accounts of each model, so we present an example for each category for illustration. For those models grounded in psychotherapy theory, we shall present person-centred and cognitive-behavioural supervision. For developmental models, we shall present the integrated developmental model (IDM). Finally, we shall present Hawkins and Shohet's seven-eyed model.

1.4.1 Psychotherapy-Based Models

Here, we introduce two psychotherapy-based models: humanistic-relationship-oriented supervision and cognitive-behavioural supervision, though there are also systemic or integrative approaches. In humanistic-relationship-oriented approaches, the focus lies in experiential awareness and using the therapeutic relationship to promote change. Thus, supervision aims to assist supervisees in developing their understanding of theory, skills, and techniques, as well as their ability to explore themselves and their use of self to create change. Being truly present, transparent, authentic, and accepting of clients is part of using oneself (i.e., use of self). In short, the psychologist uses his or her 'self' as a tool in service of clients and the therapeutic relationship. Therapeutic use of self reflects the self-aware interweaving of our professional self (one using knowledge, skills, and techniques) and our personal self (emerging from our history, beliefs, values, personality, and lived experience) (Finlay, 2022). Many relate this theoretical school to Carl Rogers and his person-centred model. Rogers' counselling theory informed his supervision, believing in genuineness, empathy, and warmth to understand oneself, understand the therapeutic process, and grow in confidence (Bernard & Goodyear, 2018).

In applied sport psychology, however, cognitive-behavioural therapies have had, and continue to have, a significant influence on the practice of applied sport psychologists. Although behavioural and cognitive therapies have separate origins and foci, their blending brought a set of propositions for the goals and processes of supervision (Boyd, 1978). For instance, to teach therapists how to behave, develop skills, apply them, and refine them in response to learning theory, supervision needs to incorporate the principles of learning theory into its practices.

In cognitive-behavioural supervision, we witness a similar structure to sessions as if we were receiving cognitive behaviour therapy, with a check-in, agenda setting, a bridge from the previous supervision session, previous supervised therapy cases, homework review, working on each agenda item, periodic summaries, homework assignment, final summary, and feedback from the supervisee (Sudak et al., 2016). This supervision session would begin with a check-in to see how the supervisee is doing and to create a safe environment for the session. Next, the supervisor and supervisee set the agenda together, with the supervisor adding to the agenda an item or items deemed relevant at that stage. The bridge represents an opportunity for the supervisee to share what was learned in the last session and how that learning was useful. Next, the supervisor will enquire about previously supervised cases, which allows both parties to acknowledge where they stand with these cases and their overall caseload. Homework is a key feature of CBT and CBT supervision. A supervisor and supervisee will set homework collaboratively for the supervisee to complete between each session. For example, a supervisee might read about a treatment intervention or attempt a new technique. Most of a CBT supervision session focuses on the agenda items. One element of an agenda might be about role-playing or direct instruction leading from an audio recording of a session with a client. Or the supervisor may use guided discovery to help a supervisee establish what to do next, having reached an impasse with a client. Once the agenda items are addressed, setting homework for the next session allows the supervisee to benefit from what emerged in the session. Next, the supervisor's capsule summaries and formative feedback reflect upon the session and what has been learned. Finally, besides opportunities to offer feedback to the supervisor during the session, the supervisor seeks feedback from the supervisee about the session and answers questions the supervisee might have from the session.

Affect is a key feature of CBT and CBT supervision. It might appear as though cognition, overt behaviour, and didactic instruction trump affect, but this appearance is a misinterpretation. After all, a supervisee might struggle with stress about their competence and effectiveness in the workplace or countertransference working in a high-performance environment. Exploring these feelings allows the supervisee to address unhelpful thoughts (e.g., I must be of immense value to the football players in this academy). Creating a safe supervisory environment, dealing with feelings, and nurturing a positive working alliance between the supervisee and supervisor have long-lasting effects on the supervisee's competence and effectiveness in applied sport psychology.

1.4.2 *Developmental Models*

Developmental models aim to clarify the evolution of professional competence during training and beyond. Stoltenberg (1981) first developed the integrated developmental model (IDM), with revisions over the next two decades (Stoltenberg & Delworth, 1987; Stoltenberg et al., 1998). The integrated developmental model illustrates four stages of growth, starting with novice and culminating in expert. Besides these developmental stages, one can assess professional growth using three organising principles: self-awareness, motivation, and independence, across eight skill domains: intervention skills competence, assessment techniques, interpersonal assessment, client conceptualisation, individual differences, theoretical orientation, treatment goals and plans, and professional ethics (Stoltenberg et al., 1998, pp. 187–199).

The four developmental stages or levels are level 1 (self-centred), level 2 (client-centred), level 3 (process-centred) and level 3i (integrated). At Level 1, the trainee/supervisee is highly motivated, and they concentrate on their own areas of weakness (self-centred). There is a noticeable lack of self-understanding, coupled with anxiety from not knowing, and supervisees seem overly reliant on their supervisors. The supervisee seeks structure and mentorship from their supervisor. In Level 2, the emphasis moves from the individual to the client (i.e., client-centred), and there is a transition period marked by autonomy and self-reliance. After experiencing moments of self-assurance, feelings of insecurity and confusion arise, followed again by periods of high confidence. When supervision cannot ease discomfort, motivation wavers, and dissatisfaction sets in. Level 3 allows for increased freedom and a stronger focus on the interaction between oneself and the client. The supervisee seeks more challenge from their supervisor. Level 3i emerges when those being supervised achieve Level 3 competence in various areas, such as assessments and interventions. This includes a customised way of working professionally in different fields and a clear understanding of abilities and areas for improvement.

1.4.3 *Process Models*

Process models blend concepts from different theoretical frameworks. The seven-eyed process model of supervision by Hawkins and Shohet (1989) identifies seven key areas, or modes, of supervision. This supervisory model considers the interplay of a supervisor, supervisee, client, work environment, and broader system, involving a dual focus (double matrix) on the client/supervisor and supervisee/supervisor relationships. Supervisors select these modes or areas of emphasis based on their preferred supervision style, the supervisee's developmental progress, and the specific circumstances of the context.

Mode 1: Focusing on the clients and what and how they present
Mode 2: Exploring the strategies and interventions used by the supervisee
Mode 3: Focusing on the relationship between the client and the supervisee
Mode 4: Focusing on the supervisee
Mode 5: Focusing on the supervisory relationship
Mode 6: The supervisor focusing on their own process
Mode 7: Focusing on the wider context in which the work happens

The first three modes explore the events unfolding during the supervisee/client's session. In the next three modes, there is a focus on the act of supervision, exploring the experiences of the supervisor and supervisee within their working relationship, potentially shaped by the dynamics of the supervisee's interactions with their clients (see parallel processes). Because the supervisor has never met the client, the supervisor depends on the supervisee to communicate information (consciously or unconsciously) about the client. The final mode offers a lens into the various circumstances that may influence the context within which the work happens (Creaner, 2014; Hawkins & Shohet, 2012).

In our work with our doctoral students training to become applied sport psychologists, we present an overview of supervision models and frameworks so trainees appreciate the various approaches supervisors might take in the supervisory process in their allotted one-to-one supervision. In group supervision sessions, however, we explore the value and complexity of supervision, leaning on the seven-eyed process model of supervision and the generic tasks of supervision (Carroll, 1996). Carroll's (1996) generic tasks model comprises seven tasks of supervision. These tasks emerged from his research with supervisees and supervisors, with a focus on what the supervisor does in supervision. This behavioural repertoire allows the supervisee to witness what the supervisor does in supervision and the responsibility the supervisor holds for undertaking these tasks. These tasks comprise (1) to set up a 'learning relationship', (2) to teach, (3) to evaluate, (4) to monitor professional/ethical issues, (5) to counsel, (6) to consult, and (7) to monitor administrative aspects. These seven spokes of the generic tasks of supervision wheel generate questions within the group about each spoke. For example, teaching (2) might raise questions like: What knowledge do you need to develop? Or which skills do you need to progress? Evaluation (3) might raise questions like: How will my supervisor evaluate my work? Or how will my supervisor help me evaluate my work? (Table 1.1).

Table 1.1 Comparison of Major Supervision Models

Model	*Core focus*	*Key features*	*Strengths*	*Limitations*	*Best used when*
Psychotherapy-based models (e.g., humanistic/ person-centred/ CBT)	Application of a therapeutic orientation to supervision	• Supervision parallels therapeutic sessions • Humanistic: empathy, genuineness, use of self • CBT: structured agenda, homework, guided discovery	• Clear structure (CBT) • Strong relational depth (humanistic) • Easy for supervisees trained in the same modality	• May over-prioritise therapeutic models instead of supervision needs • Risk of rigidity (CBT) or lack of direction (humanistic)	• The supervisee is learning a specific modality • Cases align closely with the therapeutic model • Early-stage trainees needing structure (CBT)
Integrated Developmental Model (IDM)	Developmental progression of supervisee competence and autonomy	• Four levels of development (1–3i) • Tracks motivation, self-awareness, autonomy • Eight domains of competence	• Highly adaptable to the supervisee's level • Helps supervisors pitch support versus challenge • Supports long-term growth	• Can be complex to apply consistently • Risk of over-labelling supervisees' 'stage'	• Training programmes • Long-term supervision relationships • Supervisors wanting developmental scaffolding

(*Continued*)

Table 1.1 (Continued)

Model	*Core focus*	*Key features*	*Strengths*	*Limitations*	*Best used when*
Seven-Eyed Process Model (Hawkins and Shohet)	Multi-layered view of client–supervisee–supervisor dynamics	• Seven perspectives ('eyes') including interventions, relationships, parallel process, wider context • Strong systemic lens	• Excellent for relational and systemic insight • Reveals parallel processes • Supports reflective depth	• Can be abstract for beginners • Requires supervisory skills in relational/ process work	• Complex cases • Team/ organisational sport settings • Supervisees ready for deeper process-oriented exploration
Carroll's Generic Tasks Model	Concrete tasks a supervisor performs	• Seven tasks: learning relationship, teaching, evaluating, monitoring ethics, counselling, consulting, admin • Useful behavioural map for supervisors	• Very practical and easy to operationalise • Helps supervisors structure sessions and track responsibilities	• Harder to use as a standalone conceptual model • Less emphasis on supervisee development stages	• Supervisor training • New supervisors learning their roles • Structuring group or individual supervision sessions

Model	*Core focus*	*Key features*	*Strengths*	*Limitations*	*Best used when*
Process-Oriented Models	'Here-and-now' dynamics in supervision	• Focus on interpersonal patterns • Uses moment-to-moment experiences • Strong parallels with group/team dynamics	• Powerful for emotional intelligence and relational skills • Helps reveal blind spots and parallel processes	• Requires high supervisor competence • Not always suitable for early trainees needing structure	• Advanced supervisees • Team-sport practitioners dealing with interpersonal complexity
Behavioural/ Cognitive-Behavioural Supervision	Skill acquisition through structured methods	• Agenda-setting • Modelling • Role-play • Feedback loops • Homework	• Structured and measurable • Easy to evaluate progression • Supports skill-based learning	• May under-emphasise relational depth • Can feel mechanistic if overused	• Early-career supervisees • Skill-focused training (e.g., behavioural interventions)
Humanistic/ Relational Models	Use of self, authenticity, and empathic supervisory relationships	• Emphasis on safety, warmth, congruence • Supervisory relationship as a change vehicle	• Builds a strong working alliance • Supports supervisee vulnerability and reflection	• May lack structure • Risk of avoiding evaluation or difficult conversations	• Reflective practice development • Supporting supervisees with shame/anxiety

1.5 How Supervision in Applied Sport Psychology Evolved

Applied sport psychology formalised supervision more recently than clinical and counselling psychology. Broadly, the 1980s and 1990s witnessed the first of several key developmental milestones with the emergence of applied sport psychology as a distinct professional practice area, with supervision practices borrowed largely from fields like counselling psychology (Andersen et al., 1994; Simons & Andersen, 1995). By the early 2000s, practitioners recognised the need for sport-specific supervision models that address the unique challenges of working in athletic environments. Over the next fifteen years, there were several specialised certification programmes (e.g., BPS, AASP) that formalised supervision requirements. More recently, we have witnessed the integration of technology-mediated supervision approaches and a greater emphasis on cultural competence in supervision. The evolution of supervision in applied sport psychology reflects the field's growth from focusing primarily on performance enhancement to addressing holistic well-being, mental health, and diverse athlete populations.

Training and supervision in applied sport psychology has had a 'Wild West' feel to it and, by extension, might not have prepared trainees for their careers (Tod & Lavallee, 2011). The field of applied sport psychology has boomed over the past 45 years, and with such booms, the ethics and standards of practice lagged. Codes of practice and boundaries of competence help practitioners to practise safely, ethically, and effectively; however, as the field grew, guidelines for training, supervision, and licensing were scarce, and so some practitioners taught themselves (Simons & Andersen, 1995). Although some self-taught practitioners practised safely and ethically, others did not. This 'openness' to the field meant that those wishing to practise without training and qualifications could do so and, with sufficient 'popular opinion' behind them, gathered clients whose primary concern was success rather than the practitioner's training and qualifications.

The intervening years have meant an increase in accreditation (licensing, certification) following students enrolling in undergraduate and postgraduate programmes (e.g., sport science, psychology), independent or university-directed training routes, alongside critical and reflective supervision. Although the landscape of training and supervision changes in all professions, applied sport psychology seems to have a stop-start nature to it, but travels in the right direction. It seems stop-start in the sense that some training and supervision meet the needs of future practitioners while others might not. Differences in curricula, educator training, supervision, and supervising the supervisors fortify some areas, yet leave gaps elsewhere. For instance, maybe theoretical and applied knowledge might be a strength, yet practitioner helping skills for practice with clients remain low. Another issue relates to the needs of clients in the field. Tod, Andersen, and Marchant (2009, 2011) conducted two longitudinal studies following a cohort of practitioners for six years since beginning their postgraduate training. Of those working with athletes, less than 20 per cent of their services focused on performance enhancement.

For this chapter and book, we focus on supervision. Many practitioners, past and present, recognise the specific factors (e.g., interventions) more readily than the common factors (e.g., therapeutic relationships) in applied sport psychology practice. At face value, it seems reasonable that doing something (e.g., relaxation) trumps being something (e.g., empathic). But close, caring relationships with clients help them get better at what they do (i.e., in sport and life), and the quality of the working alliance between the practitioner and client remains a consistent factor in treatment outcomes (Andersen, 2005; Sexton & Whiston, 1994). With these ideas in mind, the leanings of one's supervisor might inadvertently impress upon specific factors at the cost of common factors for the supervisee. The supervisee in practicum placement blends the art and science of applied sport psychology but often does so on the strength of the quantity and quality of supervision. With low levels of full-time employment as applied sport psychology practitioners, it seems likely that many supervisors in applied sport psychology are academics with varying levels of experience in applied sport psychology (Tod et al., 2009). In addition, despite their knowledge, skills, and experience as practitioners, they will still need to learn how to supervise (Barney et al., 1996). Supervision is not a requirement for continued registration or membership in most professional organisations, and sport psychologists rarely seek supervision following graduation (Watson et al., 2004).

With this historical backdrop of a low ratio of supervision hours to placement hours, and varying quality of supervision, one might question the effectiveness of service delivery and the helpfulness of sport psychology as a discipline amongst the sport sciences (Tod & Lavallee, 2011). Recent developments in independent training programmes, taught doctorates, and professional doctorates mean the landscape of supervision is improving. Researchers and practitioners recognise the needs of neophyte trainees through their research, which shapes our knowledge and understanding of supervisees' needs (Cropley & Neil, 2014, 2016, McEwan & Tod, 2015; McEwan et al., 2019). Yet, it remains the duty and responsibility of supervisors to bridge the gap between research and practice by keeping up to date in their knowledge and leaning on the most suitable integration of theory, research, and practice. A weight of responsibility and accountability lies with supervisors to remain current in their knowledge and practice of service delivery. Ideally, education and clinical practice would crossover each week during a trainee's learning journey to address material that is relevant at a theoretical and practical level (e.g., injury rehabilitation, career transition). Blending theory with personal, professional, and relational factors in service delivery lives week to week for those on practicum placement. And the traditional focus on performance enhancement amongst applied sport psychology practitioners has now shifted to include health and well-being (Sly et al., 2020).

1.6 What Good Supervision Looks Like in Practice

Supervisees in the helping professions report feelings of shame, worry, and incompetence in their client work, especially those early in their training, highlighting the need for improved supervision. For instance, in psychotherapy supervision, Batten and Santanello (2009) suggested trainees are likely to hold feelings of shame about making mistakes and anxiety about providing effective therapy in supervision and clinical work. One regrettable way these trainees manage these feelings of distress is to avoid exploring these shortcomings in supervision. Sometimes supervisors act as if they are without frailty or shortcomings, and emphasise their evaluative role as a supervisor, which slides the power towards the supervisor and feeds a wholly threatening supervisory environment. In short, the supervisee and supervisor collude to avoid dealing with the feelings (e.g., shame, anxiety) and challenges (e.g., confronting common problems) in their work.

If we jump back to the literature in counselling and clinical psychology, we see a wealth of psychotherapy outcome research underlining the centrality of the therapeutic relationship. Regardless of one's theoretical orientation (e.g., person-centred, psychodynamic), positive therapeutic relationships (e.g., caring, respectful) are consistently associated with positive therapeutic outcomes (Norcross, 2011). The environment for change from a person-centred perspective, as one example, depends upon the relationship conditions offered by the therapist (e.g., psychological contact, empathy, unconditional positive regard, congruence). In Carl Rogers' (1957/2007) view, all people hold the resources within for personal growth but need a warm, understanding, and non-threatening environment to empower and foster that growth.

In a similar vein, there could and (we believe) should, in supervision, be a parallel process with the therapeutic relationship in the supervisee-client dyad running alongside the supervisee-supervisor alliance (Andersen, 2021; Tracey et al., 2012). After all, common issues within therapeutic relationships are also common in supervision (e.g., issues in communication, developing relationships, and ego defences). For instance, transference and countertransference, dependence and autonomy, rights and responsibilities, and practical issues such as time constraints, financial considerations, and availability are prevalent in the supervisee-supervisor relationship (Van Raalte & Andersen, 2000). In Chapter 2, we shall explore the supervisory relationship, especially how attending to the growth and prosperity of the relationship serves all involved. Next, we will delve into theoretical models and frameworks related to supervision. This orientation will offer a foundational understanding for supervisees and supervisors in applied sport psychology, supporting better professional performance, guaranteeing high-quality service delivery, and fulfilling a gatekeeper role for the field (Poczwardowski et al., 2023).

Briefly, the four cornerstones of the supervision contract comprise (a) student's developmental needs, (b) supervisor competencies, (c) opportunities provided by the work setting, and (d) supervisory goals, methods, and focus (Rønnestad & Skovholt, 1993). We shall explore each cornerstone in the next section.

(a) *Students' developmental needs.* Each student or trainee arrives at supervision with different levels of personal and professional resources combined with their unique educational and work experiences. Considering these assets and probable expectations, alongside the perspectives and experiences of supervisors, it seems sensible to establish supervisory goals based on the unique developmental needs of each student who has yet to grasp the demands of working in the profession.

(b) *Supervisor competencies.* Though we might inadvertently expect all supervisors to hold a set of competencies commensurate with their supervisor status, varying levels of competency mean supervisees bump up against barriers to their learning because the supervisor did not outline the limits of their professional competence (McEwan & Tod, 2015). For instance, though a trainee might expect a supervisor to be competent in all aspects of cognitive behaviour therapy as a therapeutic modality because of its popularity in applied sport psychology (McCarthy et al., 2023), the trainee might witness several learning barriers because the supervisor did not explicitly outline their knowledge, understanding, and experience using CBT in sport and performance settings. It seems likely that service delivery experience and training to foster a supervisee's development will vary amongst supervisors (McEwan & Tod, 2015).

(c) *Opportunities provided by the work setting.* Drawing up a supervision contract ought to acknowledge the work setting or practicum placement, because it might not be possible to practise and meet one's competencies as expected on a training programme. One organisation might seek a battery of assessments to be administered and evaluated by a senior practitioner who presents a working formulation for the trainee to follow, preventing the trainee from gaining skills and competencies in assessment and formulation.

(d) *Supervisory goals, methods, and focus*. Perhaps the major thrust of supervision falls under goals, methods, and focus because these are signposts to guide the supervisory work. One's goals, for instance, need to be specific and measurable. As with all goal-setting processes, a fine balance or sweet spot ought to be negotiated between how broad or narrow one's goals might be and how permanent or flexible they are for the context of practicum placement. Supervisors favour specific methods of supervision involving techniques (e.g., written summaries, videotape, audiotape, one-way mirror) and interventions (modelling, feedback, confrontation, interpretation, support, or didactic instruction) and the centrality of the supervisory relationship in the change process. Finally, focus relates to the primary attentional object of the supervisor and supervisee throughout supervision. Although the sport psychology practitioner in training (i.e., supervisee), their client, and the relationship between them and their client are the focus, the supervisor is also part of these service delivery relationships, creating an instrumental focus. The instrument foci include: (a) the sport psychology practitioner (i.e., supervisee) in training, (b) the relationship interchange between supervisor and supervisee, (c) the relationship between supervisee and client, and (d) the client. Briefly, the supervisor observes the supervisee's case narratives and client relationships to acquire a comprehensive understanding of the supervisee. A supervisor may lean on one or several aspects of the supervisee's functioning, such as cognitive and conceptual, affective and relational, method and technique skills.

1.7 Where the Field Is Going

The existing research on the effectiveness of supervision within the field of applied sport psychology is still growing. We need more outcome-based studies to assess the connection between supervision quality and client results in sports environments. To advance our process research, we must deepen our understanding of supervisory alliances, feedback loops, and learning methods. There is growing evidence about how supervision contributes to the development of core competencies in those being supervised. One of the many methodological challenges of research on supervision in applied sport psychology is isolating supervision effects from other personal and professional development activities. Our understanding of how well supervision works across different cultures and with athletes from different backgrounds is also incomplete.

The needs of those stepping out on their journey towards accreditation (registration, licensing) present significantly different challenges from those further along their professional journey because they are learning how to manage ethical, intrapersonal, interpersonal, political, logistical, and organisational issues that are inherent in the helping professions (Fogaca et al., 2018). To hold, understand, and manage these needs, work is best founded on an effective working alliance between the supervisor and the supervisee (Bordin, 1983; Ladany et al., 2013). In Chapter 2, we shall explore Bordin's framework for working alliances to guide supervisees and supervisors based on goals, tasks, and bonds. For now, however, we focus on the specific supervision needs of trainees. Beginning students and advanced graduates typically request high levels of structure, a didactic (instructive) orientation, and a skill focus in their supervision, but these needs ought to be tempered with continuous reflection (Rønnestad & Skovholt, 1993). Knowing these demands and expectations fits with the developmental journey of beginning students and advanced graduates, which, outlined in a contract, addresses much of the tension and dissatisfaction experienced on the supervision journey (see Chapter 3 for details on contracting).

1.8 Summary

In this chapter, we introduced supervision as a collaborative, client-focused, and learning-oriented process central to effective and ethical practice in applied sport psychology. We outlined key functions of supervision – developmental, normative, and restorative – and highlighted how these functions support practitioner growth, safeguard client welfare, and sustain professional standards. The chapter distinguishes applied sport psychology supervision from its clinical roots by emphasising its unique performance-driven, multidisciplinary, and organisationally complex contexts.

Several theoretical models are presented, including psychotherapy-based, developmental, and process-oriented frameworks, demonstrating the varied ways supervisors structure and facilitate learning. The historical overview shows how supervision in sport psychology has progressed from loosely defined practices to more formalised, evidence-informed approaches, though inconsistencies and gaps persist.

Finally, the chapter identified the evolving needs of trainees, the variable competencies of supervisors, and the influence of practicum settings on learning. Emerging trends – such as technology-mediated supervision, cultural responsiveness, clearer competency frameworks, and supervisor training – signal a field moving towards greater professionalisation. The chapter establishes the foundation for subsequent discussions on the supervisory relationship, effective practice, and the ongoing development of both supervisees and supervisors.

Exercise 1.1: Mapping the Functions of Supervision

Create a three-column table with the headings: Developmental, Resourcing/Restorative, and Qualitative/Normative. Next, using one of your current or past client cases (real or simulated),

1. Identify one issue that fits each function of supervision.
2. Write one question you would bring to supervision under each function.
3. Explain how your supervisor could respond in a way that enhances your learning.

2 The Supervisory Relationship

2.1 Introduction

Opening this book with a chapter exploring and explaining the meaning and function of supervision leads us neatly to the supervisory relationship – the engine of change for a supervisee (and a supervisor). This engine consumes time, emotion, intellect, and money, but helps people (i.e., supervisees) gain skills and competence in what they do. A supervisory relationship, like other relationships in education and training (e.g., research, teaching), has challenges about identity and power, especially because there are strong evaluative components attached to them. It is likely that a supervisor will set various formative and summative assessments for the supervisee, and so some level of performativity inevitably creeps into the relationship (e.g., trying to please and be good for the supervisor). Trainees in applied sport psychology sense the need to 'get going' with their practicum work. They are, as Andersen et al. (2000) described, a 'galloping trainee' just waiting to get out of the gate. Drawing on this metaphor, they do not want to be held in a stable in the yard or a small paddock; they want to get out onto the gallops. The stable in the yard and paddock contains the formal education of theories, models, and research amongst other learning activities and assessments, but it is not where they want to stay. They want to work with athletes, coaches, and teams. We, as educators and supervisors, encourage trainees to work hard around the yard (i.e., learning theories, frameworks, models, practising counselling skills; engaging positively in supervision) so that when the time comes, they can be of greatest service and value out on the gallops. Part of this work around the yard also means developing one's willingness to learn, a passion for practice, honesty, self-awareness, and self-reflection. Supervising 'galloping supervisees' is costly for the supervisee and supervisor. If the supervisee has gaps in theoretical knowledge and modes of service delivery, the supervisor might need to set supervision time aside to address these because, without these basics, the supervisee will not hold a meaningful framework to work with clients.

DOI: 10.4324/9781003485667-2

Another challenge with galloping supervisees is that they have little time or interest in looking at themselves and the processes between them and their clients. Yet, without exploring their needs, personality, fears, passions, strengths, weaknesses, and how they relate to client-athletes and how client-athletes relate to them, supervisees struggle to become the 'good enough' sport psychology practitioner they sought originally. And without supervisees attending to their understanding of themselves, their needs, and their responses to the clients they work with, it seems likely they will feel more anxiety, disappointment, shame, anger, and hurt throughout their professional lives. Supervisees have shared their feelings with me (Paul) about how others did not 'thank me for my services', 'make time for me', 'recognise my contribution', 'appreciate the time to put everything together' and so forth. It seemed overwhelmingly unfair to these supervisees that they should be in the background. But these experiences are grist for the reflective mill. These thoughts and feelings tell us about ourselves in ways we may or may not wish to address; however, we can address these issues in supervision to lessen them from diminishing the quality of service you deliver to clients. In the next section, we explore the supervisory relationship, theoretical foundations, and focus intently on the supervisor attributes or behaviours that affect the supervisory alliance.

2.2 The Supervisory Relationship in Applied Sport Psychology

The supervisory relationship stands as the cornerstone of professional development in applied sport psychology, serving as the vehicle for learning and the foundation for ethical practice. Unlike traditional therapeutic relationships, applied sport psychology supervision occurs within the unique context of performance environments, where practitioners must navigate complex dynamics involving athletes, coaches, teams, and organisational structures (Andersen et al., 2001). Effective sport psychology supervision requires an understanding of the complex dynamics between supervisor and supervisee, particularly within high-pressure environments, which are characteristic of competitive sports. The supervisory relationship extends beyond simple knowledge transfer; rather, it offers emotional support, shapes professional identity, and marshals ethical guidance that ultimately influences practitioner competence and athlete welfare. The relationship, therefore, does the heavy lifting in the journey from trainee to practitioner and beyond.

2.3 Theoretical Foundations of the Supervisory Relationship

The supervisory relationship between supervisors and supervisees in applied sport psychology draws upon several theoretical frameworks that help explain its dynamics, functions, and developmental processes. These theories provide a conceptual foundation for understanding how supervisory relationships form, develop, and function effectively. Here, we briefly introduce attachment theory, the working alliance theory, and relational approaches.

2.3.1 *Attachment Theory Perspectives*

According to attachment theory (Bowlby, 1988), personality, bonding, and work habits are all intertwined (Bennett & Deal, 2009). Therefore, supervisors might apply attachment principles, such as exploring how supervisees' security-related motivations differ, to create strong supervisory bonds (Bordin, 1983) and understand behaviours like supervisee self-disclosure (Gunn & Pistole, 2012). Research on attachment theory in supervision shows a significant effect on professional outcomes, with secure attachment relationships fostering exploration, learning, and professional growth. Originally developed to explain infant-caregiver bonds, attachment theory offers valuable insights into supervisory relationships by highlighting how early attachment experiences shape adult professional relationships. In supervision contexts, the supervisor often functions as a secure base (e.g., guidance) from which the supervisee can explore challenging professional situations and develop competence. For example, the supervisor's Circle of Security model (Powell et al., 2014; Soliman, 2023) illustrates how supervisors provide an attachment safe haven (e.g., soothing) during professional distress and a launch pad for professional exploration and risk-taking. In a supervisory relationship, we might witness different attachment styles and behaviours. With a secure attachment, you might see supervisees show help-seeking behaviour, openness to feedback, and balanced autonomy. An anxious attachment may manifest as excessive reassurance-seeking, dependency, or fear of negative evaluation, while an avoidant attachment often appears as reluctance to disclose difficulties, excessive self-reliance, or emotional distance. In applied sport psychology contexts, attachment dynamics take on particular significance because of the performance-oriented culture. Supervisees may struggle to acknowledge vulnerability or uncertainty in environments that stress strength and competence. Skilled supervisors recognise these dynamics and create safe spaces for authentic professional development while respecting the performance context (Clevinger, Albert, & Raiche, 2019).

2.3.2 *Working Alliance Theory*

The working alliance theory provides a framework for understanding collaborative relationships in supervision, emphasising the importance of shared goals, agreed-upon tasks, and emotional bonds between supervisor and supervisee. Adapted from Bordin's therapeutic alliance concept, the supervisory working alliance comprises three essential components: goals, tasks, and bond (Bordin, 1983). Specifically, according to Bordin (1983, pp. 37–38), the goals of supervision relate to (1) mastery of specific skills, (2) enlarging one's understanding of clients, (3) enlarging one's awareness of process issues, (4) increasing awareness of self and impact on process, (5) overcoming personal and intellectual obstacles towards learning and mastery, (6) deepening one's understanding of concepts and theory, (7) providing a stimulus to research, and (8) maintenance of standards of service. The tasks of supervision comprise the specific activities and methods used to achieve these goals, such as case presentations (e.g., written case reports), role-playing, and direct observation (e.g., using recordings). In this way, supervisees present what they feel are issues worth exploring. The supervisor supports the supervisee with feedback, alternative perspectives, and gaps to fill. Finally, the bond refers to the emotional connection characterised by trust, respect, and shared commitment to the supervisory process. In applied sport psychology, supervision is increasingly focused on relationships, acknowledging that skills alone are not enough for successful practice (McCarthy et al., 2024). By using the working alliance, we can see how relationships play a role in making supervision successful. Research consistently shows that stronger working alliances correlate with positive supervision outcomes, including greater supervisee satisfaction, enhanced learning, and improved clinical skills (Bucky et al., 2010; Norcross, 2011). In applied sport psychology specifically, strong working alliances help supervisees navigate the unique challenges of athletic environments, including performance pressure, travel demands, and complex stakeholder relationships.

From a developmental perspective, the supervisory working alliance develops through three distinct phases (Holloway, 1995). During the initial phase, the supervisee and supervisor establish expectations, build rapport, and set preliminary goals. Then, in the middle phase, they deepen their work, addressing challenges and refining goals. Finally, in the termination phase, they consolidate learning, evaluate progress, and transition to greater autonomy. Applied sport psychology supervisors must adapt alliance-building strategies to accommodate the field's unique characteristics, including irregular schedules, seasonal demands, and integrating performance enhancement with mental health support.

In the supervision relationship, the actions of the supervisee and supervisor contribute in unique ways to the working alliance (Bernard & Goodyear, 2014). We explore a range of attributes and behaviours that affect the supervisory alliance: (a) the supervisor's style, (b) use of power, (c) ruptures and repair, (d) parallel processes, (e) psychological safety and trust, (f) relational approaches, and (g) contracting.

2.4 Supervisor Style

Supervisors hold considerable power and sway over those they oversee. There are several advantages to being aware of this power and influence. According to one study (Ladany et al., 2013), the most effective supervisors established a robust emotional connection, shared agreement on supervisory tasks and objectives, leading to a stronger supervisory relationship. They were also more interpersonally perceptive and task-focused, promoted empowerment by encouraging supervisee independence, and were receptive to supervisees' ideas (Falender & Shafranske, 2021).

The supervisor's style is defined by what (i.e., content) the supervisor focuses on in supervision and the methods they use (i.e., process) in their supervisory relationship. The supervisor's style describes the supervisor's distinct method of communicating and guiding the supervisee and implementing supervision (Friedlander & Ward, 1984). A model supervisor's personal qualities, attitudes, and behaviours reflect those we might see in the person-centred conditions in a person-centred approach to therapy.

2.4.1 Use of Power

Power dynamics represent one of the most complex aspects of supervisory relationships, requiring careful navigation to maintain a balance between authority and a collaborative learning environment (Murphy & Wright, 2005). In applied sport psychology supervision, power differentials exist on multiple levels, including professional experience, institutional authority, and gatekeeping functions. There are several sources of power in a supervisor relationship, though one might not be aware of or recognise such sources because they remain hidden as shadow motives (Guggenbuhl-Craig, 1971). In social psychology, we see references to different power types that become familiar once we see what they comprise. Expert power, for instance, reflects power based on knowledge, skills, and experience. The legitimate power a supervisor develops derives from formal roles and responsibilities overseeing supervision. The supervisor holds evaluative power because they assess competence and readiness for practice. For some supervisees, the supervisor also holds gatekeeping power, with control over access to professional opportunities and advancement. Finally, supervisors may hold informational power with access to resources, networks, and professional opportunities. Occasionally, some supervisors hold a reputation within academic and/or sports communities with influential sport organisations.

The potential for different power dynamics amongst these sources could affect a supervisee's willingness to share their challenges or errors during their practical training (Andersen, 1994). Some subordinates might hesitate to question their supervisor's views or ideas, wrongly believing their supervisor is always correct. If a relationship lacks the honesty and openness it needs, problems and anxieties might not be dealt with. It is also possible that the supervisee will resist examining and contesting the feedback given (Heckman-Stone, 2004). A supervisor might unintentionally cause a supervisee to comply without truly understanding, which can lead to a reluctance to share important information and potentially hinder learning through resentment.

Culture plays a crucial role in how power dynamics are understood, communicated, and felt within supervisory relationships. If not directly acknowledged, cultural variations in communication, perspectives on authority, and attitudes towards disagreement can cause friction or confusion. It is the supervisor's responsibility to show cultural humility when managing these situations, acknowledging how their personal cultural experiences influence their supervision and adjusting their methods to accommodate the varied requirements of those they supervise. To achieve this goal, however, one needs to acknowledge these power differentials and accept the probable influence on the supervisory relationship. Following that acknowledgement, the supervisor can foster an environment where those under their guidance can safely voice their issues. Even though the supervisor and supervisee are aware of the evaluative nature of supervision, they can still collaborate openly on decisions. The best approach for a supervisor involves finding the right mix of guidance and teamwork, tailored to the specific development level of the supervisee being supervised (De Stefano et al., 2017). Regular discussions regarding the supervisory relationship allow for the assessment and upkeep of these elements. Supervision is most effective when it uses 'power with' to foster cooperation, but it also holds authority and responsibility, rather than 'power over'

2.4.2 Ruptures and Repairs

Ruptures in supervisory relationships are inevitable occurrences that, when handled skilfully, can strengthen the relationship and provide valuable learning opportunities (Watkins, 2021). Understanding ruptures and repairs in supervisory relationships enables supervisors and supervisees to navigate conflicts constructively and maintain productive working relationships. Several types of ruptures occur in supervisory relationships. Ruptures may manifest in withdrawal, confrontation, misattunement, or cultural misunderstandings. In applied sport psychology contexts, ruptures may also arise from disagreements about intervention approaches, ethical dilemmas, or conflicts with other professionals in the sport environment. Possible indicators of a strained relationship could be shifts in the supervisee's involvement or sharing, more defensiveness or obedience, missed supervision appointments, or a decreased willingness to accept guidance. Alternatively, there could be stress or uneasiness during supervisory meetings. Supervisors must remain attuned to these signs and address concerns promptly rather than allowing them to escalate. The first step in the repair process is to identify the break. Then, the supervisor and supervisee can confirm each person's understanding and tactfully examine the reasons for the breakdown. After careful consideration, all parties can acknowledge their roles in the issue and collaborate to find resolutions. After that, they can each implement the changes and check if the repairs were successful. Every repair demands bravery, modesty, and dedication from the supervisor and the supervisee (Watkins et al., 2015). When handled effectively, ruptures provide valuable learning opportunities to deepen one's understanding of relationship dynamics. They also help each person learn how to resolve conflicts, identify trigger points, and strengthen relationships with others. These learning opportunities extend beyond the immediate supervisory relationship to enhance the supervisee's work with clients and future professional relationships (Watkins et al., 2019).

2.4.3 Parallel Processes in Supervision

Parallel process is a compelling and valuable concept in supervision, describing the unconscious mirroring of a supervisee's client's issues within the supervisory relationship. Parallel processes, like the working alliance, are two psychodynamically derived concepts, and recognising parallel processes in applied sport psychology supervision allows practitioners to understand how client dynamics can be unknowingly mirrored in the supervisory relationship. We can describe parallel processes in supervision as 'occur[ing] when (1) the therapist brings the interaction pattern that occurs between the therapist and client into supervision and enacts the same pattern but with the therapist trainee in the client's role, or (2) the trainee takes the interaction pattern in supervision back into the therapy session as the therapist, now enacting the supervisor's role'. (p. 330). It seems reasonable to assume that the needs a supervisee might have for approval, appreciation, and acceptance from the athletes with whom the supervisee works are also needs the supervisee might wish a supervisor to meet (Andersen et al., 2000; Friedlander et al., 1989).

During case discussions, the supervisee unintentionally mirrors the client's behaviours, feelings, and relationship styles, and they also unwittingly replicate supervisory relationships in their interactions with clients. Through this process, we gain insights into client experiences and relational patterns that often go unnoticed. To recognise these experiences, however, we need to recognise some indicators of parallel process. For instance, we could observe unanticipated emotional responses during supervision, relationship patterns that reflect client issues, shifts in roles, feelings of being stuck akin to client experiences, and supervisee actions that seem out of character. The supervisor should consider their emotional reactions and determine if the current supervision setup mirrors the client's situations that are under discussion.

From an applied sport psychology viewpoint, what could we see during supervision? For example, a supervisor could find that a supervisee working with a resistant athlete becomes resistant themselves during supervision. Alternatively, the supervisee could experience performance anxiety when working therapeutically with a highly anxious performer. One might witness team dynamics play out again in group supervision. Authority problems could affect the supervisory relationship between a coach and supervisee, or the supervisee might exhibit the perfectionism prevalent in high-level sports.

Parallel process allows us to examine the dynamics of supervision and understand how supervisory behaviours relate to client interactions, which is helpful for supervision. Through these connections, the supervisee can examine case conceptualisation and interventions informed by their supervision experiences. Supervisees can identify their own reactions and patterns within supervision and client casework, thanks to parallel processes. Parallel processes provide considerable educational value in terms of professional growth. Despite potential defensiveness or shame experienced by a supervisee, those who understand and apply parallel process cultivate empathy and perspective-taking, refine their case conceptualisation abilities, gain self-awareness in professional interactions, become more attuned to relationship dynamics, and deepen their comprehension of unconscious elements in clinical practice.

2.4.4 Psychological Safety and Trust

Trust and security are at the heart of any supervisory role (Vandette et al., 2019). Without these elements, those being supervised could withhold vital information, avoid tough conversations, or fail to fully participate in the supervision process. Good practice in applied sport psychology depends on professional growth via training and supervision; this is rooted in trust, which allows for authentic learning and progress. Trust is built when supervisors behave in a trustworthy and predictable manner, for example, by protecting private information, keeping their word, and showing care and consideration for their team. Trust is established and preserved through consistent supervisory conduct and perspectives in all aspects. For supervision to be effective, psychological safety is crucial; this is the feeling that you can take risks with others without worrying about being punished or humiliated. When psychological safety is present, those being supervised feel comfortable admitting they do not know something, pointing out errors, or voicing concerns. They are comfortable with differing opinions, sharing various perspectives, seeking help during challenges, and discussing their work-related feelings. To foster psychological safety, supervisors ought to show openness and honesty while upholding professional standards. This approach shows those being supervised that we expect uncertainty and errors as elements of professional growth, not as indicators of inadequacy. By keeping confidentiality, providing consistent oversight, avoiding defensiveness, being honest about their knowledge gaps, and separating developmental feedback from formal reviews, when possible, supervisors can cultivate safety and trust.

2.4.5 *Relational Approaches*

Supervisory approaches that emphasise relationships highlight the significance of the supervisory relationship as the core of professional development, serving as both the method and the outcome. These approaches recognise that supervision is not merely a knowledge transfer process but a complex interpersonal relationship that shapes professional identity and practice. Several key principles of relational supervision recognise the mutual influence of the supervisor on the supervisee and the supervisee on the supervisor in the relationship (Shaffer & Friedlander, 2017). They recognise intersubjectivity (i.e., each person brings their subjective experience to the relationship). They acknowledge the co-construction of meaning (i.e., understanding develops through dialogue and shared exploration). Finally, the process is central; therefore, how supervision is conducted is just as significant as its content. In applied sport psychology contexts, relational approaches hold value given the field's emphasis on relationship-building with athletes, coaches, and teams. Supervisees learn relationship skills not only through didactic instruction but through experiencing healthy professional relationships with their supervisors. Relational supervision approaches emphasise cultural humility and awareness, recognising how cultural factors shape the supervisory relationship and the supervisee's work with clients. This cultural attunement becomes important in sports contexts, where practitioners often work with diverse athlete populations across international settings. Integrating relational approaches with sport-specific knowledge creates supervision that addresses the technical aspects of applied sport psychology practice and the relational skills necessary for effective work with athletes and sport organisations.

2.4.6 *Contracting*

Supervisees and supervisors build an effective working relationship on their contract (Townend, 2005). Trainees usually have little experience when creating a supervision contract. In contrast, most supervisors working with trainees have their experiences from their training, experience as a supervisor to other supervisees, and their experience of their own supervision with their supervisor. This imbalance of experience often means that trainees are unsure what supervision looks like and which aspects are critical to supervision success. If a supervisor has received substandard supervision, then both parties might search in the dark for a strategy for supervision and how to put it into practice effectively.

Hewson (1999) outlined several elements that comprise contracting for supervision. The following are a sample: (1) both parties engage in developing the supervision process, (2) a vision of the end goal of supervision, (3) a guard against an abuse of power, (4) minimise covert agendas, (5) multi-handed contracts (e.g., supervisee, supervisor, and organisation), (6) contracting for content, (7) contracting about models or therapeutic approaches, and (8) teaching contracting. In the next section, we shall present a checklist with details about how to establish a contract, which elements to include, and a sample form to follow.

Supervision is relational. With their supervisors, supervisees reflect on their work with clients and organisations to learn how to practise better in their role as sport psychology practitioners. But supervision often flip-flops between formal and informal contracts with formal and informal structures for supervision meetings. Supervision involves people and processes. If we put the people first and forget the processes, we get ourselves in administrative trouble; and if we put the processes first and forget the people, we get into relational bother. People and processes each have their place in supervision to start, consolidate, engage in, service, and end supervision (Bernard & Goodyear, 2014; Hawkins & Shohet, 2012). The contractual details differ for each supervisor-supervisee relationship, but safe, ethical, and effective work with organisations depends on a good contract. But what is a contract? One definition (Sills, 2012, p. 94) is that 'a contact is an agreement between two or more people concerning the type of activity or relationship they will have with each other'. There is a 'being' and 'doing' in these supervision relationships. What a supervisee and supervisor do together matters, but what they will be for each other is just as, if not more, important (Carroll, 2014).

Caring about the supervision relationship means making promises at the beginning of the relationship and doing all we can to keep those promises. Lots of changes occur in our personal and professional lives, over which we have some control; however, other changes we do not have control over, and so we need to address these uncontrollable factors and acknowledge these changes and challenges in our supervision relationship. Written supervision agreements help establish clear boundaries and expectations. These agreements typically address:

- Frequency, duration, and format of supervision
- Goals and focus of supervision
- Evaluation procedures and criteria

- Record-keeping requirements
- Confidentiality parameters
- Emergency contact procedures
- Fees and payment arrangements (if applicable)

Regular review and updating of these agreements ensure boundaries remain clear as the supervisory relationship develops.

2.5 Key Components of Effective Supervisory Relationships

Specific elements that differentiate supervisory relationships from other professional interactions define successful supervisory relationships in applied sport psychology. These elements combine to foster environments that support learning, development, and secure ethical conduct: communication, respect, collaboration, adaptability, ethics, reflection, and cultural competence. The foundation of successful supervision is clear and consistent communication, which involves clearly outlining what is expected, providing consistent feedback, and creating open ways to discuss any issues (see Table 2.1).

In applied sport psychology, communication frequently needs to adjust to unpredictable schedules and remote work to ensure clarity and consistency. Supervisors and those they supervise build a strong supervisory relationship by valuing each other's dignity, freedom, and individual skills. It is a respect that embraces different levels of experience and influence, all while appreciating each person's unique insights and viewpoints. Good supervision means using the right amount of authority while also working together, which means involving supervisees in setting goals, reviewing performance, and finding solutions to issues. This partnership shows the advising style that those being supervised will have to use with their clients. By adapting to evolving requirements, situations, and growth phases, supervision stays pertinent and successful. This flexibility is especially crucial in applied sport psychology, given the need to adapt supervision because of seasonal pressures and competition calendars. When there is a shared dedication to ethical conduct and frequent conversations about ethics, supervision effectively protects standards while also helping the supervisee grow. The emphasis on ethics is especially critical in sports, which frequently present specific moral dilemmas. Creating space for reflection, both on clinical work and on the supervision process itself, enhances learning and professional development. Reflective supervision promotes challenging beliefs, considering different viewpoints, and connecting theory and practical application. Finally, it is crucial to recognise and be sensitive to cultural influences on the supervisory relationship and clinical practice. This involves considering variations in cultural norms, beliefs, communication approaches, and perspectives on authority.

Table 2.1 Core Traits of Effective Supervisors

Trait	*Description*	*Why it matters in supervision?*	*Examples in practice*
Self-awareness	Awareness of one's own values, biases, emotional triggers, and limitations.	Prevents blind spots, reduces inappropriate influence, supports ethical decision-making.	Notices irritation towards a supervisee and explores it in meta-supervision rather than reacting.
Reflective capacity	The ability to critically reflect on actions, decisions, and relational processes.	Models reflective practice for supervisees and supports ongoing development.	After a difficult session, writes a reflective note and identifies themes to explore next time.
Emotional attunement	Sensitivity to supervisee emotions and interpersonal signals.	Builds psychological safety and strengthens the supervisory alliance.	Pauses the agenda when noticing supervisee tension and gently explores what is happening.
Competence in theory and practice	Deep knowledge of applied sport psychology, relevant therapeutic models, and supervision frameworks is required.	Ensures accurate guidance, protects client welfare, and prevents overreach.	Helps supervisees refine a case formulation using IDM or the seven-eyed model.
Ethical sensitivity	Ability to identify ethical risks early and respond appropriately.	Protects athletes, supervisees, and organisations; upholds professional standards.	Flags a potential confidentiality breach related to a coach request and guides risk analysis.
Consistency and reliability	Demonstrates predictable scheduling, boundaries, follow-up, and professionalism.	Builds trust and stability within supervision.	Reviews previous goals and shows continuity from session to session.
Constructive feedback skills	Ability to give accurate, balanced, non-defensive, behaviour-specific feedback.	Helps supervisees grow without triggering shame or defensiveness.	Uses specific examples from recordings to illustrate strengths and areas for development.
Ability to manage power responsibly	Awareness of evaluative, gatekeeping, and expert power; transparent use of authority.	Prevents supervisee anxiety, shame, or compliance; promotes collaborative learning.	Explicitly discusses evaluation criteria and invites supervisee feedback on the process.

Trait	*Description*	*Why it matters in supervision?*	*Examples in practice*
Relational flexibility	Adapts relational style to supervisee needs and developmental stage.	Supports supervisees across novice-to-expert transitions.	Provides more structure early on, then shifts to a consultative stance as competence develops.
Cultural humility	Openness to cultural differences and recognition of systemic influences.	Enhances ethical practice and prevents culturally insensitive supervision.	Asks how cultural background influences supervisee–client interactions.
Skill in managing ruptures	Ability to recognise relational breakdowns, address them, and repair them.	Maintains trust, models healthy conflict resolution, and avoids harm.	Names tension in the relationship and invites collaborative repair.
Process awareness (parallel process insight)	Ability to notice when supervisee-client dynamics are replayed in supervision.	Supports deeper understanding and enhances case conceptualisation.	Identifies that the supervisee's avoidance mirrors the athlete's avoidance in sessions.
Commitment to development (supervision-of-supervision)	Engages in ongoing learning, meta-supervision, CPD, and reflective practice.	Prevents stagnation and reinforces supervisory excellence.	Seeks meta-supervision when struggling with evaluative discomfort.
Ability to structure and hold the frame	Establishes and maintains a clear supervision structure, boundaries, and agenda.	Ensures productive sessions, supports safety, and maintains focus on learning.	Uses agenda setting, time management, and goal review consistently.
Calmness under pressure	Maintains emotional regulation during crises or complex ethical dilemmas.	Guides supervisees through high-stress sporting environments.	Supports supervisee through safeguarding crisis without escalating panic.
Commitment to client welfare	Holds athlete well-being as a guiding anchor in supervision decisions.	Ensures supervision aligns with ethical, professional, and legal obligations.	Redirects the supervisee focus from performance-only interventions to holistic well-being.

Association for Counselor Education and Supervision Taskforce on Best Practices in Clinical Supervision (2011).

2.6 Conclusion

The supervisory relationship in applied sport psychology represents a complex, multifaceted phenomenon that serves as the foundation for professional development, ethical practice, and ultimately, effective service delivery to athletes and sport organisations. This chapter has explored the theoretical foundations, practical components, and empirical evidence supporting the critical importance of supervisory relationships in sport psychology training and practice. Integrating attachment theory, working alliance principles, and relational approaches provides a comprehensive framework for understanding supervisory dynamics and their impact on professional development. The evidence clearly shows that strong supervisory relationships serve protective functions against burnout while promoting professional growth, competence development, and career satisfaction. As the field of sport psychology continues to evolve, the importance of high-quality supervision becomes increasingly apparent. The unique challenges and opportunities present in sport environments require supervisors who can navigate complex dynamics while maintaining focus on professional development and ethical practice. The investment in supervisory relationship quality represents an investment in the future of sport psychology as a profession and in the welfare of the athletes and teams we serve.

Exercise 2.1: Working Alliance Self-Assessment

Using Bordin's *goals, tasks, bond* framework:

1. Rate yourself from 1 to 10 on your current contribution to each area.
2. Write one behaviour you currently use that strengthens each component and one that weakens it.
3. Identify one specific action that would enhance your supervisory alliance in the next month.

3 Ethics and Professional Practice in Supervision

3.1 Introduction

Whenever an ethical issue emerges, it is likely that some legal considerations sit just around the corner. Sometimes acting ethically means one breaks the law, and when acting lawfully, one might not act ethically. Our legal liabilities as professionals mean we need to be aware of choices and actions while also acknowledging our ethical responsibility to others (e.g., supervisees, supervisees' clients, professional bodies). In supervision, the supervisor faces challenges related to informed consent, competence, dual roles, due process, evaluation, and vicarious liability (Borders & Brown, 2022). These challenges weave across the supervision term, bringing us back to our standards and ethics for applied sport psychology practice to guide our choices and actions.

As practitioners, most will be familiar with their responsibilities to the client, such as safety, respect for client autonomy, competence, non-exploitation, confidentiality, privacy, record-keeping, evaluation of services, and supervision. Regrettably, attending to the safety and well-being of the client often slips from its primary position. Sometimes this slip-up happens because we need to decide who receives our services when the demand exceeds supply. At other times, we may sit at the foot of an organisation whose primary interests diverge from the client's safety and well-being, or the sport psychology practitioner's needs supersede those of the clients. One critical goal of supervision and professional practice remains to stay on track with constructive support for ethical challenges, challenge and support colleagues to maintain safe practice, and remain ethically mindful (Reeves & Bond, 2021).

In practical terms, ethical and professional practice in supervision in applied sport psychology requires supervisors and supervisees to gather a comprehensive knowledge of professional codes and regulatory frameworks that govern supervisory relationships. The unique nature of sport environments, with their emphasis on performance, competition, and public visibility, creates distinct ethical challenges that supervisors and

DOI: 10.4324/9781003485667-3

supervisees must navigate skilfully. In short, effective supervision in applied sport psychology means adhering to established ethical principles and effective practices while adapting to the dynamic and often unpredictable world of athletic performance. For these reasons, the intersection of ethics, professional practice, and sports creates unique challenges for supervision relationships, particularly when working with high-profile athletes, team dynamics, and organisational pressures (Andersen, 1994). Professional ethical guidelines in applied sport psychology provide the foundation for responsible supervision practices, yet their application requires a nuanced understanding of theoretical frameworks and practical realities.

This chapter explores the complex landscape of ethical supervision in applied sport psychology, examining foundational principles, regulatory requirements, and practical strategies for maintaining the highest standards of professional practice. From managing dual relationships to navigating confidentiality concerns, supervisors must develop sophisticated ethical reasoning skills that protect supervisees and the athletes they serve.

3.2 Ethical Frameworks and Codes of Conduct Governing Supervision

Multiple overlapping frameworks also ground ethics in applied sport psychology supervision and offer comprehensive guidance for professional practice. The British Psychological Society (BPS, 2021), for example, has established a foundational ethical framework built on four fundamental principles that govern all psychological practice, including applied sport psychology supervision: respect, competence, responsibility, and integrity. These principles form the cornerstone of ethical practice and serve as the primary reference point for supervisory decision-making. The principle of respect encompasses recognition of the inherent dignity and worth of all individuals involved in the supervisory process. This principle includes respect for supervisee autonomy, cultural diversity, and individual differences in learning styles and professional development needs. In applied sport psychology contexts, respect extends to understanding the unique pressures and demands faced by supervisees and the athletes they serve. Supervisors must show cultural competence and sensitivity to the diverse backgrounds and experiences that characterise modern sports environments. Competence requires supervisors to practise within their areas of expertise while continuously developing their knowledge, skills, and attitudes (Goldberg et al., 2016). This principle expects supervisors to maintain a current understanding of applied sport psychology practice and supervision methods. The rapidly growing nature of psychology, sport science, and coaching requires ongoing professional development to ensure that supervision remains relevant and effective. Supervisors must honestly assess their limitations and seek consultation or refer supervisees to more appropriate supervisors when necessary. The principle of responsibility emphasises the supervisor's obligation to promote the welfare of supervisees, clients, and the broader profession. This principle includes creating safe learning environments, providing appropriate support and challenge, and maintaining awareness of the broader effects of supervisory decisions. In applied sport psychology, responsibility extends to understanding how supervision quality affects not only individual practitioners but also the athletes, teams, and organisations they serve (Ooijen & Spencer, 2017). Integrity requires honesty, transparency, and consistency in all professional interactions. Supervisors ought to model ethical behaviour, acknowledge mistakes, and maintain clear boundaries between personal and professional relationships. The high-visibility nature of sports environments makes integrity particularly crucial, as ethical lapses can have far-reaching consequences for both individuals and the profession.

Besides the British Psychological Society, the Association for Applied Sport Psychology (AASP) provides additional ethical guidance specifically tailored to applied sport psychology practice. The AASP Ethics Code tackles specific issues in sports, such as multiple relationships, confidentiality within team settings, and the relationship between performance improvement and mental health care. These guidelines emphasise the importance of clear role definition, appropriate boundary management, and ongoing ethical reflection in supervisory relationships. The International Society of Sport Psychology (ISSP) provides international perspectives on ethics in sport psychology supervision, emphasising cultural safety, inclusive practice approaches, and recognising diverse perspectives in supervision. The ISSP position highlights the importance of culturally appropriate supervision methods and the need for supervisors to develop cultural competence that extends beyond their own cultural backgrounds (Poczwardowski et al., 2023).

Professional ethical guidelines in applied sport psychology also cover the unique challenges of working in performance environments that may test traditional therapeutic boundaries. The emphasis on winning, public scrutiny, and organisational pressures creates ethical dilemmas that require sophisticated reasoning and clear professional guidelines. Supervisors must help supervisees navigate these challenges while maintaining their professional identity and ethical commitments. Integrating multiple ethical frameworks requires supervisors to develop a nuanced understanding of how different codes (e.g., APA, BPS) and principles interact in practice. When conflicts arise between different ethical guidelines, supervisors need to engage in careful ethical reasoning that considers the specific context, stakeholder interests, and potential consequences of different courses of action. This process often involves consultation with colleagues, ethics committees, or professional organisations to ensure that decisions align with the highest standards of professional practice.

3.3 Legal and Regulatory Considerations

Applying ethical standards in psychology to sport contexts requires specialised knowledge of the legal and regulatory landscape that governs professional practice. The Health and Care Professions Council (HCPC) provides the primary regulatory framework for practitioner psychologists in the UK, establishing mandatory requirements that directly affect supervision practices in sport psychology. The HCPC Standards of Proficiency require practitioners to practise within their scope of competence, regularly assess their practice limitations, manage their workload effectively, and maintain appropriate professional boundaries. These requirements create specific obligations for supervisors, who must ensure that supervisees understand and comply with regulatory expectations while developing their professional competence (Reeves & Bond, 2021).

These professional regulations form part of the overall legal and regulatory landscape, but legal considerations in applied sport psychology supervision also include broader legal frameworks governing privacy, data protection, and duty of care. The General Data Protection Regulation (GDPR) (2016) creates specific obligations for how one collects, stores, and shares personal information in supervisory relationships. Supervisors need to ensure that they and their supervisees understand these requirements and implement safeguards to protect sensitive information. Duty of care represents a fundamental legal principle that shapes supervisory relationships. Supervisors have legal obligations to provide competent supervision, monitor supervisees' practice, and intervene when necessary to protect client welfare. This duty extends to ensuring that supervisees are adequately prepared for their responsibilities and that appropriate support is available when challenging situations arise. The legal framework surrounding confidentiality in applied sport psychology supervision is complex because of the team-based nature of many sport environments and supervisees working within different organisational settings (e.g., Olympic sport, professional sports team). Legal requirements for maintaining confidentiality need to be balanced with practical needs for communication and coordination within sport organisations. Supervisors should help supervisees understand when they can breach confidentiality legally and ethically, and how to navigate these situations professionally.

Professional indemnity insurance represents another crucial legal consideration for applied sport psychology supervisors. Insurance requirements vary depending on employment status, practice setting, and specific roles and responsibilities. Supervisors must ensure that they and their supervisees maintain insurance coverage and understand the limitations and requirements of their policies. Legal considerations also extend to the documentation and record-keeping requirements that govern supervisory relationships. Legal standards for documentation vary depending on the setting and nature of the supervisory relationship, but generally require clear, accurate, and timely recording of supervisory activities. These records may be subject to legal scrutiny in cases of professional misconduct or malpractice claims. The intersection of legal and ethical requirements sometimes creates tensions that supervisors must navigate carefully. Legal compliance represents the minimum standard for professional practice, while ethical guidelines often require higher standards of care and responsibility. Supervisors must help supervisees understand these distinctions and develop the judgement necessary to exceed legal minimums while fulfilling their ethical obligations. International legal considerations become relevant for supervisors working with supervisees who practise across national boundaries or with international athletes and teams. Different countries have varying legal frameworks governing psychological practice, confidentiality, and professional responsibility. Supervisors must be aware of these differences and help supervisees navigate the complex legal landscape of international sport psychology practice.

3.4 Dual Roles

Dual roles comprise multiple relationship types, which may compromise one's professional judgement or the professional role itself (Corey et al., 1998). Borders and Brown (2022) outlined three types of dual roles: social, sexual, and therapeutic. In applied sport psychology, especially those in training in a university doctoral programme, will likely encounter a university supervisor with overlapping social roles. For instance, a university supervisor will likely teach a supervisee, perhaps supervise a research project, and act as a coordinator for practicum placements. Though a supervisor might hold these roles, it is possible to separate them and minimise conflict. The APA Ethics Code offers guidance on how to handle multiple relationships, accentuating the importance of carefully examining professional connections, assessing any potential imbalances of power, and periodically reviewing the limits of those relationships. Outside university doctoral programmes, those undertaking independent routes of training are also likely to meet a supervisor with dual roles. What matters most is maintaining objectivity regarding the knowledge, skills, and attitudes of the supervisee. After all, a supervisory relationship focuses on the personal and professional development of the supervisee.

Though a supervisor and a supervisee might develop a friendship because of their common interests (e.g., profession, sport, sports team), the possibility of a sexual relationship means supervision has taken a wrong turn and ought to be examined. A supervisor might be attracted to a supervisee, or a supervisee might be attracted to a supervisor. At that point, exploring those feelings in supervision helps assess their origin and learn from them (e.g., transference or countertransference), allowing the supervisor and supervisee to assess the status of their supervisory relationship and how to avoid this type of dual relationship.

Therapeutic dual roles find their way into supervisory relationships, especially because personal issues crop up in supervision for professional growth. It seems natural for a supervisor to respond to a supervisee as one might in therapeutic work with a client without realising it. The guidance, however, is that this relationship is supervisory, not therapeutic. A supervisor's counselling skills might form part of a self-awareness process to understand how one's personal issues might influence professional working.

These dual roles mean the supervisor and supervisee need to consider the potential for exploitation, impaired judgement, or harm to the supervisory relationship. For instance, supervisors hold significant authority over supervisees' professional development, and power imbalances are likely to crop up. Where the power imbalance tips overwhelmingly towards the supervisor because of an additional relationship with the supervisee, a supervisee might feel reluctant to share concerns, offer feedback, or disagree with their supervisor. A sensitive supervisor creates opportunities to allow the supervisees to share concerns about the supervisory relationship and untangle any issues with other roles. Maintaining an open dialogue will allow supervisors and supervisees to maintain boundaries for each role and resolve conflicts as they arise.

On other occasions, a supervisor might employ or share roles with a supervisee within an organisation (e.g., professional football academy). This dual role needs to be clear and separated from the processes of supervision because the financial dependency created by employment could raise conflicts of interest that compromise the supervisor's ability to offer clear, honest feedback and recognise and report on the supervisee's competence.

Applied sport psychologists represent a small community relative to other professions (e.g., coaching, physiotherapy, medicine) and a few qualified supervisors within a region might mean multiple relationships are inevitable. When faced with these scenarios, supervisors should clearly define limits, get advice when issues arise, and explore different ways of managing the work if needed. To address some of these challenges, supervisors need support because navigating these challenges alone can be overwhelming. By consulting professionals within the field, seeking peer supervision, and using ethics committees, supervisors can gain helpful viewpoints on handling challenging dual relationships, all while adhering to ethical guidelines and providing effective supervision.

3.5 Competence

A primary role of a supervisor in a supervisory relationship is to address the competency level of the supervisee (Gaete & Strong, 2017). Equally, this responsibility means that the supervisor ought to assess and reflect upon their experience and training within these competency limits. Some supervisors might feel their experience as a practising sport psychologist means they meet the competencies to supervise. Yet, on further exploration, without a clear and detailed knowledge of supervision, its processes, and responsibilities, one cannot serve their supervisees appropriately (Fogaça et al., 2020). Within the British Psychological Society, for instance, competency remains a fundamental principle with an obligation for supervisors to assess, develop, and maintain competency in themselves and their supervisees. A snapshot of the technical competencies related to assessment, formulation, intervention, and evaluation will also include ethical reasoning, cultural awareness, and professional communication. The supervisor must source and administer reliable methods to assess competencies and track supervisee competency development. The developmental nature of competency also means skills develop gradually through experience, reflection, and guidance, requiring supervisors to scaffold and support at the beginning of a supervisee's training and prepare for greater supervisee responsibility and autonomy.

On a broader note, supervisors and supervisees need to attend to cultural competency, ethical reasoning, boundaries, communication, self-awareness, record-keeping, and professional development. We shall briefly explore these competencies here and expand upon them in other chapters within this text. To begin, given the diverse backgrounds of athletes, coaches, and support staff in sport settings and the international nature of sport itself, supervisors need to assess and develop their own cultural competence while helping supervisees develop awareness of their cultural biases, knowledge of diverse cultural perspectives, and skills for working effectively across cultural differences. To make ethical decisions, supervisors should recognise ethical problems, consider conflicting values, and find suitable solutions to ethical challenges. Together with a supervisee, they might choose case discussions, role-playing, or guided discussions to develop reasoning skills, especially in complex and uncertain situations.

Setting boundaries means one ought to acknowledge the challenges of relationships with clients and organisations and an awareness of power dynamics, conflicts of interest, dual roles, and so forth. Competent supervisors display healthy boundaries, helping supervisees to gain an awareness of their boundaries and how to manage them. Aligned with healthy boundaries are skills to communicate effectively with various stakeholders, such as athletes, coaches, parents, and organisational administrators. Ethical communication thrives with honesty, respect, cultural sensitivity, and the professional skills to explain complex psychological concepts in accessible language. At the heart of the supervisee's development lies self-awareness, which involves understanding one's own values, biases, limitations, and emotional reactions in professional situations. A lack of self-awareness might mean one is likely to impose their values on clients, miss important cultural dynamics, or become involved in boundary violations.

From an administrative level, keeping records of supervision, competencies achieved, and professional development activities means meeting professional requirements and providing evidence of competency for regulatory bodies or employers. In brief, supervisors and supervisees need to consistently learn, ask for guidance when facing challenges, and acknowledge their own shortcomings. Keeping up with the changes in applied sport psychology, codes of conduct, and professional standards requires ongoing learning to ensure competence and ethical service delivery.

3.6 Informed Consent

In supervision, the client and the supervisee must give their consent to the supervisory process (Ellis, 2017). First, the client should be informed about the supervision process, and second, the supervisee should know the expectations and duties involved in the supervisory process. In the therapeutic process, the informed consent process establishes clear expectations, boundaries, and agreements between the client and the psychologist. In a similar vein, the supervisory process also outlines essential elements of informed consent, such as a clear service description, risk and benefit disclosure, and documents that reflect the characteristics of the service. Informed consent and contracting serve several purposes, such as establishing clear expectations for the relationship, mitigating misunderstandings, and for both parties to recognise their rights and responsibilities. The consent process is ongoing rather than a one-off event, with lots of opportunities to review and update agreements as the relationship develops. Contracts typically include details about session frequency, length, and structure, and outline what supervisors expect supervisees to prepare, participate in, and adhere to regarding supervision recommendations (Townend, 2005). The process of obtaining consent should include details about the supervisor's credentials, experience, and supervisory methods.

Because supervision encompasses evaluation (i.e., formative and summative), supervisees need to know about the process of evaluation. For instance, how will my supervisor assess my performance as a supervisee working with clients? Which criteria comprise my evaluation? How will my supervisor document and communicate my progress and any outcomes from our supervisory relationship? This information allows a supervisee to make an informed decision about their supervision (Falender, 2014). In line with this outline, supervisors need to share what supervision and the supervisor can offer, and what it cannot. One might assume that as a supervisee, one will develop knowledge, skills, and attitudes to perform well in service delivery, yet overlook potential conflicts with a supervisor, stress of evaluation, feeling unsupported, and so forth that can arise in a supervisory relationship. The consent process should also detail the actions taken if the supervisory relationship fails, including how to request a different supervisor, the procedures involved, and how to move to a new supervisor.

When training with regulatory bodies and organisations, supervisees understand they will keep some supervision information confidential and disclose other information. Supervisees must understand what information will be shared for organisational, legal, and professional purposes, which may affect the privacy of confidential information. Supervision usually means a financial commitment for the services of the supervisor. These fees must be transparent during the consent process, with the usual policies for payment, missed sessions, and any additional costs of supervision. Some supervisors do not charge for their services, but each party should know the challenges of such commitments in time and emotional labour as part of the supervisory relationship. The consent procedure should explain how to reach a supervisor outside of normal working hours. For instance, this contact agreement could have an emergency plan. Supervisees need to know what constitutes an emergency and which resources are available if one's supervisor is unavailable. When regular supervision is not in place, these emergencies may happen in applied sport psychology, such as during training, travel, or competitions.

Written agreements between a supervisor and a supervisee capture the key elements of a supervisory relationship. When each party signs the written agreement, they do so with an understanding of their commitments. These agreements are not static and can change according to the needs of the developing supervisory relationship. Supervision often incorporates technologies for scheduling supervision, videoconferencing, and digital record-keeping systems, so each party needs to know how electronic communications are shared and stored.

3.7 Evaluation

Supervisors play a critical evaluative role in the supervisory process to allow supervisees to grow personally and professionally as applied sport psychologists. A central feature of this evaluative role is to provide feedback on the principles and practices of the supervisee's work. Formative and summative evaluations are typical for those in training and form part of the assessment process for those seeking accreditation. To achieve these aims, however, supervisors meet regularly with their supervisees (e.g., face-to-face, online) to allow supervisees to review and discuss their client work. These meetings offer a conduit for constructive feedback, integrating formative evaluations as supervisees work through their tasks to achieve their goals. Oral and written feedback to the supervisee, structured around personal and professional strengths and areas of development, allows supervisees to practise safely within their current abilities in service delivery. From an ethical standpoint, supervision notes allow the supervisor to track changes over time in the supervisee's personal and professional development. At the end of the supervisory period, a paper trail of supervision and its processes allows the supervisee and supervisor to observe the professional, responsible, and accountable standards undertaken. If one were to legally account for their actions during supervision, this documentation would attest to the process.

3.8 Consultation

Working as a supervisor might amount to a significant proportion of one's working week. Supervision, alongside one's therapeutic practice, might mean a slide towards professional isolation for the supervisor – something to avoid proactively (Borders & Brown, 2022). One way to reduce professional isolation is to connect with fellow supervisors regularly to maintain safe, ethical, and professional standards in training and supervision. It is likely that from time to time a supervisee will present complex client cases, or perhaps the supervisee is not setting and maintaining ethical and professional standards. Consultation with a peer offers perspective on the content of the problem and the process between the supervisor and the supervisee that a supervisor might not see. Peer supervision of supervision might involve a peer supervision group where supervisors share experiences of supervision with peers, offer constructive feedback and suggestions for intervention. Maybe the supervisees have specific training needs, but also the supervisor gains insight into supervisory skills they need to develop themselves.

3.9 Managing Ethical Dilemmas and Violations

Examining ethical issues in applied sport psychology reveals the intricate nature of dilemmas supervisors face, encompassing everything from minor boundary issues to significant breaches that jeopardise a client's well-being and a professional's reputation (Moore, 2003). To manage these situations successfully, logical procedures, proper consultation, and decisive action when needed are essential. Supervisors in applied sport psychology often face ethical challenges, such as the conflict between protecting a client's privacy and sharing information with a team, the distinction between improving performance and providing mental health support, and the complexities of managing various relationships within the close sport environment. In any of these situations, an ethical dilemma brings a tug-of-war amongst ethical principles and professional obligations, and any decision means a compromise of ethical values. Above all, thorough analysis, consultation, reflection, and documentation of how we decide are crucial.

Supervisors are responsible for addressing ethical violations that are reported, but they must also remain aware of potential ethical concerns while fostering a safe environment for supervisees to voice their worries. This secure environment enables the early detection of ethical concerns, allowing for proactive collaboration to prevent situations from escalating into severe breaches. For supervisees in training, supervisors could offer education about common ethical warning signs and highlight procedures and protocols for raising and managing ethical concerns.

Ethical concerns range from minor (e.g., boundary confusion) to serious (e.g., sexual misconduct). While most minor concerns offer a chance to learn for supervisees and prevent escalation, some serious ethical violations will involve reporting to professional bodies or legal authorities. Addressing small ethical dilemmas happens during supervision or further training to foster a helpful educational space; however, immediate interventions are necessary for serious ethical violations such as breach of confidentiality, practising beyond one's competence or sexual misconduct. It is the responsibility of supervisors to know their reporting duties for ethical issues and to act even if it means damaging the supervisory relationship or the supervisee's career.

The process for reporting ethical misconduct is determined by your professional organisation (such as BPS, HCPC, or APA) and the policies of your workplace. Client safety is paramount, and this includes reporting the issue to the appropriate agencies, as well as keeping a record of the breach and the response. Due process dictates supervisors must treat a supervisee accused of ethical breaches justly when they face this kind of situation. This means that the supervisor informs the supervisee of the accusations, the supervisee responds, and the supervisee receives adequate representation or support. It is the supervisor's job to protect clients and their profession, to be fair to those supervised, and to foster supervisee professional growth.

3.10 Conclusion

The ethical landscape of applied sport psychology supervision represents a complex intersection of professional principles, legal requirements, and practical challenges that require a sophisticated understanding and skilful navigation. This chapter has explored the foundational frameworks that guide ethical practice, from the fundamental principles established by professional bodies to the specific challenges created by sport environments and technological innovations. Integrating multiple ethical frameworks – including principle-based approaches, virtue ethics, and care ethics – provides supervisors with comprehensive tools for addressing the diverse challenges they encounter. The application of these frameworks, however, requires ongoing development of ethical reasoning skills, cultural competence, and practical wisdom that can only be developed through experience, reflection, and consultation with colleagues. The future of ethical supervision in applied sport psychology will require continued attention to cultural competence, international practice standards, and emerging technologies. Professional bodies, training programmes, and individual practitioners must work together to develop and maintain ethical standards that protect clients, support practitioner development, and advance the profession's commitment to excellence and integrity.

Exercise 3.1: Ethical Dilemma Walkthrough

Choose one ethically complex situation common in sport (e.g., a coach demands confidential information, a dual relationship in an academy, or performance pressure from a director).

With the six-step ethical reasoning model:

1. Identify the ethical principles involved.
2. Map the stakeholders and potential harms.
3. Identify constraints (legal, organisational, cultural).
4. Propose three actions.
5. Describe the supervision conversation you would start.
6. Conclude with the *most defensible* ethical response.

4 Being a Good Enough Supervisee

4.1 Introduction

Reaching the stage of engaging in supervision signals that the supervisee already possesses, in Herbert's words, a *capacity* for learning. With any new role, an element of learning and adaptation is required. The role of the supervisee is no different. Although the importance of developing the *ability* to learn within the supervisory relationship is well documented, limited guidance about how to do this exists, particularly in sport and exercise settings (Enlow et al., 2019; Hutter et al., 2015; Oddli et al., 2021).

Supervisees will often enter their applied training (and supervision) following a long journey through education, where traditional 'student-teacher' relationships characterised by authority, expertise provision and hierarchy are dominant. Parallels exist between this student-teacher and supervisee-supervisor relationship; however, notable differences also emerge, often representing a period of transition for the supervisee. Crucially, supervision demands a more active and engaged approach to learning from the supervisee. For example, in student-teacher settings, learning content (e.g., topics) and delivery style (e.g., presentations) are predominantly selected by the 'teacher'. Supervisors may at times guide conversations towards core themes (see Chapter 10); however, it is broadly the responsibility of the supervisee to identify learning needs, developmental goals and session content and manage the learning relationship. Proctor (1994) highlighted the value of developing such supervisee know-how for becoming an effective applied practitioner, especially given the high presence of performative anxiety and role confusion that is likely to accompany the process of beginning applied and supervisory practice.

So, what constitutes a 'good enough' or, dare we say it, 'good' supervisee? And how can you explore learning in supervision? In this chapter, we address these questions by outlining the core components of effective supervision from the supervisee's perspective. We explore how to consider one's developmental stage, identify learning goals, and consider the contextual factors that help to establish the scaffolding to learn how to use

DOI: 10.4324/9781003485667-4

supervision. We will focus on developing a learning agreement, establishing boundaries, and preparing for supervision sessions.

4.2 Writing a Learning Agreement

A useful starting point is collaboratively creating a learning agreement. Here the onus is shifted from the formalities and administrative aspects of contracting to the practicalities of establishing what the supervisee is seeking from the supervisory relationship. Investing time in learning agreements provides several benefits:

1. Practical experience: Like several supervisee-supervisor processes, the learning agreement process mirrors that of the client-psychologist. It provides an opportunity to develop a therapeutic relationship, gather and establish needs and effective ways of working, and identify any potential barriers to learning and development.
2. Setting yourself up for success: Research has highlighted that supervisees who complete this process report greater satisfaction in the establishment and maintenance of the supervisory relationship, motivation, and engagement – in their own development and interaction with relevant material (Watkins & Scaturo, 2014). Factors that combine are predictors of the development into an ethical, effective, and successful applied practitioner.
3. Accountability: Establishing a clear learning agreement provides a reference point for both parties, hopefully instilling a sense of ownership in the supervisee. Further, it ensures there is a mutual understanding of needs and expectations, increasing the likelihood of congruent behaviour and reducing the probability of any rupturing events (e.g., incongruent expectations) (Watkins et al., 2024).

There are differences between a learning agreement and a contract. Learning agreements are not intended to be rigid, binding ways of working. Instead, we view learning agreements as a facilitative framework to situate supervision, acting as a prompt for relational development and understanding. Both parties should feel they can adapt, deviate, and evolve to improve the learning experience, regularly attuning to changes in developmental needs. The point, therefore, is to emphasise the relevance of asking questions and begin developing the self-awareness and reflection-based skills that guide applied practitioner development, while empowering the supervisee to shape their environment.

4.2.1 Learning Goals

Identifying learning goals, or intentions, helps establish what you are trying to get out of this relationship. Learning needs of applied sport and exercise psychologists differ significantly based on the psychologists' developmental stage and prior experiences (McEwan & Tod, 2015). Early literature on psychologists' developmental stages in sporting contexts emanated from counselling and clinical models (Tod, 2007). However, recent trends in sport psychology literature argue that significant differences in developmental trajectories exist between the respective fields (McEwan et al., 2019; Fogaca et al., 2020). Exploring the full range of developmental models is beyond the scope of this chapter. In light of this, we will provide a brief overview of Fogaca et al.'s (2024) model of development for sport psychology. Fogaca et al.'s paper represents their synthesis of psychologist developmental models and therefore may also act as a reference point for further reading and exploration. We will then consider some more general recommendations for considering developmental stages in supervision originating primarily from counselling sources.

Following a systematic review, Fogaca et al. (2024) identified four key developmental phases, namely introduction, exploration, solidification, and fulfilment. To progress through each phase, practitioner psychologists are required to engage in four inter-related processes: supervision, reflection, learning by doing, and connections and networking with peers. Within each process, some argue nine core elements (purpose, confidence and anxiety, focus, awareness, adaptability, independence, philosophy/congruence, professional identity, and the individual) should be attended to. A progressive model within each element is indicated corresponding to a phase of development. For example, in relation to dependence, in the introduction phase practitioners are perceived as dependent. In this early phase, practitioners will often seek direct guidance or feedback around elements of service delivery, utilising more information-provision or practitioner-led approaches. As the practitioner progresses into the exploration stage, a degree of ambivalence is suggested to emerge, internalising their supervisor's voice. In the subsequent phase, practitioners are considered independent – they may have trust in their own capabilities to operate functionally in the environment, seeking a combination of autonomy and flexibility alongside supervisory observation and guidance (Quartiroli et al., 2019). In the final phase, fulfilment, practitioners are argued to come full circle, possessing a capacity to offer mentoring and support to other young professionals.

Intriguingly, linear pedagogical models are often presented, despite growth and development rarely being a linear process. Supervisees should be cautious of addressing learning goals associated with any length of engagement or based on 'experience level', taking developmental stages with a pinch of salt, and being willing to move forwards or backwards based on their current setting and circumstances. The requirement to take stead is exacerbated by the individual nature of developmental progression; supervisees may find themselves highly competent in one 'theme' or 'trait' or lagging on another based on factors such as age, cognitive capacity, and previous learning (McEwan et al., 2019). Developmental models, while helpful in providing guidance, are presented rigidly, often obscuring the individual perspective of the trainee. A simplistic counterbalance to this is Hawkins and Shoet's (2000) four-tier offering based on Stoltenberg and Delworth's (1987) work.

Level 1: self-centred ('How do I make this work?')
Level 2: client-centred ('How can I support the client to create change?')
Level 3: process-centred ('How are the client and I relating to one another?')
Level 4: process-in-context-centred ('How is the environment impacting our work?')

This model, while simplistic, highlights that while the *learning goal* of the supervisee may not differ substantially, it is their focus that will. It is also implied that learning, development, and experience elicit changes in the questions supervisees can explore.

The initial process of formulating and expressing functional learning goals has been observed as challenging for supervisees, particularly early in their supervision journey (Carroll, 1996). Common challenges include a general ambiguity and vagueness e.g., 'I would like to be a great psychologist' or a naivety or lack of awareness around the complexity or time required for the task at hand e.g., 'I want to become an expert in injury'. This is often coupled with an understandable lack of certainty, particularly for new supervisees, as without a clear awareness of the landscape, it is difficult to determine how to progress. To counteract this Gonsalves and Calvert (2014) proposed a competency-based framework to developing learning goals, utilising SMART (specific, measurable, achievable, relevant, and time-bound) goal setting, a way of operating highly familiar to those in sport and exercise contexts (Bird et al., 2024). Learning goals will likely therefore be tied to intended developmental outcomes or end-of-service competencies (i.e., knowledge acquisition) or regulatory guidelines from relevant institutions (i.e., HCPC or BPS), while providing coverage of a comprehensive range of personal and professional development themes.

4.2.2 Learning Preferences

Having established learning goals 'the what', a second consideration is your learning preferences and how these might play out in supervision 'the how'. In entering a supervisory dyad, both individuals bring with them a range of delivery preferences, and it is beneficial to tailor the relationship towards these, regularly gathering feedback (Norcross & Wampold, 2011). While not the critical determinant of supervisory development, compatibility in learning and supervisory style (i.e., approaches and interpersonal attitudes) can enhance the supervisory relationship and, in turn, the effectiveness of the supervision process (i.e., competency acquisition). To a certain extent, compatibility will emerge organically, with the supervisee and supervisor attuning (or not) to one another's style and way of being.

However, initially the responsibility lies with the supervisee to express their preferences, sharing their story through learning (or at least snippets of it)! Learning preferences exist in relation to numerous components of learning, including learning style and directiveness, engagement and interpersonal style, structure and organisation, degree of care and support, and feedback mechanisms and challenge. For example, Lochner and Melchert (1997) illustrated that task-oriented supervision is preferred by behaviourally oriented supervisees, while relationship-oriented supervision was more effective for those with stronger interpersonal orientations. Providing this initial feedback on learning preferences then gives the supervisor a guide on where to interact from. The following exercise presents reflective questions designed to promote learning preference identification.

4.2.3 Administrative, Contextual, and Cultural Influences

A final component of a learning agreement entails reflections on the administrative, contextual, and cultural influences (or demands) perceived by the supervisee, considering any impact these might have on supervision. For example, being an applied sport and exercise psychologist (in training or once qualified) is rarely a role that occurs in silos, with practitioners often undertaking numerous roles (directly relevant to supervision or otherwise) simultaneously (Waumsley et al., 2010). In doing so, supervisees may compromise their capacity to source relevant or applied career progression opportunities (Fitzpatrick et al., 2016), face challenges with boundary blurring or role clarity (Jones, Evans & Mullen, 2007; Williams & Andersen, 2012), or become overwhelmed by organisational demands (Chandler et al., 2016). Such influences may disrupt a supervisee's capacity to engage meaningfully in supervision because of the availability of relevant content or holding the emotional bandwidth to engage with material purposefully.

Supervisees are people too – holding a range of different contextual markers and experiences that enter the supervisory dyad. Hindes and Andrews (2011) review of gender in the supervisory relationship highlighted differences that occur in supervisory interactions based on the gender of the supervisor and supervisee. Similar findings have been identified in limited explorations of other socio-cultural and contextual variables (i.e., ethnicity, age, and religion). However, variable impact is observed to be negated when open discussions are facilitated (Cheon et al., 2009). Proactively considering these influences is therefore a critical feature of becoming a good enough supervisee. This section by no means provides an exhaustive list of considerations for a learning agreement. It is hoped, though, to provide a framework that enables open, honest and authentic conversations between supervisee and supervisor, while opening the door for vulnerability. Throughout your engagement in supervision, it would be typical to re-visit learning agreements, tailoring them to suit your changing development needs.

4.3 Boundaries

Applied psychology practice requires practitioners to establish and maintain clear, professional boundaries. In sport and exercise contexts, endeavours (both inadvertently and maliciously) to blur and stretch boundaries are commonplace, rendering boundary issues a common ethical dilemma attended to in supervision (Stapleton et al., 2010). The responsibility with the supervisee in the first instance, then lies with understanding boundaries in the applied context. Boundaries particularly tested in applied sporting contexts include the management of time, space, and communication. Sport psychology practice often occurs in non-traditional counselling environments (i.e., occurring pitch-side vs in a traditional office setting), varies significantly in duration (i.e., rarely the 50-minute therapeutic hour), and includes more informal communication opportunities (i.e., updates/messages). These discrepancies are often expectations of effective consulting in the sporting environment and thus require additional caution and attention to detail. Failure to maintain boundaries constitutes a breach of regulatory guidelines and is therefore imperative for practitioners. Supervision can then be utilised as a platform for monitoring boundaries, proactively considering areas in which they may be compromised by either yourself or the client. It is the supervisee's responsibility to endeavour to set boundaries effectively, alongside proactively raising concerns for discussion should they arise.

A secondary exploration of boundaries for the supervisee is how they are maintained in the supervisory relationship. Psychologist development requires the continual pursuit of both personal and professional exploration. Personal development can naively be interpreted as unnecessary for effective practice; however, with our personal qualities and characteristics underpinning the delivery of ethical effective practice (i.e., enhanced therapeutic relationships, therapeutic outcomes and decision making) and, to, unethical or compromised practice (i.e., transference/countertransference, inappropriate boundary maintenance; Verner et al., 2021; Winstone & Gervis, 2006). In allied psychology professions, trainees are often required to undertake personal therapy (i.e., UK counselling psychology trainees are required to complete 40 hours of personal therapy; British Psychological Society, DATE). Despite the benefits, mandates on personal therapy are currently not extended to sport and exercise psychology training routes (Kumari, 2011). A proverbial gate is opened, with greater personal exploration facilitated in applied sport supervision. Supervisees are thus tasked with considering areas in which their personal characteristics or experiences are influencing their practice, contemplating the appropriateness of exploration in their supervisory relationship, and engaging in discourse on seeking personal therapy themselves.

4.4 Preparation for Supervision

In preparing to prepare for supervision, it is important to establish supervisee responsibilities and their manifestation in supervisee behaviour. Preparation for supervision is documented as a critical determinant of effective supervision and primary supervisor expectations (Creaner, 2014; Meijen & Manley, 2010). Guidance about what 'preparation' entails is woven through narratives concerning supervision and includes topics such as the maintenance of progress notes, critical reflection and examination of one's own strengths and weaknesses and the honest provision of information regarding content or ethical dilemmas (Poczwardowski et al., 2023; Van Raalte & Andersen, 2021). Here, we will break preparation into three concepts; practical preparation - the organisation of resources and content, psychological preparation – the readiness to engage in supervision and distinguishing between 'wants' and 'needs' – the capacity to balance your own desires from supervision with your supervisors' perspectives on your development.

4.4.1 Practical Preparation

The focus of supervision is on you and your work. Ensuring the practicalities of supervision are met ahead of time thus provides the opportunity to address relevant content in a comprehensive and efficient manner. Simplistically, this involves tasks such as

- Creating and sharing an agenda for the session.
- Organising appropriate content (e.g., intervention designs or client session recordings).
- Engaging in reflective practice (e.g., reflecting on the processes involved in your practice or facets of the therapeutic relationship).
- Evidencing engagement in your development (e.g., exploring relevant literature).

4.4.2 Psychological Preparation

The psychological facet of preparation entails ensuring your readiness for the opportunities and challenges of supervision. You will be expected to bring a psychological openness, demonstrate a capacity to take initiative, an interpersonal curiosity, a degree of psychological flexibility (personally and professionally) and a reflective or introspective capacity (Berger & Bucholz, 1993). Psychological readiness for supervision therefore necessitates engagement in reflective practice (Knowles et al., 2007). For example, to successfully bring the required degree of openness and authenticity, supervisees will need to explore their own utilisation of strategic withholding – a deliberate non-disclosure because of perceived consequences, alongside their strategies to combat the experience (Gibson et al., 2019). Supervisees often receive supervision 'in-house' (within their educational training programme or organisational contexts), where strategic withholding is suggested to be more prevalent because of implications on educational or career progression. In these settings, closer consideration of potential withholding behaviours and mitigating approaches should be completed by the supervisee.

It is here that the concept of being 'good enough' may challenge the supervisee. Supervisees may regularly question: *what am I bringing to the table or am I enough?* Regularly challenging oneself on how successfully one is truly engaging in learning and development, bringing an appropriate attitude and responsibility for learning, and criticality to their practice is part of the professional development process. Supervisees will make mistakes! Perfectionism is a trait that practitioners regularly support clients with (Watson, 2025). Psychological preparedness may include un-burdening oneself of the metaphorical shackles themselves. Instead, supervisees may seek to ask themselves: Am I doing the best I can?

4.5 Distinguishing between 'Wants' and 'Needs' and Vice Versa

A third skill for effective preparation is developing the capacity to distinguish between one's 'wants' and 'needs' and vice versa. The learning agreement will have helped establish the learning goals. Balancing needs and wants allows the supervisee to accelerate the mechanism of achieving these. Competently addressing the supervisees' wants is logical from a relational and pragmatic perspective. Relationally, a lack of want-oriented support may elicit disillusionment, impede continued engagement, and reduce supervisee motivation. Pragmatically, the supervisee is the only one truly experiencing their work and so is best positioned to offer purpose and direction; however, stagnation phases are a natural component of applied practitioner development, suggesting this may not in and of itself be sufficient (Carlsson, 2016). Stagnation phases are hypothesised to be in part a product of supervisee 'blind-spots' in which a lack of knowledge or awareness of one's competencies or deficiencies in either a personal or professional capacity emerges (Hutter et al., 2015; Loganbill et al., 1982). In these instances, the supervisor may offer additional themes to be explored in supervision that are incongruent with the supervisee's own desires. Supervisees may recognise a misplacement in supervision spotlighting themselves. Opportunities to challenge how actively one's 'wants' from supervision are accurately targeting their development occur regularly. For example, supervisees may begin to identify patterns, be that in their cognitive processing, emotional experience, or behavioural responses to specific content or themes that are incongruent with desired goals. Re-occurring patterns highlight an experiential gap that would benefit from the critical yet compassionate eye of supervision.

4.6 Case Study: Zoe

> Somewhat unsurprisingly, my expectations for supervision contrasted with my actual experience. I had anticipated the content to revolve around placement content and 'applied knowledge' (and had prepared accordingly) and not, well, *me*. Having discussed the importance and associated intricacies of managing session time.

The above extract is from my (Zoe's) supervision notes during my professional doctorate. At this point in my training, I was still heavily drawn towards the acquisition of knowledge. My 'want' therefore was to engage in conceptual and theoretical conversations, enhancing my knowledge of. My supervisor, however, directed our focus elsewhere, having recognised a parallel 'need'. I had sufficient knowledge to deliver the intended intervention but lacked the application skills that would influence its efficacy. While I initially left this supervision session perplexed and frustrated, this highlighted the importance of contending between what was wanted, needed, and any incongruence between the two.

4.7 Summary

In this chapter, we have explored some tasks and skills that facilitate being a 'good enough' supervisee. Given the distinct learning mechanisms that come with engaging in supervision, particularly for new supervisees, it is not surprising that challenges in engagement often arise. In providing a scaffolding for some of the essential skills from a supervisee's perspective, it is hoped prospective supervisees will use supervision in a way that is effective for their development and practice. A thread woven throughout all aspects of using supervision effectively is the requirement for supervisee personal accountability and motivation. Turning up will not achieve learning goals and enhance practice.

Exercise 4.1: Identifying and Creating Learning Goals

1. What are you looking to achieve from supervision, and what would be a determinant of success?
2. What are the key areas or competencies that you need to develop?
3. Are there any specific areas of competency that you are finding challenging right now?
4. How will you know if you are progressing towards achieving these goals?
5. What formality do you want in relation to your learning goals and the monitoring of progress?

Exercise 4.2: Establishing and Communicating Learning Preferences

1. How do you learn most effectively? (i.e., learning by doing, discussing, knowledge acquisition, watching, reflecting).
2. What are your preferences for structure? (i.e., highly structured or concrete agendas vs. more flexible agendas with space for fluid and emergent conversations).
3. What are your preferred feedback mechanisms? (i.e., timing and frequency, focus, format, and delivery).
4. How do you communicate/interact most effectively? (i.e., requirement for time/space to reflect vs. comfort with direct engagement).
5. How can you work together to accommodate those learning preferences? (while being flexible) (i.e., creating structured feedback plans, appropriate resource creation).

Exercise 4.3: Exploring Your Context and Impact on Supervision

1. How do you typically manage the demands of client work and academic load, a combination of the above?
2. What challenges exist in your environment (e.g., time, finances, availability of client hours, family commitments) that may influence your ability to engage in supervision?
3. What expectations, biases, experiences, or cultural influences (e.g., gender or religion) may impact your ability to work effectively with this supervisor?
4. Which additional learning needs do you have (e.g., dyslexia) and what accommodations can be made to best support you?
5. When administrative, contextual, and cultural challenges arise – what is the best way to support you? What self-care activities work for you?

5 Being a Good Enough Supervisor

5.1 Introduction

The title of this chapter and the previous chapter raises the notion of what it means to be 'good enough'. The concept of 'good enough supervisee' we borrowed from Donald Winnicott, a British paediatrician and psychoanalyst, who introduced the concept of the 'good enough mother' and the 'good enough environment'. For most trainees in applied sport psychology, the first step on their training journey is to get their heads around what doing sport psychology is all about. And because doing sport psychology comprises countless facets, they are stunned before they begin. When we pile supervision on top, it often feels like the knockout blow. Getting to our feet, we need to grab hold of a few books to steady us. It might be the opening chapter of Mark Andersen's Doing Sport Psychology (2000) or Basch's Doing Psychotherapy (1980).

5.2 Supervisor Competencies

The purpose of supervision is to foster good practice, defined by the professional guidelines of an awarding body (e.g., APA, APS, BPS, 2024) to meet client needs. But what if supervisor competency does not meet adequate standards in universal and specific terms? What if supervisory sessions do not fulfil their purposes? There are competencies relevant to every supervisor in the health professions to communicate a standard of practice, reflect upon and develop one's supervisory practice, ensure supervision sessions meet their intended goals, and evaluate whether the supervisee's performance is adequate for their therapeutic modality (e.g., CBT). For example, Kennerley and Clohessy (2010) presented general guidelines for good supervision practice in CBT. To evaluate a supervisor's performance, the supervisor needs to submit a recording of a session, ideally a video recording, supervisees' feedback form, and a reflection of one's supervision to encourage self-reflective practice (Hill et al., 2016). The areas of practice under scrutiny included structuring sessions, enhancing learning,

DOI: 10.4324/9781003485667-5

the supervisory relationship, other process issues, professional and ethical practice, and reflective practice. In the next section, we shall outline some specifics of each of these elements.

Structuring the session: The structure of a session should meet the needs of the supervisee and supervisor, which means supervision ought to fit within the allocated time boundaries and follow an agenda or at least negotiate a change to the arranged agenda. The goals of the session ought to be set collaboratively to reflect the original supervision contract and progress at a pace that allows for reflection and learning.

Enhancing learning: Supervisees learn in practicum placements and, although some supervisors offer 'live' supervision on placement, others depend on, for example, role play, Socratic methods, and case discussion to bridge the gap between what happens in practice and what the supervisee presents in supervision. In these methods, the supervisor can appraise and evaluate the supervisee's skills and knowledge while recognising the developmental needs and learning orientation suitable for the supervisee. Sometimes supervisees need resources to guide their learning alongside sensitive and constructive feedback to challenge and support the supervisee. One critical foundation of supervision is the theory-to-practice link, to bring, for instance, theory from sport and exercise psychology, link it with research and sound service delivery to reflect coherently on one's practice. Reflective practice is a key component of applied sport psychology training programmes and usually appears in a logbook of one's training.

Supervisory relationship: Good supervision depends upon a collaborative and engaging relationship following the tasks, goals, and bonds displayed in the contract (Bordin, 1983). Acknowledging that most supervisees in training seek a safe, supportive, non-judgemental environment in which to learn, supervisors ought to lead in respectful, supportive, and sensitive communication, yet it needs to focus on the education of the supervisee. The educational boundary allows for feedback to travel in both directions so that supervisors offer guidance towards clinical goals and supervisees request the support and guidance they need based on the feedback received and the supervisee's sense of the direction of their supervision.

Other process issues: Exploring processes between the supervisee and client and between the supervisee and supervisor are central to good supervision. Relationship ruptures and repairs are common in the practitioner-client relationship and the supervisee-supervisor relationship. Because the supervisee usually operates in several wider systems (e.g., domestic, occupational, institutional) and so does the client (e.g., domestic, occupational, institutional), relationship issues work their way into practitioner-client relationships and then into supervisee-supervisor relationships. Dealing sensitively with problems that arise and setting healthy boundaries to prevent other relationship problems from developing and escalating are all part of the process issues in a supervisee-supervisor relationship.

Professional and ethical practice: A good supervisor works within their boundaries of competence and acknowledges the limits of their knowledge, skills, and experience. The values of respect, responsibility, integrity, and competence ought to be seen and felt in sessions. For example, the supervisor ought to respect client confidentiality, promote safe, ethical, and professional practice, and encourage safe case management so that the supervisee's caseload fits with their knowledge, skills, and experience.

Reflective practice: A critical review of one's current practice as a supervisor means one can learn from, and through, the experiences of supervision of others. Though this process might unsettle some supervisors, it allows the supervisor to learn by critically reflecting on the feedback from supervisees. The supervisor, regardless of their stage of development, learns from each supervisee about how to supervise better. But this improvement does not happen by accident; rather, it needs to be translated into challenging but realistic goals. A supervisor might benefit from supervision of their supervision (i.e., meta-supervision) or learning to manage the pace of supervision sessions or attending CPD sessions related to gaps in knowledge, skills, or experience.

In summary, a curiosity and passion to develop oneself as a supervisor means openly and non-judgementally accepting feedback and steering from trusted others. When we avoid this self-exploration of our supervision practices, we deny ourselves the opportunity to learn and grow as supervisors and practitioners in the field, set an unbalanced example to our supervisees about continuous professional development, and push the development of our profession a little further down our list of priorities. Investing time in self-reflection benefits everyone involved.

5.3 Models and Modes of Supervision

Several models of supervision abound through various professional fields in psychology (e.g., clinical, counselling) and beyond (e.g., social work). Perhaps, as Barney and Andersen (2014) noted, there could be a similar number of models of supervision as there are models of psychological treatment. We explored three models in Chapter 1. Cognitive-behavioural supervision was introduced for models rooted in psychotherapy theory. Next, we introduced the integrated developmental model (IDM) for developmental models. We concluded with Hawkins and Shohet's seven-eyed model, used for process models.

Van Raalte and Andersen (2000) presented the relationship in supervision between processes and outcomes. If supervision is the process, then competence and better care of the client are the outcomes. Supervision processes could include planning athlete cases, learning cognitive-behavioural techniques, internalising the supervisor, making and learning from one's mistakes and learning one's limits, recognising one's own needs, knowing how one relates to athletes, coaches, and supervisors. These processes and outcomes fit into several models of supervision, such as behavioural, cognitive-behaviour models, phenomenological, psychodynamic, and developmental models, which we described in Chapter 1. Phenomenological models of supervision emerged from the research and theory in humanistic and existential psychology. One influential example of humanistic psychology applied to the supervisory experience is Carl Rogers' work (1957/1961). Like therapeutic work with a client, a supervisor in phenomenological supervision creates the conditions for the supervisee to grow. Empathy, unconditional positive regard, and congruence provide the necessary and sufficient conditions to guide one's own learning at one's chosen pace. At one level, a supervisee might flourish with such autonomy, yet for a beginning trainee, the lack of other-directed (i.e., supervisor) structure and direction rouses anxiety.

5.4 Using Recordings and Observational Materials

What happens during a session with a client? This tale often depends on the tales shared by the practitioner, but one can imagine the gap between what happens in a session with a client and what a practitioner says happened. This gap is not a criticism; rather, it is an inevitable consequence of storytelling. Trying to be as objective as possible, one still leans heavily on a one-sided view of events. When we can listen to an audio recording or watch and listen to a video recording, we realise the tale's completeness or incompleteness (Neenan & Dryden, 2021).

These recordings offer a clearer picture beyond the practitioner's description. For a supervision session, one might listen to an excerpt and focus on it to identify strengths and areas for improvement. The supervisee and supervisor can explore and discuss the blind spots, difficulties, mistakes, vulnerabilities, and dilemmas that arise. Trainees often share their reluctance to record (e.g., Oh, it is not very good at all) and share recordings of their work with clients; however, the ensuing recordings often highlight a higher level of competence than calculated by the trainees. Without these recordings and supervision as a process to help the supervisee, one cannot monitor the quality of the service (e.g., CBT) being offered to the client. The competence domains of core CBT skills, for instance, would include (a) agenda setting, (b) formulation, (c) CBT interventions, (d) homework, (e) effective two-way communication, (f) fostering the therapeutic relationship, (g) effective use of time, and (h) assessing change (Muse & McManus, 2013; Muse et al., 2016).

5.5 Common Problems in Supervision

A supervision session in CBT might follow a predictable format of a CBT session with agenda-setting, bridging items, main topics, homework, and review. As a trainee following a CBT modality, these items will seem familiar yet unversed if a supervisor travels a different route through supervision. It may have been difficult to secure regular, competent supervision, or after securing supervision, it might not meet your precise needs. Self-supervision fills a gap here while you search for another supervisor. Many of the problems arising in supervision arise from poorly designed or rushed contracts, or ones created at the outset of supervision that do not adjust to the changing needs of the supervisee or supervisor. The problems in a supervisory relationship might relate to a poor match between the supervisee and supervisor or a lack of commitment from the supervisor to meet the basic requirements of supervision (e.g., attend on time, avoid interruptions, focus on the supervisee). Often, supervisees are reluctant to raise issues with their supervision and 'make do' or 'withdraw' from the process. Sometimes, the demands from a supervisee are unexpressed or overwhelming and ought to be brought to personal therapy rather than supervision. Returning to the contract allows each party to address some basics of supervision. For example, which needs are being met or unmet? Is it possible to meet these needs? Are expectations reasonable for the supervisory relationship? Is further training necessary? Is there extra time to meet the training needs required? (Kennerley et al., 2017). Whichever problems arise in supervision, we can often trace their origins to issues in training supervisees to use supervision.

5.6 Training Supervisees to Use Supervision Effectively

Courses for training supervisors vary in the scope and specificity of their learning outcomes. Some supervisors invest heavily to meet these learning outcomes and continue to learn and reflect on their practice as supervisors throughout their careers. Supervisees, under their tutelage, grow and prosper in this positive learning environment because these supervisors know supervisees need to learn how to use supervision at developmentally appropriate levels from their first days in practicum placement until their supervision contract ends. Some supervisors, however, assume supervisees are familiar with using supervision. It might appear axiomatic that adults, having progressed through primary, secondary, and tertiary education, would appreciate a supervision process and liken it to the educational process, especially in more independent forms of training and education in undergraduate and postgraduate courses. This leap, however, often presupposes a baseline of understanding and skills on the supervisee's part that is usually missing. (Inkskipp, 1999) suggested three reasons supervisors ought to train supervisees in using supervision. First, training empowers the supervisee because the supervisee's expectations can be explained and explored alongside the supervisor's expectations of the supervisee. This openness means the power imbalance reduces and the collaborative ethos can flourish. The supervisee's personal and professional development becomes a shared activity for the ultimate protection and support of the client. Second, good supervision depends heavily on supervisees feeling safe in sharing themselves and their work. If supervisees do not feel safe or feel as though they cannot request their needs to be met, supervision lurches along unsatisfactorily. Helping a supervisee to create a contract for this working alliance helps because the contract acts as the map for the territory the supervisee will enter. The map can be updated with the supervisor as the territory becomes more familiar. Finally, the working or supervision alliance is the driving force behind mutually beneficial supervision (Watkins, 2014). As with all healthy alliances, all parties need to engage actively and intentionally, acknowledging their boundaries, accepting their roles, rights, and responsibilities. At this level of detail, precision brings clarity and a sense of unity to proceedings in the working alliance.

The skills, knowledge, and attitudes expected at this level of training and scholarship overwhelm some supervisees. Based on Inskipp (1999), we present a story arc to capture these competencies during a training programme. We do not expect supervisees to hold these competencies at the outset of supervision; rather, we acknowledge how training and supervision weave them strategically into one's development as a supervisee.

In this section, we present an outline for teaching supervisees how to use supervision, blending our experiences as practitioners, educators, and supervisors with the guidance from other researchers and supervisors (Inskipp, 1999; Carroll, 1996). Before we begin, however, we wish to present two pathways for training supervisees: (a) doctoral training and (b) independent training. For those on doctoral training programmes, training supervisees to use supervision usually fits within a series of modules, for example, within professional development modules across their three years of training (e.g., in the UK). In this scenario, trainees learn about the goals, tasks, bonds, and boundaries of supervision while developing a sense of efficacy and motivation to use supervision to their advantage. In a professional development module, for instance, students develop skills as a supervisee that run alongside their training in counselling skills classes and theory classes to (1) define learning needs and explore supervisory models, (2) negotiate a contract, (3) build and maintain a working alliance, (4) record client case notes and reflect upon client sessions, (5) prepare and present in supervision, (6) collaborate on a supervision agenda and seven ways of focusing, (7) receive and give feedback during supervision, and (8) handle challenges and conflicts in supervision.

For those training independently with a supervisor, the time spent guiding supervisees on how to use supervision presents a few challenges. First, the supervisor and supervisee will need to devote the early part of their supervision programme to content and methods to develop the skills listed in the previous paragraph. Second, the supervisor and supervisee will need to dedicate ongoing supervision time to upskill on content and methods usually presented in a training module separate from supervision. Finally, some supervisors will not wish to undertake these developmental tasks, such as how to use supervision, and recommend trainees upskill as part of their independent learning. Although this method seems possible, our experience shows that supervisees struggle in supervision and practicum placement because they have a blurred understanding of how to use supervision to their advantage. Whether training alone or in a doctoral programme, these steps provide a roadmap for successful supervision.

1. *Define learning needs and explore supervisory models*: Most supervisees do not know what they do not know, especially as they begin their journeys as trainee sport psychology practitioners. Supervision will probably be a new process to them, and without a defined supervisory process and model, supervision can feel muddled. Supervisees normally attend counselling skills triads, lectures, and seminars to understand the theory and practice of a therapeutic modality (e.g., a person-centred approach; cognitive behaviour therapy) and share their learning experiences with peers in professional development classes, for example. Learning how to practise as a sport psychology practitioner also means learning about oneself, one's internal processes, thoughts, feelings, bodily sensations, and critically learning to describe these to oneself and others (e.g., clients, peers, and supervisors). Based on these experiences, some supervisees will have different learning needs from others; however, they all need to follow a supervision model that is developmentally appropriate for them (see more about supervision models in Chapter 1).
2. *Negotiate a contract*: A contract for supervision needs to define supervision and outline goals, tasks, bonds, and boundaries for all involved. Without roles, responsibilities, and rights openly discussed, the power imbalance between the supervisor and the supervisee remains with the supervisor. Presenting a safe, ethical, and professional standard in one's supervision practices means the supervisee learns by example. Most supervisors begin with a general contract as a starting point and adjust it to meet the needs of the supervisee. Such a proforma (Kennerley et al., 2017; Ellis, 2017; Townend, 2005) usually contains statements about confidentiality, content of supervision (e.g., acquiring knowledge, conceptualisation, and clinical skills), practicalities (e.g., time, dates, venue, fees), methods and content (e.g., exploring working alliances, case presentations, assessments, formulations, interventions, homework, observing practice, reviewing service user safety, clinical guidelines, current theory and practice), aims and goals

(e.g., gathering knowledge, refining one's attitude, and developing skills), anti-discriminatory practice and which steps to follow in the breakdown of these arrangements for supervision (see Chapter 3 for details).

3. *Build and maintain a working alliance*: The primacy of a mutually beneficial working alliance cannot be emphasised enough in applied sport psychology practice and supervision. With this prominence established, we need to attend to the working alliance through all stages of supervision. The supervisor and supervisee need to cultivate the skills and qualities of a good alliance, each playing their part, acknowledging issues of power, boundaries, roles, responsibilities, rights, and accountability throughout.
4. *Record client case notes and reflect upon client sessions*: These realities serve ethical, legal, and professional standards in work undertaken with clients. Client records follow different systems depending on the organisation, but privacy and confidentiality remain paramount. Recording content and process is necessary for training, reflective learning, and supervision. Most supervisees need guidance and exemplars to follow to undertake client records that are meaningful to their personal and professional development.
5. *Prepare and present in supervision*: Each supervision session with a supervisor presents a boundaried time for the supervisee to learn and reflect upon their development and their developing relationship with their supervisor. To use this time well, however, also means leaning on one's awareness (e.g., cognitive, emotional, physical) and the interpersonal process to be fully present for the session, prepared and ready to engage. One's 'internal supervisor' reflects how the supervisee internalises and uses the supervisory relationship for self-support and self-review (Casement, 1985, 1990). Choosing what to bring to supervision requires the supervisee to ponder which cases, issues, and dilemmas to share with a supervisor. Maybe a supervisee could reflect on those sessions that went well with a client (or clients) and those that did not. Perhaps some uncertainties arose and are still with you. Perhaps you hold doubts and anxieties about your work with a client, or maybe you are looking forward to opportunities in your work with clients in the weeks ahead.
6. *Collaborate on a supervision agenda and seven ways of focusing*: Setting an agenda for each session means that the supervisee and supervisor can focus on the goals for supervision, methods, and content established in the supervision contract. A proposed agenda clarifies and records the content and processes covered in supervision over the period of a contract. Hawkins' concept of the Process Model of Supervision (1989) and the related seven-eyed supervisor (Inskipp,

1999). The seven-eyed supervisor comprises: (1) the client's life and experience, (2) the practitioner's interventions and techniques, (3) the process and relationship between client and practitioner, (4) the internal experience of the practitioner, (5) the here-and-now relationship and the process between practitioner and supervisor, (6) the internal experience of the supervisor, and (7) the systems which may affect any of the others above (see Chapter 1 for details).

7. *Receive and give feedback*: Feedback in all its forms, whether formative or summative, presents opportunities to learn. Viewed in this way, the supervisee and supervisor are always learning together. A supervisee might receive feedback about the content of a session (e.g., client's presenting issues, precipitating factors, the choice of interventions and actions by the supervisee) and the process of the session (i.e., the interaction and relationship between the supervisee and client and the internal processes of the practitioner). Making sense of the feedback might happen in the supervision session or form part of a reflective process after the supervision session. A good supervisor will also request feedback about the content and process of their supervision from the supervisee.
8. *Handle challenges and conflicts in supervision*: Inevitably, challenges and conflicts will arise in supervisory relationships. Sometimes supervisees approve strategies that they ultimately do not agree with, or partially meet, or undertake to be most agreeable to their supervisor. Dealing with these issues of incongruence saves much anguish all around. One example might relate to audio recordings. Both parties recognise their necessity and value, but the supervisee is reluctant to audio record sessions because of a fear of negative evaluation by their supervisor. Or the supervisee diligently audio records sessions, but the supervisor pays little attention to them. Each party in the supervisory relationship ought to focus on helping the supervisee get better at what they do and so help clients more effectively. In this supportive stance, supervision is an opportunity to learn rather than a wielded threat (Kennerley et al., 2017).

The concept of being a 'good enough' supervisor in applied sport psychology draws inspiration from Winnicott's (1953) notion of the 'good enough mother' – one who provides sufficient care and responsiveness without attempting perfection. This framing acknowledges that effective supervision is not about flawless performance but about creating conditions that facilitate growth while modelling authentic professional practice. In sport psychology, where practitioners navigate complex ethical terrain and diverse performance environments, the good-enough supervisor balances structure with flexibility, challenge with support, and expertise with humility (Goldberg et al., 2016). In this chapter, we explore the competencies, approaches, and developmental processes that enable sport psychology professionals to become effective supervisors. It examines how supervisors can develop their craft, teach effectively, manage the complex dynamics of the supervisory relationship, and sustain their own well-being. The chapter aims to demystify supervision by presenting it not as an innate talent but as a learnable skill set that strengthens through intentional practice, reflection, and ongoing development.

5.7 Case Study: Dan

In supervisee training, part of Dan's doctoral training programme, Dan began by sketching the tasks, roles, and boundaries of supervision and drawing these up in a contract to build a sustainable working alliance with his supervisor (Watkins, 2014). Dan attended counselling skills triads, lectures, and seminars to understand the theory and practice of a person-centred approach and shared in professional development classes with his peers. Not only was Dan learning how to become a sport psychology practitioner, but he was also learning about himself, his internal processes, thoughts, feelings, and bodily sensations, acquiring the capacity to describe them to himself, his peers, and his supervisor. When Dan passed his fitness to practise assessment, he was ready to begin practicum placement. The course guidance stipulated a one to six ratio in which Dan received one hour of supervision for every six hours of practicum placement. Through ongoing counselling skills classes, Dan developed an awareness of the moment-to-moment interaction between himself and his peers, which allowed him to work safely and meaningfully on placement. This moment-to-moment awareness of the processes between Dan and his clients, alongside conscious and unconscious processes, became a primary feature of supervision. As part of the supervision contract, Dan accepted responsibility to bring and share work with his supervisor, acknowledging the boundaries between service delivery and supervision, and taking time to reflect on which needs are being met or unmet in the supervisory process. Part of this sharing process meant Dan would audio-record sessions with clients and share these with his supervisor. Dan also wrote process reports and client case studies as formative and summative assessments, receiving feedback in supervision on the competencies met and unmet in these assessments. Dan learned how to gather informed consent from his clients to share recordings while addressing any organisational processes and ethical issues. A central feature of Dan's unfolding development was to keep records of case (or progress) notes and reflections upon his development in a logbook. All of Dan's work with his supervisor and more broadly on the doctoral training programme meant formative and summative assessments and feedback, and for Dan, it meant learning how to accept, reflect, and learn from these experiences. Dan also needed to acknowledge through self-assessment where he felt he needed to develop his competencies and continually explore these with his supervisor while leaning on his supervisor's guidance and experience. Dan had to give feedback to his supervisor about her supervision of his work. He also realised the primacy of respect, responsibility, integrity, and competence as the ethical pillars of his work with clients. Over three years, Dan developed the skills and competencies to work safely, ethically, and professionally in several organisations. This section will explore the story arc elements and how to integrate them into training and supervision.

5.8 Developing Supervisor Competence and Identity

Effective supervision in applied sport psychology requires a distinct set of competencies that extend beyond clinical expertise or sport science knowledge. These competencies develop progressively through education, experience, and deliberate practice (Rousmaniere et al., 2017). Using Falender and Shafranske's (2012) competency-based supervision model as a foundation and applying it to the applied sport psychology domain, several key spheres come into focus. The areas of expertise encompass knowledge, skills, and attitudes/values. To illustrate knowledge competencies, a supervisor should possess extensive knowledge and comprehension of applied sport psychology's theory, research, and practical application. This knowledge should also incorporate ethical, legal, and professional principles, along with an understanding of the different sports environments and cultures within which applied sport psychologists operate. A supervisor should also have a comprehensive understanding of supervision models, their practical use, and knowledge of the stages of professional development. Skills competencies should include the ability to build and maintain strong supervisory relationships, the ability to adjust supervision based on the supervisee's needs, determined by evaluating their skills, and the capacity to establish and maintain boundaries in both supervisory relationships and the wider sporting world. We expect strong abilities in providing helpful criticism to those supervised. Finally, attitude/value competencies would include a commitment to ethical practice and supervisee welfare. A good supervisor would appreciate the intricate nature of applied sport psychology and respect individual variations and cultural backgrounds. We would also see a strong endorsement of reflective practice, evidence-based methods, and a commitment to continuous professional growth.

Supervisors commonly progress through developmental stages comparable to those experienced by supervisees. Drawing from Stoltenberg and McNeill's (2010) Integrated Developmental Model, supervisors may move through the novice, intermediate, and advanced stages. In the novice stage, supervisees focus on 'doing it right', anxiety about evaluation, and reliance on structured approaches to supervision. Next, increased confidence marks the intermediate stage, greater flexibility in approach, and the development of an awareness of the relational aspects of supervision. Finally, supervisors in the advanced stage integrate their personal style, feel comfortable with complexity and ambiguity, and can tailor supervision to diverse supervisee needs. In applied sport psychology, this development often occurs without formal training in supervision, as practitioners assume supervisory roles based on experience in the field rather than specific supervision credentials. This reality underscores the importance of intentional development of supervisory competencies through continuing education, mentorship, and reflective practice.

5.9 Ongoing Development as a Supervisor: Meta-supervision or Supervision-of-Supervision

The journey towards becoming a good enough supervisor continues throughout one's professional life. Meta-supervision or supervision-of-supervision (SOS) – receiving supervision on one's supervisory work – provides a structured approach to ongoing development (Power, 2013). Defining supervision, as we explored in Chapter 1, is a complex process because of its dimensions and variables. Underlying everything is the practitioner's commitment to the safety, well-being, and physical and mental health of their clients (Van Raalte & Andersen, 2000). In practical terms, supervision is two people, a supervisor and a supervisee, meeting to discuss the supervisee's professional work, sharing experiences, and analysing cases. Meta-supervision, or supervision of supervision, is two people discussing the supervision practices and experiences of one of them (Barney & Andersen, 2014). Meta-supervision helps supervisors to identify and work through their supervisory practices to ensure their supervision is ethical, professional, and valuable to supervisees. In applied sport psychology settings, not only do we need supervision, but we also need supervision of supervision, which means the training of practitioners to become competent supervisors. Watson et al. (2004) reported that 47 per cent of the membership of the Association for Applied Sport Psychology had received no training in supervision. Ten years later, Vosloo, Zakrajsek, and Grindley (2014) called for more training in supervision processes together with suggestions for new supervision training models. More recently, researchers exploring supervision and professional development highlighted the benefits of supervision to professional growth (Fogaca et al., 2020; Haluch et al., 2022; McEwan et al., 2019).

With a scarcity of training models for novice supervisors in applied sport psychology, there is much to be learned about the role and goals of a meta-supervisor. A supervisor-in-training would benefit from the support of a meta-supervisor to attend to the personal and professional needs of the supervisor-in-training. A primary goal of meta-supervision would be to enhance the quality and efficacy of the supervisory process (Andersen et al., 2014). Depending on the quality of one's training and supervision to attain accreditation (registration), it is possible to dodge self-disclosure and evade personal exploration by, for example, leaning on the psychologist's toolkit on theories, therapies, and interventions through one's training. Without sinking a spade into one's disappointments, prejudices, biases, progress, conflicts, strengths, pride, shame, and embarrassment, it is likely that pains from one's past are present heavily in work with clients and supervisees.

The concept of the 'good enough' supervisor acknowledges that perfection is neither possible nor necessary in supervision (Knox et al., 2011). Rather, effective supervision in sport psychology requires ongoing development of specific competencies, thoughtful pedagogical approaches, balanced challenge and support, ethical modelling, reflective practice, self-awareness, and sustainable self-care. Through intentional development in these areas, supervisors create conditions that facilitate supervisee growth while continuing their own professional evolution. The good-enough supervisor demonstrates competence without claiming omniscience, provides structure without rigidity, offers challenge balanced with support, and models ethical practice while acknowledging the complexities of real-world application. This approach creates a learning environment where supervisees can develop not only technical skills but also the professional judgement, ethical reasoning, and reflective capacity essential to effective sport psychology practice.

As the field of sport psychology continues to evolve, so too will approaches to supervision. The good-enough supervisor commits to ongoing learning, adaptation, and development, modelling for supervisees the lifelong professional growth that characterises excellence in practice. Whichever way we cut it, endings feel different to supervisees and supervisors. These feelings might swing from sadness and loss to relief and excitement on both sides. But one element of the supervisory process seems to remain from the beginning to the end, bringing with it an undercurrent of worry and uncertainty: evaluation. Evaluation, added to formative assessments and feedback, serves critical purposes for those in training and those qualified, to know where they stand in the landscape of professional practice as a sport psychology practitioner. Ultimately, how does a supervisee learn, grow, and practise safely, ethically, and professionally without evaluation?

Supervisors are gatekeepers of their profession. Though they might not hold ultimate responsibility for the outcome (i.e., who qualifies and who does not qualify) of supervisees on a training programme, their assessment, feedback, and evaluation of knowledge, skills, and abilities are their ethical responsibility. Supervisees, though they might wince at the thought of assessment, feedback, and evaluation, also seek these estimates because they reassure them about their progress and offer directions on how to practise more effectively in their profession. Equally, evaluation seems at odds with one's practice as a professional working with clients, offering empathy, avoiding judgement, and allowing them to determine their paths towards their therapeutic goals. Initially, these requirements seem ill-fitting and clearing a space to fit supervision into one's services to potential supervisees often requires open discussion with peers, one's supervisor, and with the supervisees to find a place for the evaluative component of supervision (Borders & Brown, 2022).

5.10 Conclusion

In this chapter, we delved into several dimensions of being a good-enough supervisor. Here, we view the supervisor as someone who facilitates growth, upholds standards, and serves as a role model for reflective, ethical practice. Being a 'good enough' supervisor means embracing humility, structure, relational depth, and continuous development. Effective supervision, ultimately, strengthens the profession and ensures high-quality support for athletes, teams, and organisations.

The parameters of supervision ought to be ordered from the outset of supervision, with regular updates to ensure supervision meets the needs of all parties. These parameters mean the supervisee and supervisor witness their roles and responsibilities with a clear sense of direction and proportion to their working alliance. In an autonomy-supportive environment, undertaking assessments, receiving feedback, and undergoing evaluations appear less daunting. Sometimes, however, the supervisor might not notice the sense of threat and judgement in their relating to a supervisee. Unbeknownst to the supervisor, their perception of a positive, supportive, respectful, yet challenging approach to supervision lands heavily on the supervisee, which increases the supervisee's sensitivity and defensiveness. This defensiveness seems reasonable at the beginning of a supervisory relationship because supervision can be threatening if one feels threatened by it. Building a feedback mechanism into supervision sessions allows the supervisee and supervisor to reflect upon their ways of relating and adjust as necessary for a positive learning environment.

Exercise 5.1: Supervisor Competence Audit

On a scale of 1 to 10, please rate yourself in the following categories:

- Structuring sessions
- Enhancing learning
- Managing process issues

- Feedback skills
- Ethical/professional practice
- Reflective practice

Choose your two lowest scores. For each, write a three-step development plan that includes:

1. A resource (training, reading, supervision-of-supervision)
2. A specific behavioural change
3. A timeline for implementation

6 Supervision in Practice

Choosing a Style

6.1 Introduction

Supervision in applied sport psychology represents a critical bridge between theoretical knowledge and applied practice. The supervisory style adopted by practitioners significantly influences the quality of training, professional development, and ultimately, service delivery to athletes and teams (Hawkins & Shohet, 2012). The supervision experiences – uplifting and challenging – during an applied sport psychologist's education, training, and early career mould their supervisory style. Selecting and refining a successful supervisory style in applied sport psychology reflects constant evolution, not a fixed endpoint. The best supervisors use a flexible, integrative strategy based on strong theoretical knowledge, addressing their supervisee's growth and adjusting to specific sport and exercise situations. By carefully examining and refining one's supervisory style, supervisors enhance the development of competent practitioners while also contributing to the advancement of the field and the quality of services provided to athletes and clients. In this chapter, we shall explore the various approaches to supervision in applied sport psychology, examining how theoretical orientations, supervisee needs, and contextual factors shape effective supervisory relationships.

6.2 Theoretical Orientations and Supervisory Style

The theoretical foundation on which a supervisor operates shapes their approach to supervision. Each orientation provides a unique lens through which to understand client-athlete behaviour, psychological processes, and the supervisory relationship itself (Falender & Shafranske, 2021). We shall briefly explore five approaches: psychodynamic, cognitive-behavioural, humanistic and person-centred, systemic, integrative, and eclectic.

6.2.1 Psychodynamic Approaches

Psychodynamic supervision in sport psychology emphasises understanding unconscious processes, transference, and countertransference that

DOI: 10.4324/9781003485667-6

may emerge within the supervisory relationship and the supervisee-athlete relationship. Supervisors sharing this perspective might prioritise guiding supervisees to understand how their own lingering concerns might affect their work with athletes. They might also explore parallel processes between supervision and client work, sensing the subtle emotional undercurrents in competitive environments and team dynamics (Jacobsen, 2007). Supervisees might help athletes understand how formative experiences sculpt their reactions to the intense pressure of performance, the friction of team conflicts, and the dynamics of coaching relationships. In the sports context, psychodynamic supervision proves valuable when working with athletes battling the icy grip of performance anxiety, grappling with the shifting sands of their sports-related identity, or struggling to navigate the turbulent waters of career transitions.

6.2.2 Cognitive-Behavioural Approaches

Cognitive-behavioural supervision focuses on structured learning, skill development, and interventions based on evidence. This approach is common in sports psychology because of its practical and goal-focused design, which complements the improvement of athletic performance. Supervisors in this orientation often show techniques and interventions like imagery, changing self-talk, or setting goals. The supervisee receives tangible feedback regarding their application of the techniques. They often emphasise outcomes and performance indicators that are impartial and quantifiable. Session recording, role-playing, and behavioural rehearsal are examples of tools they might use for supervision. They also highlight the scientific practitioner model, focusing on contemporary research. For those new to sport psychology, this approach provides a well-defined structure that complements the performance-oriented nature of many sports settings.

6.2.3 Humanistic and Person-Centred Approaches

Humanistic supervision in applied sport psychology prioritises the supervisee's personal and professional development, fostering a relationship built on empathy, unconditional positive regard, and authenticity. This approach commonly sees supervisors building a safe environment for supervisees to delve into their work with athletes. This supervisor-supervisee relationship allows the supervisor to affirm the supervisee's knowledge gained through intuition and experience, promote their independence and self-guided learning, and consider the supervisee and the whole athlete. The person-centred approach is valuable because it addresses the overall well-being of athletes, not just their performance; helps supervisees deal with complicated ethical problems; and encourages athletes to be independent even when their sport is highly controlled.

6.2.4 Systemic Approaches

When approaching systemic supervision, supervisors and supervisees analyse athletes in their wider relationships, teams, organisations, and cultural systems. The supervisor in this structure supports supervisees in contextualising athlete issues within team, organisational, and cultural settings. They also explore the influence of various stakeholders, such as coaches, parents, and teammates, on athlete experiences and examine the influence of sport organisations and competitive structures on psychological processes. Instead of focusing only on the individual athlete, they lead interventions that tackle broader, systemic issues. In applied sport psychology, this approach is relevant because team dynamics, organisational culture, and various stakeholders significantly affect how well athletes perform and feel.

6.2.5 Integrative and Eclectic Approaches

Experienced supervisors in sport psychology often take integrative approaches, using different theoretical orientations depending on the supervisee's individual needs, the athlete population's characteristics, the challenges encountered, and the work context. To be an effective integrative supervisor, you need a firm foundation in various theoretical orientations and well-defined reasons for using each approach. This adaptability enables supervisors to handle the various problems that arise in sports and exercise settings.

6.3 Matching Style to the Supervisee's Developmental Needs

Effective supervision in applied sport psychology requires adapting one's approach to the developmental stage of the supervisee. For instance, if we draw from Stoltenberg's Integrated Developmental Model (Stoltenberg & McNeill, 2010), which we referred to in Chapter 5, for novices (Level 1), supervisors might consider providing more structure, direction, and positive reinforcement while helping supervisees manage anxiety and develop basic competencies in sport psychology techniques. Supervisors at Level 2 (intermediate) should balance support with challenge, as supervisees may experience fluctuating confidence and motivation. They should encourage greater autonomy while remaining available for consultation. Finally, at Level 3 (advanced), a supervisor might adopt a more consultative approach as supervisees develop their own integrated style, focusing on refining advanced skills and addressing complex cases.

The developmental approach recognises that supervisees' needs evolve, requiring supervisors to change their level of directiveness, structure, and focus progressively (Rønnestad et al., 2019). In applied sport psychology, a crucial element of supervisory style is the continuum between directive and non-directive supervision. One example of a directive method includes providing explicit instructions, demonstrations, and feedback, much like one might experience in cognitive-behavioural therapy. The supervisor might focus on acquiring and implementing skills by establishing clear expectations and structure. It is common to use this approach in high-pressure scenarios or when guiding beginners. A non-directive approach, however, might feature techniques like Socratic questioning and reflection. By encouraging self-discovery and problem-solving, the supervisor can help the supervisee concentrate on developing their personal style. This method often works well with experienced professionals or when dealing with complicated ethical dilemmas. Effective supervisors are adaptable and can navigate the balance between providing clear instructions and fostering independent exploration in their supervisees (Carroll, 1996).

6.4 Balancing Structure and Flexibility

Finding the right balance between structure and flexibility in applied sport psychology supervision is complex and depends on several variables (Andersen et al., 2001). Structured elements can involve things like regular meeting schedules, standardised case presentation formats, systematic reviews of video recordings, or competency checklists, while flexible components may encompass responsiveness to developing problems, receptiveness to topics brought by the supervisee, and flexibility according to preferred learning methods. Applied sport psychology supervisors who are effective balance clear structural guidelines with adaptability to the evolving world of sports and the increasing needs of their supervisees. The importance of this balance is clear in sports because competitions, travel, or the quickly changing nature of team situations can throw off schedules.

6.5 Evaluating the Effectiveness of Your Supervisory Style

Seeing yourself in the mirror can represent confronting the fear of being judged. Without consistent evaluation, supervisors cannot improve or offer meaningful support to their supervisees (Reiser & Milne, 2017). Overcoming this challenge does not require one giant leap; rather, it means choosing different tools for the job. These tools vary from formal assessments – for instance, using a standardised instrument to evaluate supervision – to the collection of structured feedback. Reflective practice enables a supervisor to engage in a systematic self-assessment of their supervisory relationships and the resulting outcomes. Alternatively, one could monitor the supervisee's skill development, client outcomes, and professional growth (Bell et al., 2016). These performance indicators give a real-time sign of change in supervisees. Aside from the supervisor-supervisee context, you can discuss methods, difficulties, and prospects with your peers. Lastly, further education helps one remain informed about the latest best practices in supervision. Supervisors who are effective prioritise seeking feedback, being open to change, and always improving their supervisory style to best support those they supervise, as well as the athletes and clients they work with.

The process of choosing and developing an effective supervisory style in applied sport psychology is a journey, not a destination. Supervisors who excel adopt an adaptable, comprehensive method built on a firm grasp of theory. They understand their supervisees' developmental needs and adjust their approaches to suit specific sports and exercise environments. When supervisors thoughtfully examine and refine their supervisory style, they enhance practitioner development, contribute to the field's advancement, and improve the quality of services offered to athletes and clients.

6.6 Core Tasks of Supervision

The supervisory process in applied sport psychology encompasses several fundamental tasks that, when skilfully executed, ensure the comprehensive development of practitioners and quality service delivery to athletes and sport organisations.

6.6.1 Case Conceptualisation and Formulation

Case conceptualisation represents a cornerstone of effective supervision in applied sport psychology. Those who have studied cognitive behaviour therapy, for instance, will be familiar with the facets of case conceptualisation. Case conceptualisation involves guiding supervisees to organise client information into coherent frameworks that inform subsequent interventions (Callahan et al., 2009). Once the supervisee gathers client information, the supervisee and client can explore patterns in presentations within the context of performance demands. The supervisee can organise and understand how various factors (e.g., biological, psychological, social, organisational) interact in athlete issues. Rather than being limited by one's perception or perspective, case conceptualisation encourages multiple perspectives and alternative formulations to avoid premature closure or narrow thinking. The good-enough supervisor communicates case conceptualisation or formulation as an ongoing process rather than a one-time event, adapting as new information emerges through the service delivery process. For example, a supervisor might help a supervisee reconsider an initial formulation of an athlete's performance anxiety when new information about team dynamics, coaching pressure, and organisational changes emerges. The unique demands of sport contexts mean case formulation needs to consider the wider landscape, such as the psychological and performance demands specific to the sport (e.g., motorsport vs. snooker), team dynamics, organisational challenges, competition schedules, periodisation, and the competing roles athletes hold (e.g., student and athlete).

6.6.2 Intervention Planning and Implementation

Supervisors provide direction to those they oversee on how to convert case formulations into successful intervention strategies, informed by the supervisee's therapeutic approach (e.g., ACT, CBT, PCT, and REBT). The supervisor and supervisee contribute their combined theoretical understanding, research, and practical skills to this collaborative endeavour. Planning and implementation involve decisions about what to do, the order of actions, adjustments, demonstrations, and how to resolve problems. As an example, the supervisor and supervisee can place the athlete's needs and background on a conceptual workbench. They could then explore multiple methods supported by research, which are fitting for athletes, and possibly arrange these procedures to match the competition timeline or meeting plans. The supervisor could adjust common psychological methods to suit specific sports and show intervention techniques through examples, role-playing, or recordings. The supervisor and supervisee can collaboratively resolve implementation issues specific to sports settings. Sometimes, as supervisors, we may lose sight of the practical challenges of implementing interventions in the fast-paced world of sports, where we have limited access to athletes, must work around training schedules, and face pressure to get results quickly (Poczwardowski et al., 2023).

6.6.3 Facilitating Professional Development

Although a supervisor and supervisee might earnestly begin their work together with a needs analysis (i.e., to understand what the supervisee needs) and then focus on the content of cases in subsequent meetings, the broader lattice of professional development helps acknowledge the parts and the whole. Professional development, in a broader sense, involves identifying and addressing gaps in knowledge or skills and encouraging exploration of relevant literature and continuing education (McLeod & McLeod, 2014). It also involves supporting ethical choices in challenging sports environments, encouraging self-care and sustainable practices in demanding athletic settings, and assisting the development of a professional identity for sport psychology practitioners. In short, successful supervisors are attentive to the changing needs of those they oversee, and they adapt their support as their supervisees advance in skill, moving from less to more self-sufficient work. For example, it might include giving progressively harder cases to those being supervised or pushing them to learn specialised skills in certain parts of applied sport psychology (e.g., psychometric assessments).

6.6.4 Evaluation and Assessment

Supervision means judging and measuring the progress of the person being supervised, while also focusing on how clients are affected. If you are in a specialised training programme like the British Psychological Society's Stage Two training or a university doctoral programme, your evaluation must align with the requirements set by the training organisation or university, including competencies and assessment methods. The supervisee needs frequent, developmental feedback on their practice to reach these goals. They also need help in choosing and using suitable methods for measuring outcomes. By working together, the supervisor and supervisee can analyse the success of the intervention and simultaneously maintain records for their professional accreditation. Applied sport psychology supervision must acknowledge the specific difficulties in assessing outcomes in sports settings, given that factors other than psychological help (e.g., coaching, environmental constraints) often influence athletic performance. Considering these nuances, supervisors help practitioners develop advanced methods for measuring their influence.

6.7 Essential Supervisory Skills

To be a good supervisor, you need to have certain skills that help those you supervise learn and grow in applied sport psychology. The abilities mentioned are comparable to those used in a professional environment, including listening carefully, using questioning methods, providing feedback, establishing goals, observing progress, and overseeing groups in a supervisory capacity (Bernard & Goodyear, 2019; Falender & Shafranske, 2021). Let us briefly examine these crucial supervisory skills.

6.7.1 Active Listening and Questioning Techniques

Communication is at the heart of supervision. To communicate effectively, you need to improve your presence and engage actively in supervisory meetings. The ability to ask open-ended questions encourages the supervisee to engage in reflective thought regarding the conversation. People who have experience with cognitive behaviour therapy will recognise the benefits of Socratic questioning in helping clients discover things on their own, rather than being given the answers. The supervisor could also consider the content and emotional aspects of casework to help the supervisee better understand what might happen for the supervisee and the client. Thinking relies on strategic silences to prompt further discussion and contemplation. In more complex situations, supervisors should especially attend to countertransference issues linked to athletes' successes or their sense of self within their sport. The supervisee may have failed to recognise ethical issues particular to sports contexts (like confidentiality within teams) and the systemic influences affecting athlete behaviour.

6.7.2 *Providing Constructive Feedback*

A careful equilibrium between supportive connections and constructive feedback is crucial for supervisors. Therefore, our goal is to recognise assets and pinpoint those aspects needing improvement. In this scenario, supervisees typically need to know what their supervisor wants, not just a general idea of it. Supervisees can get feedback from a supervisor or assessment team through formative and summative assessments; nonetheless, supervisees may find value in feedback on audio recordings as they go through their training. This method of providing staggered feedback through audio recordings of client sessions gives the supervisee targeted, behavioural feedback suitable for their stage of development, facilitating acceptance and reducing defensiveness (Avent et al., 2015). You could make the case that all feedback fosters development, not simply an evaluation. One method for attaining this aim is to show receptiveness to feedback by actively seeking input from those you supervise regarding the supervisory approach. In applied sports psychology, supervisors will appreciate how performance-driven cultures can affect how those they supervise react to feedback because it could cultivate perfectionism or fear of judgement, mirroring the challenges athletes face.

6.7.3 *Goal Setting and Progress Monitoring*

Setting goals to achieve goals allows the supervisory process to progress along desired lines. Well-defined supervision goals help the supervisor and supervisee stay aligned by identifying their respective goals within the supervisory dynamic and by presenting suitable challenges that foster growth without being excessive. Achieving these aims boosts confidence, and consistent evaluations permit modifications. Modifications might be needed because of new requirements, changes in practicum locations, organisational difficulties, and similar factors. Progress notes aid in documenting accomplishments and progress made, including any achievements to date, and this information can be logged in professional development records. Supervision in applied sport psychology works best when it is like the performance-improvement methods used with athletes, creating a link between the supervision itself and what is being done in practice.

6.7.4 Managing Group Dynamics (for Group Supervision)

Supervising groups in applied sport psychology offers distinct advantages and difficulties. To account for some difficulties in group supervision, university programmes offer students guidance through group sessions and one-on-one supervision. To ensure group supervision is productive, the leader or facilitator must manage member involvement to encourage contributions from everyone. Competition is possible in all groups, and although it can be helpful, it usually harms the open, cooperative dynamic of group supervision. A key advantage of group supervision lies in the countless viewpoints that improve understanding of cases. Psychological safety, which is necessary for vulnerability and learning, is another advantage of group supervision. Within applied sport psychology, group supervision leverages group processes to exemplify team dynamics pertinent to athletic settings. In short, group supervision can be useful in applied sport psychology. It allows for the exploration of team and organisational issues through observing the parallel processes occurring within the supervision group.

6.8 Reflective Practice Frameworks

For sport psychology practitioners, it is vital to engage in reflective practice to grow professionally (Tod & McEwan, 2023). This claim is supported by the observation that processing experiences, whether cognitive or emotional, can lead to changes in how practitioners understand, know, and apply their skills in practical contexts. Reflective practice helps one understand and accept themselves as individuals and professionals as they strive for individuation, a process of aligning personal traits like values and beliefs with their professional identity, encompassing theoretical orientation and therapeutic methods (Tod et al., 2017). Becoming an expert in sport psychology involves diverse routes for practitioners. We are not advocating for one controlled journey for all; instead, we appreciate and welcome the individuality and resonance of one's personal journey. According to Skovolt and Rønnestad (1995), a key element in a practitioner's professional growth is professional reflection. Those who maintained their professional growth as therapists were differentiated from those who stalled and experienced burnout through professional reflection. Let us shift our focus to organised methods for practising reflection.

Structured approaches to reflective practice, using various frameworks, are the basis for continuous professional growth in applied sport psychology supervision. Here, we will give a quick overview of two frameworks. To begin, Donald Schön's framework differentiates between reflection-in-action, which is the real-time awareness and adaptation during supervision sessions or interventions, and reflection-on-action, which involves a retrospective analysis of supervision or intervention after it has finished. In applied sport psychology supervision, reflection-in-action could entail recognising, as it is happening, similarities between a supervisee's annoyance with an athlete and the athlete's relationship with their coach. Structured reflection-on-action could involve a post-supervision analysis of how the supervisor dealt with this parallel process and what different approaches were possible (Jacobsen, 2007). Through reflection, supervisors can go beyond using technical methods and tackle the intricate, individual, and value-driven scenarios that define practical sport psychology.

The experiential learning cycle developed by Kolb offers a framework for learning from experience that includes four stages: concrete experience, which involves the supervision session or intervention; reflective observation or considering what happened; abstract conceptualisation, which involves making sense of the experience through theories; and active experimentation, where insights apply to future practice. Applied sport psychology supervisors can lead supervisees through this process, ensuring that they learn fully from every significant professional situation. Following a difficult team intervention, a supervisor could lead a discussion about the events, link the experience to team dynamics concepts, and help prepare for the subsequent team meeting using these understandings.

6.8.1 Critical Incident Analysis

By analysing critical incidents, you can reflect and learn, making this a useful practice for understanding significant events from sport settings. The process includes pinpointing key moments in supervision or practice, evaluating them from different viewpoints, scrutinising the beliefs behind reactions, linking these moments to theories, and creating guidelines for future application. Some critical incidents in applied sport psychology could involve ethical issues about confidentiality within teams, difficult interactions with coaches or sport organisations, or unforeseen reactions from athletes to treatments. Analysing these occurrences systematically promotes professional advancement.

6.8.2 Facilitating Supervisee Reflection

Reflective skills in those supervised develop slowly, and supervisors use different approaches to cultivate these skills (Hill et al., 2016). The most effective method for fostering this reflective ability involves demonstrating reflective practice by openly sharing one's thought processes. Supervisors can set aside time for reflection in their meetings and use questions that prompt reflection, challenge viewpoints, and explore other possibilities. The supervisor's acceptance of uncertainty and the continuous nature of professional growth foster this transparency. Training programmes frequently use structured reflective assignments, which are beneficial during and between supervision sessions. Supervisors who are good at their jobs know that the ability to think reflectively grows slowly and needs a psychologically safe space. In applied sport psychology, where there is a lot of focus on quick solutions and getting results fast, supervisors could benefit from explicitly recognising the value of time for reflection, seeing it as something that goes together with a focus on action.

6.8.3 Tools for Enhancing Reflective Practice

All professionals gain from strategies and methods to strengthen their ability for reflective practice. Structured techniques have the potential to boost reflection within applied sport psychology supervision, and we have several methods available to us. Some of the most frequently used methods are reflective journals (i.e., using guided writing prompts about specific practice elements), reviewing audio and video recordings (i.e., a systematic analysis of recorded athlete sessions), and case presentation templates. Other structured methods to encourage diverse viewpoints include metaphor analysis (e.g., examining the hidden metaphors supervisees use to describe their work), role-playing and simulations (e.g., hands-on activities that provide material for reflection), peer consultation protocols (e.g., organised formats for colleagues to discuss cases), and reflective team approaches (e.g., using multiple observers to gather varied perspectives). Applied sport psychology supervisors pick suitable tools based on the learning styles and developmental needs of those they oversee, progressively implementing more complex reflective methods as abilities increase (Milne, 2009; Watkins, 2021).

6.8.4 Balancing Reflection with Action

Although reflection is crucial, successful supervision in applied sport psychology should integrate reflection with tangible skill enhancement and practical application. Supervisors and supervisees need to be aware of the line between thoughtful consideration and dwelling on problems or avoiding decisions. The purpose of reflection should be to provide insights that can be put into practice, not just remain abstract. This aim can be met by incorporating skill-building exercises alongside reflective practices. Supervisors should acknowledge sports' emphasis on action while also allowing time for contemplation, assisting those they oversee in finding their ideal equilibrium between thinking and doing. In applied sport psychology, this balance is crucial, as professionals usually function in quick environments that emphasise concrete results and workable approaches. Supervisors assist professionals in cultivating reflective practices that improve rather than hinder their ability to react to the urgent demands of athletic situations.

6.9 Conclusion

The tasks, skills, and reflective practices outlined in this chapter form the foundation of effective supervision in applied sport psychology. By mastering these elements, supervisors create optimal conditions for developing practitioners who can navigate the complex demands of supporting athletes and sport organisations. Integrating structured supervision tasks, refined communication skills, and systematic reflective practice enables continuous professional growth and ultimately enhances service delivery to athletes and teams. As the field of applied sport psychology continues to evolve, supervision that balances practical skill development with critical reflection will remain essential to advancing individual practitioners and the profession. Through thoughtful attention to these supervision processes, the field strengthens its capacity to meet the diverse and changing needs of athletes and sport organisations across competitive levels and contexts.

Exercise 6.1: Supervision Style Case Interview

You are assigned one scenario (pick or create):

- A novice trainee beginning a practicum placement.
- A mid-career practitioner in a high-performance environment.
- A supervisee struggling with countertransference.
- A supervisee requiring advanced case conceptualisation support.

For your scenario:

1. Choose the most suitable supervisory style (CBT-based, humanistic, systemic, integrative, etc.).
2. Justify your choice using theory.
3. Identify the risks of misalignment.
4. Outline how you would adapt if the style was not effective.

7 Shaping a Supervision Session – Structure and Purpose

As previous chapters have shown, supervision is critical to the professional development of sport and exercise psychologists. For supervision to fulfil its key developmental role, it must be purposeful and well-structured. Effective supervision serves as a bridge between the theoretical knowledge gained in the classroom or from books and its practical, ethical, and effective application in professional practice. Supervision is not just a passive process or a casual relationship, but instead it is structured, has purpose, and can be hugely influential in professional activities, providing a cornerstone of competent ethical practice.

Supervision is intentional and grounded in theory and evidence. It is not an ad hoc or reactive process but is theory-driven and structured. We are not seeking to impose rigid rules within our supervision but instead need to offer a safe and predictable space where the supervisee can explore whatever they need to in relation to their client work and their own personal and professional development. This supervision acts as a key contributor to practitioners developing professional identity. Ensuring supervision is structured and purposeful allows the supervisee to experience growth in their insight and skills.

In this chapter, we will explore the core elements of structured and effective supervision, beginning with the practical elements of how to build an effective supervisory session with a clear structure. We will then examine the models and theories underpinning supervision in sport and exercise psychology before considering the functions of supervision and the methods and techniques used within supervision, finally drawing the chapter to a close with some common session challenges.

7.1 Structure of Supervision Sessions

This subsection examines a framework for organising individual supervision sessions into different phases. This type of framework can be considered in your contracting (see Chapter 8 for more on this).

DOI: 10.4324/9781003485667-7

Well-structured supervision sessions are required for effective supervision, and following this type of structure provides a clear map of the sessions for the supervisor and supervisee, managing expectations and paving the way for targeted discussion. Without this type of session structure, supervision can wander and become aimless. Creating a stable structure for sessions can help the supervisor and supervisee ensure they are covering the 'what', 'how', and 'why' of supervision. Following a clear structure allows supervisees to incorporate reflection into the process; for example, Driscoll's reflective cycle (Driscoll, 2007) asking 'What?'; 'So What?'; and 'Now What?' could easily be incorporated within the following stages. This enables the supervisee to learn from experience and the supervisor to track their progress (see McCarthy et al. 2024 for additional detail). Furthermore, this aligns with one of the three functions of supervision: education, and we will cover more on this in Section 8.4. For now, though, we will focus on the phases contained within a single supervision session. Structuring supervision using this type of phased approach helps ensure that the time is used effectively, developmental goals are met, and ethical/professional standards are maintained. What follows is a recommended structure that you could adapt for use with one-to-one or group supervision:

1. The Opening: Checking-in

The session should start with a personal check-in, which should be brief but will benefit both parties. It can help the supervisee transition from whatever they were doing to being focused on the supervision space. It can also help the supervisor gain a sense of the supervisee's emotional state. Having this brief check-in helps to acknowledge that both parties see the other as a person and not just as a facet of the supervisory session or a means of discussing case material. Through this brief check-in, rapport can be established and developed.

2. The Map: Agenda Setting

We will talk more about this in Section 7.2 below, but this is a means by which the supervisor and supervisee can work together to establish the 'road map' they are following. It should be co-created, and agreement should be reached on what the focus of the session will be. It might be a specific case presentation or an ethical issue that has arisen, or it might involve skill building or professional development. Explicitly making time to set an agenda feeds into the time management aspect of supervision and facilitates the organisation of thoughts and key issues and development needs within the supervisee.

3. The Core: For example, Case Presentations

A single case presentation often sits at the heart of a supervision session. The supervisee might choose to detail their work with a specific client, outlining their professional competencies, alongside any challenges, successes, or feelings of uncertainty. This core work should enable the supervisee to reflect deeply, facilitating a greater understanding of the application of theory to practice. The supervisor uses active listening and questioning to encourage reflection. Previous learning goals can be revisited if relevant to make connections to ongoing developmental trajectories.

4. The Experiential Element: Building Skills

Practical elements are also an integral part of supervision, and these lend themselves well to supervision within sport and exercise psychology. Many approaches can be used here, including but not limited to role-play and rehearsal. Role-play can be effective in the development of key communication skills for example, whereas rehearsing specific skills such as progressive muscle relaxation can also contribute and help the supervisee move from having the knowledge of what to do to feeling confident in doing that.

5. The Motion Momentum: Goal Setting

Towards the end of the supervision session, time should be given to collaboratively setting goals for the supervisee to work on before the next supervision. This can help ensure smooth progression towards larger professional goals, can offer a sense of continuity, and can provide forward momentum. Setting goals provides reinforcement to the idea that learning is ongoing and continuous and that development occurs between and not only within sessions.

6. The Close: Wrapping Up

In the last few minutes, it's important to summarise key points and to confirm the next session time. This can be accomplished through questioning, e.g. 'What is one thing you're able to take away from our supervision session today?' which can also enable reflection and integrating supervisory content into the field.

7.2 Creating Effective Session Agendas

This part addresses collaborative approaches to determining session content. It explores methods for prioritising topics, balancing supervisee and supervisor agenda items, and ensuring coverage of essential areas despite time constraints.

Setting an agenda for supervision is vital to avoid feeling as though you are navigating a ship through uncharted territory; it acts as a guide and a boundary-setting mechanism (Milne, 2009). Supervision is most impactful when it is an intentional, structured yet adaptable activity. A central method to ensure sessions are focused and productive is to have a clear agenda and agreement on how the items on the agenda are chosen and moved through.

Agendas in supervision are collaborative and powerful, helping to avoid supervision being seen as 'tick-box' or superficial, and essentially creating a dynamic tool that affords reflection and accountability. The following functions are fulfilled through agenda setting: structure and focus; shared responsibility; and continuity. Although these are key in any supervisory setting, in sport and exercise, they are vital because of the high-pressure environments often encountered and the likelihood of important issues emerging quickly and where supervision contributes directly to shaping professional identity (Foltz et al., 2015). Having a clear and well-defined agenda can prevent supervision from being reactive. As highlighted in Section 8.1, agenda setting should be collaborative and a shared activity between supervisee and supervisor, a way in which both parties can contribute to the learning process. This is a two-way process where the supervisee and supervisor contribute (Callahan et al., 2019). Collaboration can be based on pre-session reflections where the supervisee might identify key issues ahead of time; through co-construction at the start of the session itself; through having rolling agenda items that allow evidence of continuity and accountability, and sometimes, through the development of non-negotiable agenda items that can ensure ethics and safeguarding for example are consistently addressed (British Psychological Society [BPS], 2017).

Between these different methods, maybe there are too many items to include, and so methods for prioritisation become key. This allows supervisees to engage in depth with the topics that are significant rather than the time being spread too thinly across less significant issues. At a basic level, this can be done by allocating timings to each item to enhance efficiency. Alternatives, though, include employing urgency-importance frameworks such as the Eisenhower Matrix (Abdulrahman & Alzayed,2025); or using a thematic clustering approach where similar topics are grouped (Bernard & Goodyear, 2019). Models can also be employed here, such as the Integrated Developmental Model (Stoltenberg & McNeill, 2010) and allow topics to be aligned with the supervisee's stage of development.

To ensure professional development and oversight, there should be a balance of agenda content from both parties. As a supervisor, leading content ensures adherence to ethical, cultural, and professional standards. Because of the importance of safeguarding, ethical and competency-related criteria, this type of structured, time-limited approach is necessary (BPS,

2017). Including set agenda items covering ethical and professional standards, with a rotating agenda allowing broad competency coverage, you can keep sessions focused, ensure depth and safeguard against the pressures of practice and development. Finally, while it is vital to have and follow an agenda, supervisors must be ready to adapt should a critical issue arise during the session.

7.3 Time Management in Supervision

This segment explores strategies for the efficient use of limited supervision time. It examines approaches to pacing, prioritisation, and focus that maximise learning opportunities while addressing necessary administrative functions.

Setting and following a clear agenda will help with time management, but given the time constraints usually placed on supervision (typically a 50-minute window), efficient time management is a key skill for supervisors as it is for practitioners. Having prioritised agenda items, it is important to monitor session progress and ensure that they do not become aimless and that topics that were identified as important to the agenda are not left unexplored. Managing time well within a supervision session is vital to creating focus and intention.

As a supervisor, you want to create a shared sense of responsibility for time management and provide a way of doing that. One method is for the supervisor to be strategic and propose a time limit for each agenda item. For example,

> We've identified several important agenda items here, I suggest we use 20 minutes on the case presentation you mentioned, then move onto discussing ethics for 15 minutes, then we could take 10 minutes to discuss your professional development and awareness of your competencies saving the final five minutes for reflection and wrap-up.

This allows the supervisee to suggest alterations based on their perception of the importance of each and sets a clear shared awareness of the time you have for each item. You do not want to be rigid in following this, but you will both have a shared understanding of the pace of the session and what you want to cover within each time block. As a supervisor, you might, during a conversation, decide you need to extend the timing of a particular item on the agenda as you both learn more about it. This can be facilitated within this model, and if anything is not covered that was intended, you can consider it within the wrap-up and add it to the agenda for the following session.

A key skill for a supervisor is to keep the conversation on time. There are many ways to do this, through, for example, intentional redirection when the session is not following the agreed timings. You might do this by using a reminder such as, 'We have about ten minutes left on this agenda item', which can help to move the conversation forward. Or you could choose, in collaboration with your supervisee, to have a clock or other visual timer between you. There will be times when the supervisor needs to redirect the conversation back to the agreed item, and you can do that directly, for example, 'This is a really interesting point that you're making, so perhaps we can schedule time for this during our next session, but for now let's get back to the agenda item we agreed on'.

Finding a way that works for you and your supervisee is key to success here, and a certain trial and error will be required.

7.4 Balancing Administrative, Educational, and Supportive Functions

This subsection applies Proctor's tripartite model to session planning, although there are others you can use (e.g., Kadushin's model, Pawar & Anscombe, 2022). It examines approaches to integrating multiple supervision functions within sessions and across the supervision relationship, with attention to appropriate weighting based on context and need.

As its definition suggests, supervision can serve many functions. One way to balance these functions and ensure adequate coverage of them within supervision is to apply a model such as Proctor's tripartite model both to the development of your supervisory contract and to your session structure.

Proctor's model is widely used in supervision across fields, including, for example, nursing (Scottish Government, 2021) and counselling (Litherland et al., 2023). Originally developed by Brigid Proctor in 1986 (Proctor, 1986) it breaks supervision into three core functions, each of which is a separate aspect or element of professional development. These are, first, a normative function (based around accountability); second, a formative function (based around education or development); and third, a restorative function (based around support and emotion). When supervision is within the normative function, the focus would be on ensuring ethical, legal, and professional standards are upheld. Here, supervisors monitor performance, ensure safe practices, and provide feedback, checking that work is quality assured and adheres to policies. The formative function of supervision is where knowledge can be enhanced and skills can be developed. The supervisor's contribution in this function is to help supervisees learn from their experiences, to set goals, and to develop as professionals. Reflective practice is encouraged here, as is critical thinking. Finally, the restorative function of supervision is where the supervisor provides emotional support, helping to prevent burnout and support stress management. The supervisor would aim to identify any early signs of burnout and would also help the supervisee develop their resilience and reflect within a safe space about any challenges or concerns they have.

A skill required of supervisors is to balance the three functions within supervision and not to lean too heavily into just one or two. This can be facilitated through carefully establishing supervision contracts defining roles, expectations, and boundaries, and through the fostering of trust and accountability. The three functions can also be tailored as needed to individual supervisees. For example, the emphasis could be on the normative function for more experienced supervisees and on formative and restorative functions for those new to practice and supervision.

Recent research has examined the development of a questionnaire that could facilitate the construction of a supervisory contract based on this model and that includes a reflective component. This work by Fagernas et al. (2024) resulted in the creation of an instrument that can assess preferences for key supervisory functions aligned with an extension to Proctor's model, which includes reflection.

7.5 Methods for Case Presentation and Discussion

This part explores various approaches to case review, from informal discussion to structured formats like the Consultation Model or SOAP framework. It examines the advantages of different presentation methods for specific learning objectives.

A key component of supervision in sport and exercise psychology is the case review. This provides a structured method through which to reflect on and learn from applied practice. Supervisees are accountable to themselves and their clients, and by discussing client work in supervision, they enable their ability to refine their informed decision-making, their ethical reasoning, and their ability to integrate evidence-based knowledge into their work (Anderson et al., 2002; Milne, 2009). There are several ways to do this, ranging from informal conversations to the use of formal frameworks like the Consultation Model or SOAP (Subjective, Objective, Assessment, Plan) framework. We will briefly consider these along with their advantages and objectives within supervision now.

Informal case discussions are minimally structured and flexible, which could feel natural in the supervisory relationship, mimicking the flow of reflective conversation. Relational aspects of supervision are brought to the fore here (Hawkins & Shohet, 2012; Chidiac et al., 2018) prioritising open communication and consideration of the supervisee's emotional responses within their client work. We suggest informal case discussions are valuable early in the supervisory relationship, where trust and confidence in the supervisory process are being built. Informal communication allows supervisees to verbalise any uncertainties they have encountered and to reflect on their own biases and reactions during their client work. Its efficacy is seen in enhancing self-awareness and relational understanding; however, the informality and lack of structure here can limit and detract from in-depth exploration of professional competencies that the supervisee needs to develop. Informal discussions can also benefit experienced practitioners who may be comfortable with less prescribed means of reflection, evaluation, and development.

Structured case review approaches bring systematic frameworks, providing scaffolding for client presentations and discussions. The Consultation Model, adapted from Caplan's theory of mental health supervision and developed through applied psychology and counselling contexts, encourages a collaborative, problem-solving stance in supervisory meetings (Mendoza, 1993; Anderson et al., 2002). The process typically involves a series of stages or phases, such as developing and maintaining a relationship, clarifying the supervisee's needs, assessing the problem or issue by gathering relevant information about the client and context, and identifying possible interventions or solutions. This structured model emphasises critical and analytical thinking alongside collaborative working, shared formulation, and consideration of the case from multiple perspectives. This can be beneficial in promoting interprofessional consultation, vital to applied work as a sport and exercise psychologist working, for example, with teams and coaches.

An alternative structured model is the SOAP framework, which prioritises the concise and evidence-based presentation of cases. The model originates in clinical contexts and was then developed within counselling contexts (Cameron & Turtle-Song, 2002) and aims to enhance communication amongst professionals by taking a considered, concise and detailed approach to each client's case. SOAP is an acronym for subjective, objective, assessment, and plan, and each initial represents one section of the client case notes:

Subjective: the client's reported experiences, thoughts, plans, and perceptions
Objective: observable or measurable data that is written in quantifiable terms
Assessment: the supervisee's clinical thinking, interpretation, or formulation linking information to psychological theory
Plan: proposed intervention or action plan or supervision goals.

SOAP allows logical organisation of material and encourages the supervisee to integrate empirical evidence alongside their personal reflections. Within sport and exercise psychology, this could assist with moving away from informational peer supervision and focusing on outcome monitoring and systematic evaluation of practice to enhance professional development (Tod et al., 2017).

No one approach seems better than the others, and the choice of approach needs to reflect the supervisee's and supervisor's preferences. Whatever model or approach is adopted, it is vital that all professional practitioners develop their supervision skills (Bernard & Goodyear, 2019) and that trainees or neophyte practitioners use supervision. Structured models may benefit neophyte practitioners, providing a road map for analytical and ethical reasoning, whereas more experienced practitioners may find more freedom and growth through exploratory dialogue that supports nuanced reflection. Effective supervisors can move between informal and structured case review styles, ensuring they adapt their approach to optimise the professional development of their supervisees.

Overall, the format used is pivotal in shaping the learning environment that is inherent within supervision. Open approaches and more structured models help session flow, help those involved know what to expect, and allow supervisees to integrate their reflections, their reading, and theoretical knowledge into their practice, facilitating the development of competent, ethical practitioners.

7.6 Live Supervision Techniques

This segment examines approaches such as bug-in-ear, reflecting teams, and one-way mirror observation. It explores the theoretical foundations, practical implementation, and evidence base for various live supervision methods.

To enable direct observation, allowing immediate feedback and real-time skill development, live approaches can be implemented within supervision sessions. The techniques used here such as bug-in-ear communication, reflecting teams, and one-way mirror observation originate within counselling and related contexts but are relevant within applied sport and exercise contexts too (Nottingham, 2018; Bernard & Goodyear, 2019). These techniques facilitate supervisees to integrate theoretical understanding with applied skills and can enhance confidence in trainees by providing a bridge between learned skills and the inherently complex practice environments they will encounter (Nottingham, 2018; Maaß et al. 2022).

The bug-in-ear method involves the supervisor communicating live but discreetly with the supervisee via an earpiece during a session. This technique is rooted in social learning (Bandura, 1977) underpinned by the knowledge that observation and guided practice lead to the development of professional competencies. It aims to improve the supervisee's abilities, offering immediate support and corrective feedback to the supervisee

(Wark, 2017). It can also help reveal blind spots (DeRoma et al., 2007); however, it might alter the supervisee's behaviour in session, increase their anxiety and disrupt the session, so collaborative planning is necessary before using this technique.

Reflecting teams, an integral part of family therapy teams in the UK, were developed to prevent therapeutic sessions from becoming stuck. They were developed by Andersen (1991), who observed that allowing families access to therapists' discussions expanded their perspectives and enabled their thinking to move on (Shah, 2019). In this technique, observers listen quietly to a session and then offer reflections while the supervisee listens, encouraging multiple viewpoints (Constable et al., 2022). This is not evaluative but should work to enhance reflexivity and critical thinking, key to professional judgement (Hawkins & Shohet, 2012).

In one-way mirror live supervision, the supervisor observes often without direct participation, allowing for detailed analysis of key session components such as interpersonal dynamics, communication, and intervention strategies. This technique allows evidence-based feedback and enhances supervisee awareness of their level of competence; however, ethical considerations around consent and confidentiality must be negotiated carefully. This technique has been developed into technological setups for internet-based use (Rousmaniere & Frederickson, 2013).

Live supervision has support from empirical studies showing it is more beneficial than no supervision and equally beneficial as delayed supervision. It offers several benefits over delayed supervision (Rousmaniere & Frederickson, 2013) and can enhance supervisee confidence and skill acquisition (Maaß et al. 2022). In sport and exercise psychology, combining immediacy with reflection can be vital, as the context of sport and exercise practice is fast-paced and requires competence in reflection and ethics. For these reasons, live supervision can be valuable.

7.7 Troubleshooting Common Session Challenges

Both structured and live supervision models and techniques support professional development within sport and exercise practice, but the supervisory process rarely unfolds smoothly because of its inherent complexity. In applied settings inhabited by sport and exercise practitioners, unpredictable challenges arise frequently. This necessitates a balance of structure with flexibility and an expectation that sessions will deviate from the plan. Being able to manage these complexities is a supervisory skill required by the nature of applied sport and exercise practice. This subsection addresses frequent obstacles such as unprepared supervisees, crisis interruptions, and session drift. It provides strategies for maintaining productivity despite challenges, while using difficulties as learning opportunities. As we will see, supervisory challenges can also be viewed as opportunities to model key core competencies such as reflective practice, ethical reasoning, and adaptability (McEwan & Tod, 2023; BASES, 2018).

There are many reasons supervisees attend supervision unprepared. This includes confusion or lack of clarity around expectations, a lack of confidence, and an excessive workload. Should supervisees attend without being adequately prepared, for example, with no reflections, notes or data, this can affect how meaningful the supervision can then be. In these cases, supervisors should set clear expectations and reinforce preparation as a professional obligation and competence (Milne, 2009). Supervisees may experience self-doubt relating to supervision, which can lead to avoidance or lack of preparation, and power dynamics within the supervisory relationship should also be considered (Wilson et al., 2016). It may be helpful in these circumstances to link preparation for supervision to athlete welfare and overall service delivery to show the practical significance of supervision. Resistance to supervision could also be a reason for lack of preparation (Bernard & Goodyear, 2019).

Crisis interruptions for trainee psychologists include unexpected and urgent situations that occur during their applied practice work and require immediate, focused attention. These interrupt the planned content of supervision and include things such as client mental health emergencies, risk and safeguarding concerns, and ethical issues around dual relationships or breaches of confidentiality. While they are challenging and require prioritisation, they can also be powerful learning and teaching moments that can help trainees build their confidence and ethical awareness, honing their ability to face future incidents. The importance of contingency planning and procedures to follow for emergencies should be considered within the supervisory agreement at the stage of contracting.

Another common challenge is session drift, which happens when there is a gradual move away from the intended content. Discussion can deviate from the objectives set and can dilute the impact and value of supervision. It could be a lack of focus that creeps in, allowing unrelated topics to be discussed, sometimes because the supervisor and supervisee become familiar and relax boundaries. Properly organising the supervisory experience and maintaining that organisation through clear co-construction of agendas, the use of summaries and agreed goals can help to reduce drift and preserve focus (Bernard & Goodyear, 2019).

Recognising when these challenges occur and navigating them constructively strengthens the supervisory relationship and aids professional development. They provide opportunities for reflection and ethical and evidence-informed considerations that provide the foundation for effective sport and exercise psychology practice.

7.8 Summary

This chapter has explored core elements of structured and effective supervision, including practical planning elements, theoretical approaches alongside the functions of supervision, and has introduced methods and techniques that could be used within that. It finished by exploring common session challenges. The next three chapters will consider in more depth the important elements of supervision, moving from beginning to middle to endings.

Exercise 7.1: Build a Supervision Session Plan

Design a 50-minute supervision session using:

- Opening check-in
- Agenda setting
- Core case discussion
- Experiential skill component
- Goal setting
- Closure

Use a real or simulated case. Then highlight where you would incorporate:

- Reflection
- Ethics
- Feedback
- Parallel process awareness

8 Beginnings – Key Elements of Starting a Supervisory Relationship

In this chapter, we will consider the key elements of beginning a supervisory relationship. We will focus on initial contracting and setting expectations, how to conduct a needs assessment, and collaboratively setting goals. We will consider the importance of individualised learning plans and touch briefly on how best to evaluate within supervision. The need to create a psychologically safe environment, build the supervisory alliance, and reduce resistance and anxiety in the supervisee will also be considered.

This initial phase of supervision is key to setting the tone and direction for the entire supervisory relationship. Investing time and effort to consider this phase correctly lays the foundation for a productive and meaningful relationship.

8.1 Initial Contracting and Setting Expectations

This subsection examines the critical first phase of supervision, focusing on establishing clear parameters for the working relationship. It explores contract elements including roles, responsibilities, meeting structure, and communication expectations, with attention to both formal and psychological contracting.

There are clear reasons why in this initial phase of supervision, you would need to establish defined working rules, or a clear sense of how your supervisory relationship will work. These are to ensure that your supervision meets the formal and psychological functions required to be effective. As outlined by the HCPC (2025a), supervision has significant benefits for the supervisee, supervisor, and the wider service and service users. Establishing a clear contract fulfils formal and psychological purposes (Amaro et al., 2020). As a formal function, it serves to outline roles and responsibilities and cover key areas like the structure of meetings and the way communication will work within supervision. As a psychological function, the contract can help to develop trust within the working alliance; it can set and clarify expectations and reduce uncertainty.

DOI: 10.4324/9781003485667-8

Supervision facilitates the development of the supervisee, socialising them into the profession (Amaro et al., 2020) and as such helps build skills and professional identity. Because of this, setting clear expectations via a contract at the start of your work is vital.

There is a lot to do at the start of the supervisory relationship when contracting, including: establishing the groundwork for a positive and productive supervisory relationship; agreeing a framework or structure for supervision; and setting developmentally relevant goals for the supervisee. There are templates and contract examples or suggested content available for use (see, for example, Bernard & Goodyear, 2014; HCPC, 2025b; Gonsalvez, 2014) and these are worth reviewing when developing your own agreement. The first key area to include within your contract is roles and responsibilities. Barney and Andersen (2014) highlight the need for role clarity, listing it as one of the core conditions required for supervision, regardless of the theoretical model used. The roles and responsibilities of each person, supervisor and supervisee, should be listed. For the supervisee, this can include attending meetings prepared and open to feedback and agreeing to action items between sessions. The supervisor should monitor applied practices, offer constructive feedback, and help the supervisee develop as a practitioner. Should there be confusion over the roles and responsibilities, this can be detrimental to the supervision experience and outcomes, so working on clarity and ensuring there is no ambiguity is vital (Meijen & Manley, 2010).

The contract between a supervisor and a supervisee should also clearly outline the logistics of supervision. For example, how often will you meet? Will this be in person or online? And how will sessions be documented? Providing clarity in these areas means misunderstandings can be avoided, and by defining the focus of supervision, the continuity and effectiveness of supervision are supported (McCarthy et al., 2024). Research suggests that regular meetings, feedback, and opportunities for self-reflection contribute to supervisees' growth, so they should be considered within the scope of contracting (Tod et al., 2021).

Another consideration at this early stage is how communication between the supervisor and supervisee will occur outside of formal meetings. Will this be via email or messaging, for example, and are there clear expectations around response times? How will supervisees be able to contact the supervisor should there be an emergency, and how should disagreements be resolved? Clarity on these elements helps establish supervisees' perceptions of psychological safety (Fogaca et al., 2018).

What we are suggesting here is formal contracting – a clear written agreement outlining the operational parameters of your supervisory relationship. It is also important to be mindful of the psychological contracting that can occur – those less explicit factors that can affect the relationship.

Andersen (2012) highlights the importance of considering the interpersonal elements within supervision and offers insight into how mindfulness could be considered. The psychological contract underlies the formal contract, and together they help build trust in the relationship.

Contracting is key to building a solid scaffold for the supervisory relationship and to allay concerns and provide clarity of expectations. Contracting allows us to formally and informally set expectations and implement supervision in a way that is central to the development of professional sport and exercise practitioners, ensuring ethical practice and client safety (Poczwardowski et al., 2023).

8.2 Conducting Supervisee Needs Assessments

This subsection explores methods for evaluating supervisee strengths, growth edges, and learning preferences at the outset of supervision. It examines structured assessment tools, interview approaches, and self-assessment methods that provide the foundation for tailored supervision.

To set individual learning goals, it is necessary to conduct a supervisee needs assessment. This is a fundamental step at the beginning of supervision that allows the co-construction of a developmental plan (Johnson, 2017). It allows both parties to have a clear and shared understanding of the supervisee's current level of competency, their strengths, learning preferences, and their growth edges. A good starting point is for the supervisee to reflect on their perceived strengths across core competencies such as ethical reasoning and communication. This can be enhanced by examining any previous placement or work experience and gaining an understanding of their previous academic qualifications too. A supervisor can also use their observations to gather information on the supervisee's interpersonal skills, confidence, and ability to take initiative.

Considering baseline competencies (for example, from the BPS key roles and HCPC standards) helps to understand the supervisee's current position and identify any gaps which can then feed into the statement of developmental goals. This also allows us to establish whether the supervisee is where they should be relative to their stage of professional development. Examples of how to do this are offered by authors such as Johnson (2017) who provides a worksheet for needs assessment and goal setting.

Growth edges can be identified by using competency checklists in combination with self-assessment tools. These can highlight areas for development or improvement in, for example, ethics, communication, or performance enhancement. A key role of the supervisor is to assess supervisees' knowledge and experience in specialist settings to identify their developmental needs. A further means of doing this can be through the presentation of hypothetical or real cases to observe how the supervisee approaches these, and feedback from previous supervision can also be requested and can, where available, provide further insight into the supervisee's current competence and their previous progress.

Psychometric tools can explore, for example, resilience or emotional intelligence, and these can be combined with interviews where open-ended questions offer information on supervisees' motivations, expectations, and self-perceptions. Using interviews also ensures that supervision is tailored to the individual and not seen as generic or prescriptive by those seeking supervision. Reflective questionnaires and skills inventories can also help supervisees gain a sense of agency and control regarding their development, promoting their understanding of their own strengths and areas for development. 'What am I doing well' can be as important as 'What do I need to improve?' so strengths should be highlighted at this stage, not just growth edges. An understanding of both is needed to promote supervisee growth and their development into a competent practitioner (Poczwardowski et al., 2023). Taking a broader strengths-based approach to supervision is also possible; see, for example, Wade and Jones (2015).

Learning preferences should be considered, and this can be from the perspective of inventories (such as VARK or Kolb) to establish an understanding of the supervisee's learning style and preference but can also focus on how the supervisee likes to receive feedback and how they have learned best in the past.

Strengths form the bedrock or foundation for progress and growth; edges are then targeted considering learning preferences to increase engagement in the supervisory process, motivation, and, as a result, professional practice. The needs assessment phase ends with a co-created and jointly agreed learning plan that fits with the proposed methods of supervision. This is not a static document and will require regular review as the work progresses.

8.3 Collaborative Goal Setting

This segment addresses approaches to establishing meaningful, specific objectives for the supervision process. It explores frameworks for ensuring goals are developmentally appropriate, measurable, and aligned with professional competency standards.

Many authors have written about goal setting within supervision (Bernard & Goodyear, 2019; Corey et al., 2020) and agree that these goals, when agreed on collaboratively, can act as both a foundation for and a clear marker of evaluation within supervision (Wade & Jones, 2015). Milne et al. (2008) identified goal setting as one of the most successful supervisory interventions. In fact, to orient the process of supervision towards growth, it is necessary to set meaningful, specific goals or objectives early in the supervisory process, ensuring accountability is prioritised and that work is aligned with professional competency standards.

As highlighted by Reiser and Milne (2017a), goal setting is not merely an administrative task but one that helps form and build the supervisory alliance and working relationship between supervisor and supervisee. Competencies for sport and exercise psychology practitioners are often complex, and goals need to be adequately broken down to align with these. Goals help to scaffold sessions, providing what Vygotsky (1978) referred to as a zone of proximal development and empowering supervisees.

Using SMARTER goals can be a key approach to framing supervision goals. These are Specific, Measurable, Achievable, Realistic, Time-bound, Evaluated, and Recorded. These should then be reviewed and refined regularly. Setting goals this way ensures that measurement of progress is possible, and that progress is grounded in specifics that can be measured and evaluated. Setting collaborative goals, aligned with relevant competence frameworks and appropriate to the supervisee's stage of development, facilitates the supervisee's movement from foundational awareness to autonomous practice and competence (Poczwardowski et al., 2023).

In summary, setting goals should be collaborative and take into consideration the supervisee's learning preferences and the contextual and organisational systems within which they are working. The process of negotiation enhances engagement and ownership of the goal, and setting SMARTER goals can form the foundation of meaningful supervisory planning and evaluation.

8.4 Developing Individualised Learning Plans

This subsection examines the creation of structured development plans based on assessments and goals. It explores methods of sequencing learning experiences, identifying resources, and establishing timelines that support systematic competency development.

Using the previously discussed needs assessment, trainee self-assessment and reflection, and consideration of the supervisee's placement on competency development, an individualised learning plan or ILP should now be co-created. This should outline how the supervisor and supervisee will work to address the growth edges and build competence in the supervisee.

Through this, short- and longer-term developmental objectives are set, and a clear structure or scaffold for the supervisory content is established. These plans help the supervisee gain a sense of their professional development over time, and align well with the recognition in the literature that development can start with a focus on observation and guided practice, moving through a series of increasingly independent and focused work to create individualised development in sport and exercise practitioners

(Tod et al., 2009; McEwan et al., 2019). An ILP should include timescales too and allow for the evaluation of goals and their refinement as the supervision progresses. Realistic timelines should be included in the ILP, with short, medium- and long-term review points being clearly defined. The type of evidence required to demonstrate attainment of developmental milestones should also be stated, e.g. supervisor ratings using the CTS-R if the supervision is CBT-based, or case study write-ups.

The supervisor and supervisee can use the ILP to make explicit the expectations of and sources of development opportunities. For example, reading can be set; observational and modelling opportunities identified; and peer learning and placement opportunities should also be included. The aim is to include a range of activities that can support development against specific competencies, bridging theory and practice and ensuring a variety of learning opportunities which are identified in the literature as being key to practitioner development (McEwan et al., 2019; Cushion et al., 2010).

8.5 Establishing Evaluation Criteria

This subsection addresses approaches to creating transparent evaluation processes. It examines the establishment of clear performance expectations, assessment methods, and feedback mechanisms that will be used throughout supervision.

Without clear evaluation criteria, supervisees will struggle to understand performance expectations, how to operationalise the ILP, and will not understand how their work is being assessed and judged. Feedback is crucial to evaluation, and discussions should occur between the supervisor and supervisee outlining how feedback and evaluation will be given. Formal evaluations can be anxiety-provoking (for supervisor and supervisee), so as a supervisor, it is helpful to consider evaluation even before the first meeting with the supervisee. Knowing what criteria you will use and how you will evaluate and present that evaluation to the supervisee increases the chances that opportunities for the supervisee to develop will be thoughtful and well planned.

Johnson (2017) outlines the importance of setting clear expectations around feedback and the need for it to be fair and respectful. He suggests immediate feedback on any area falling below the expected level, allowing for refinements and corrections to be made. Additionally, offering feedback on any areas where expectations have been surpassed is good practice to maintain a balanced view of the supervisee's development.

Effective supervision requires continuous monitoring of the progress the supervisee is making and the communication of feedback that is constructive, positive, and aligned with goals and competencies (Falender, 2014).

Setting key dates for feedback with regular formative feedback and an end-point summative feedback session ensures both parties understand how and when the evaluations will be presented. The processes surrounding both formative and summative feedback should be transparent to ensure the supervisee knows the views and appraisals of the supervisor (James et al. 2007). Having regular formative evaluations allows future planning and alterations to be made ahead of summative evaluations, ensuring the supervisory process remains on track and aids the supervisee in their practitioner development. As Borders et al. (2014) highlight, providing feedback and conducting evaluations are elements included in best practice guidelines for supervision. Supervisors can use recognised checklists as part of their evaluation or could choose to employ techniques such as interpersonal process recall or IPR (Kagan & Kagan, 1997) which allows for additional positive outcomes for the supervisee including reducing evaluation anxiety (James et al., 2007). Depending on the modality being used, there are further considerations around evaluation and feedback. For example, see Reiser and Milne (2017b) for detailed information on evaluation in CBT supervision.

To cultivate a supervisory environment where openness and continuous learning are at the forefront, you need to have transparent evaluation criteria and consistent assessment practices. Without that, it would be difficult to justify any judgements around competency development. To support supervisees in the progression of their practice as sport and exercise practitioners, assessment, evaluation, and feedback mechanisms must be agreed in advance and kept, allowing ongoing refinements and development.

8.6 Creating a Safe Learning Environment

This segment explores techniques for establishing psychological safety in the supervisory relationship. It examines approaches to normalising learning challenges, managing performance anxiety, and creating conditions that support appropriate vulnerability and risk-taking. It provides help in distinguishing between developmental anxiety and problematic resistance.

Creating a psychologically safe environment within supervision is key to effective learning and professional development in sport and exercise psychology (Chircop Coleiro et al., 2023). Supervisees must feel able to express their doubts, report any concerns or mistakes, and reflect honestly within the session free from fear of judgement or reprimand (Edmondson, 2018; Liu et al., 2016). Interpersonally risky behaviours such as disagreeing with the supervisor and others, asking questions, bringing ethical dilemmas, perceived failures, and reporting mistakes must be seen as normal developmental activities to create an efficacious learning environment (Lee et al., 2022). Without this atmosphere of acceptance and safety, supervisees will lack the ingredients they need to develop their own reflective competence and improve their ethical awareness.

To create this psychological safety, supervisors need to behave intentionally. This can be considered during contracting, where expectations are clearly spelled out, and feedback and its developmental role are highlighted, leading to a sense of comfort and safety (Milne et al., 2008). To promote psychological safety, supervisors can normalise challenges encountered by their supervisees, reframing them as opportunities for growth, not evidence of incompetence. This can help to address developmental anxiety experienced by supervisees.

Anxiety negatively affects learning in supervision (Kuo et al. 2016) and as Bernard and Goodyear (2019) highlight supervisors act as gatekeepers for the profession that supervisees ultimately want to join, so ethically they need to provide a safe learning environment within which to grow and develop professionally. Anxiety is one of the most recognised and prevalent emotions within clinical supervision (Kuo et al. 2016) and has the power to enhance or impede learning. If we assume an inverted U-shaped relationship between anxiety and learning to follow the Yerkes and Dodson (1908) model, then anxiety itself appears not as something to be avoided or eliminated but as something to be recognised and managed so that it results in positive learning and development. The ways this can be enacted within a supervisory relationship require a safe environment and can be enhanced using tools and measures such as those outlined by Kuo et al. (2016). Recognising and managing anxiety well within supervision can strengthen the working alliance and benefit communication and performance. Supervision should also differentiate between developmental anxiety, where a supervisee is being pushed slightly out of their comfort zone to enhance their competence, and problematic resistance, which can impede development and stem from areas such as perfectionism or the rupture of the working alliance.

By working explicitly on psychological safety and the productive use of anxiety for professional development, we are mirroring within supervision how we expect practitioners to behave.

8.7 Building the Supervisory Working Alliance

This subsection considers Bordin's working alliance theory (goals, tasks, bond) and Holloway's tripartite theory in the establishment of effective supervisory relationships. It considers the importance of developing rapport, trust, and collaboration from the earliest interactions.

Developing and maintaining the supervisory relationship or working alliance is widely recognised as being crucial to the effectiveness of supervision (Beinart, 2014). Often, there are power differentials between supervisor and supervisee, and as a result, the onus is often on the supervisor to create the right atmosphere for a positive working alliance. Supervisors might assume that they will naturally create a positive working alliance as they do this with clients; however, that does not always follow – in part because of the evaluative element of supervision (Johnson, 2017). As Chircop Coleiro et al. (2023) found, there are helpful supervisory behaviours which underlie this and strengthen the working alliance, increasing disclosure and confidence of supervisees. These include aspects such as the supervisor being able to facilitate learning, to recognise differences, and to establish psychological safety. In a good supervisory relationship, the supervisor creates a secure base from which supervisees can explore and develop their competencies.

The first model to consider is Bordin's (1983) model of the working alliance, and it is the best-known example of supervisory relationship models. This model offers a framework comprising three elements: goals, tasks, and bond. The goal element is where developmental objectives are collaboratively constructed and jointly agreed upon. In sport and exercise psychology, they may refer to specific intervention techniques or to the enhancement of ethical decision-making skills. The task element of the framework refers to the actual activities through which the supervisee can meet the goals, for example, case discussion, live observations, or self-reflective journalling. The bond underpins the framework and is based on trust and respect gained through perceptions of psychological safety. This framework has a research evidence base; however, it lacks the scope to include the broader elements of education and evaluation, which are key to supervision within sport and exercise (Cliffe et al., 2016). In fact, Watkins and Milne (2014) provide a nuanced understanding of the difference between the supervisory working alliance and the supervisory relationship. They explain that although the terms tend to be used to have the same meaning, the supervisory working alliance can be seen to be more theoretically based and arising from Bordin's working alliance theory comprising goals, tasks, and bond (Bordin, 1983). The supervisory relationship, however, is broader in definition, including educational and evaluative aspects.

This brings us to a second model, Holloway's (1995) model, where there are three essential elements to successful supervisory relationships. The first is the interpersonal relationship between the supervisor and supervisee, where both parties influence the relationship and the development from formal to informal over time. The second is the phase of the relationship moving from beginnings to maturation to termination as supervisee autonomy increases over time. The third is the supervisory contract, where goals and tasks are negotiated and expectations and relational aspects are clarified (Fleming & Steen, 2012). However, although clear, the model lacks empirical support.

Both these models and others (see for example Beinart, 2012) provide clear, coherent structures for developing and growing collaborative and growth-focused supervision. Through intentionally strengthening the supervisory working alliance and supervisory relationship, supervisors in sport and exercise psychology can aid supervisees in their development of competence and their autonomy, and in their future applied practice.

8.8 Summary

This chapter has considered elements that are key to the beginning phase of supervision and are important considerations for supervisors and supervisees. We have covered the importance of contracting; expectation setting and needs assessment. We covered collaborative goal setting and the ILPs that follow needs assessment and goal setting. We considered the importance of evaluation (both formative feedback and summative evaluation) and covered the need for psychological safety within a supervisory relationship alongside the need for supervisors to intentionally provide the right aspects for the development of a sound supervisory working relationship. While not an exhaustive list of key considerations at the start of supervision (for example, orienting to organisational context and requirements and practices for documenting supervision could also be important here), we have considered many of the key introductory foundations of effective supervision. In the following chapter, we will consider the aspects key to the middle phases of supervision.

Exercise 8.1: Contracting Simulation

In pairs, role-play a contracting meeting:

Supervisor role:
Introduce expectations, boundaries, evaluation procedures, confidentiality, and communication norms.

Supervisee role:
Ask clarifying questions, express concerns, negotiate needs, identify potential challenges.

After 15 minutes, reflect on:

1. What was easy/difficult to discuss?
2. Any unspoken expectations?
3. How will this conversation shape future supervision?

9 Middles – Navigating the Core of Supervision

9.1 Introduction

In Chapter 8, we explored the initial phase of a supervisory relationship and the factors within that are vital to establishing a strong foundation. During the initial phase, you need to establish expectations, assess needs and align these with competencies to create a shared vision of the path to professional development. Once you have successfully navigated that phase, you can move to what is arguably where the real work begins. That is the middle phase of supervision – the longest and most sustained period of supervision. This chapter considers the key elements within this middle phase, where the goals from the initial contracting are translated into skills, where initial theoretical knowledge is given real-world application, and where the supervisory working relationship or alliance is deepened and strengthened.

What you are aiming for during this phase is a consistent approach that enables the momentum you gather in your work together to continue, and for stagnation to be avoided. By putting in a degree of intentionality into the supervisory role, the supervisor can help to scaffold and direct supervision, helping the supervisee to navigate plateaus and facilitate meaningful, lasting learning and development. There is a danger at this phase of the process that supervision loses momentum and becomes a repetitive chore rather than a more dynamic and purposeful experience.

This chapter offers ideas on how to navigate this core phase of supervision. We will start by presenting some guidance on maintaining forward momentum, managing the balance between consistent and predictable structures with sufficient variation to maintain interest and learning. We shall then move on to explore experiential learning and examples of supervision techniques that align with that. This leads us into a discussion of feedback and how to manage challenging conversations that are often necessary in supervision. We also consider how to address plateaus and regression before ending the chapter with some information on revising goals and approaches during supervision. In sum, this chapter covers key

DOI: 10.4324/9781003485667-9

elements of the middle phases of supervision, highlighting that this phase is about actively building, refining, and developing professional competence and skill.

9.2 Maintaining Forward Momentum

This part addresses the tension between consistency and novelty in supervision sessions. It explores techniques for establishing predictable structures while introducing sufficient variation to maintain interest and address diverse learning needs. It also considers the supervisor's ability to provide clear signposting and navigate the often complex content of supervisory meetings. Finally, it examines how supportive interventions appropriately shift as supervisees progress, with attention to recognising regression during stress and adjusting support accordingly.

As we have demonstrated so far in this text, supervision in sport and exercise psychology functions as a critical developmental mechanism and enables supervisees to progress from neophyte to autonomous practitioners (Bernard & Goodyear, 2019; McCarthy et al., 2024). It also allows for professional development in experienced practitioners and is a key requirement of safe, effective practice, contributing to the supervisee, supervisor, and client/organisation. During the middle phases of supervision, the key tension involves finding a good enough balance between predictability and novelty in supervision. We want supervision to be consistent and to meet the expectations of both the supervisor and supervisee; however, we also want there to be sufficient novelty, variability, and adaptation within supervision to ensure that it does not stagnate. As mentioned in Chapter 8, we are trying to create a safe and predictable space for supervision, and creating and maintaining this structure can prevent supervision from drifting (more on that later). However, to stop supervision feeling repetitive and stagnant, we need to also introduce novelty, as that is vital to engagement and to addressing developing and changing needs as supervision progresses. One role of the supervisor is to manage that balance. We can do that by retaining the clear check-in, agenda setting, discussing current cases, and setting next session intentions. Then, within that structure, we can alter different elements. For example, we can alter the content by changing the topic area, switching between ethics, professional identity and specific intervention skills, or we can change the format by changing between didactic methods such as case studies, recorded sessions and role play (Poczwardowski et al., 2023). The skill the supervisor needs is to balance this and provide the right degree of structure alongside flexibility. If sessions seem too improvised, they can lack psychological safety, but if they are too structured, they can feel constricting.

Clear signposting during supervision is needed to manage this balance. The content of supervision can be complex, and without clear signposting, i.e. being explicit about how individual components of the supervision align with overarching goals, it can seem unfocused. Supervisees need to see how individual discussions or the review of, for example, a live session relates to their broader goals and development. Clear signposting also helps structure the session e.g. 'We'll consider this case study, then we'll move to your live recordings, and finally, we'll set our intentions for the week' and allows the supervisee to orient themselves. Finally, clear signposting enables reflection, and reflection is key to supervision in sport psychology (Knowles et al., 2007) supporting applied practice. Reflection also enables a deeper understanding of one's professional identity, personal and professional philosophy (Poczwardowski et al., 2004). Existing models of reflection, such as Gibbs' reflective cycle and Driscoll's model, can be incorporated into sessions to enable this reflection (Gibbs, 1988; Driscoll, 1994).

Without some degree of structure and consistency, supervisory drift can occur (Roscoe, 2021) in the middle phase of supervision. Supervisory drift is defined as 'instances in which core components of supervision (e.g. outcomes monitoring, direct observation, mutual feedback) are omitted, avoided or deprioritised, resulting in a gap between supervisory theory and practice' (Pugh & Margetts, 2020, p. 5). This mirrors the concept of therapist drift (Waller, 2009) where practitioners diverge from evidence-based practice, and movement can occur from 'doing' to 'talking'. Both supervisor and supervisee need to be cognisant of when the drift from being a 'doing' process occurs and work to bring it back, or supervision will not be creating development opportunities for supervisees. Supervision will essentially move from being about 'showing' to 'telling'.

Interventions need to be adjusted as supervision progresses too, recognising the stage the supervisee is at and their developing competence. Developmental supervision models allow an individualised approach to be taken where the supervisee's stage of development is recognised, and interventions adapted accordingly to prioritise the relevant learning needs of the stage (Poczwardowski et al., 2023). There are two models that could be followed to enable this, the integrated developmental model (IDM; Stoltenberg & McNeill, 2010) and the six-phase model of supervision by Rønnestad and Skovholt (2003). These developmental models, which enable the adjustment of interventions, apply to experienced and novice supervisees. Supervision can progress from being more directive or hands-on to being more collaborative as needs change. Earlier supervision may require direction and scaffolding that in later phases makes way for more facilitative methods to match the supervisees' development needs.

As we progress through the middle phase of supervision, it is also good to be mindful that development is not linear and that challenges such as ethical dilemmas encountered by supervisees can result in reduced confidence, increased anxiety, and the need for supervision to revert to being more supportive and directive.

9.3 Experiential Learning Methods

This section considers the movement through Kolb's learning cycle and aligns that with supervision. Using a variety of techniques and approaches during supervision is key to embedding experiential learning within the process effectively (Milne & Reiser, 2017). Therefore, this section considers experiential learning with a focus on role-play and simulation, live supervision, and journalling as examples.

As practitioners develop, they need to manage the tensions between being expected to learn by doing and to learn from mistakes, while also working to ensure that they are prioritising client safety and outcomes (Ilgen et al., 2021). Supervision can help to manage or navigate these uncertainties and tensions, and one way to do this is by providing an approach based on experiential learning methods. Experiential learning helps with the move from the supervisor leading the initial early stages of contracting to a more balanced, facilitative role.

Although not originally conceptualised as a model for supervision, embedding experiential learning allows supervisors to be active agents in the development of supervisees' skills through structured experience, reflection, and conceptualisation. Using Kolb's (2014) experiential learning cycle, both supervisor and supervisee can engage in the structured process of moving from early verbal discussions of cases to more active, experimental, real-time practice. Kolb's well-known model contains four phases: concrete experience, reflective observation, abstract conceptualisation, and active experimentation.

According to experiential learning, change and growth occur through this four-phase process (Abbey et al., 1985). During the first phase, concrete experience, the supervisee is engaging in a specific task or situation. Moving into phase two, they then think back or reflect on that experience, taking time to notice any patterns and their own processes or reactions. This facilitates the move to abstract conceptualisation where together the supervisor and supervisee can identify key learning points, make clear links between theory and practice, and consider potential alternative approaches. Finally, active experimentation allows the supervisor and supervisee to plan how these learning points can be embedded in future practice and can set goals around this, allowing the supervisee to try new strategies and develop new approaches to their practice. In this way, using experiential learning within supervision supports critical thinking and self-awareness while highlighting the need for evidence-based reflection and aligning that with professional development goals. Both the supervisor and the supervisee have input in terms of individual learning styles and the time allocated to each phase. Some will prefer more reflection time, while others prefer more action. This allows the co-creation of a method that works for both supervisor and supervisee, giving both a sense of joint working and engagement with the process. See McCarthy et al. (2024) for a review of the importance of reflective practice within training and supervision in sport and exercise psychology.

As mentioned above, incorporating multiple techniques for experiential learning is important. Role-play and simulation are two of the most used techniques within supervision (Pugh & Margetts, 2020). They can be used for a variety of purposes, including rehearsal, where the supervisee can practise techniques, and modelling, where the supervisor can demonstrate specific skills, techniques, or interventions. Common scenarios within sport and exercise psychology supervision also include its use to experiment or test new techniques or to re-enact something that happened in the supervisee's practice to learn and acquire alternative perspectives. Supervisees can also use role-play to practise difficult conversations. This highly versatile technique serves a variety of purposes and allows the immediate sharing of in-the-moment feedback within a psychologically safe environment. It works through the supervisor and supervisee agreeing on a specific scenario to practise and agreeing on the roles to be taken by each. For example, a supervisor might role-play an athlete who is particularly resistant to change or one who is frustrated following an injury. A key element of role-play is a de-brief at the end to allow both parties to reflect on what went well and what was challenging. Ensuring the supervisee offers their reflections first is important.

New advances in technology are currently changing the way role-play can be used within supervision. For example, Maurya and DeDiego (2025) have written about the ability of AI to offer support by providing simulated case studies for role-play. Maurya (2023) also found in a content analysis of ChatGPT's client simulation role plays that it can effectively simulate the role of a client in counselling practice, and this could provide opportunities for use within sport and exercise settings too.

Live supervision is another technique aligned with experiential learning. This was discussed in Chapter 8, where we discussed how direct observation, allowing immediate feedback and real-time skill development, could be implemented through live approaches. This is an impactful method of experiential learning, to allow in-the-moment or real-time feedback and facilitating the observation of more nuanced elements of the supervisee's practice that can be missed in mere verbal summaries (Maaß, et al. 2022). Live supervision can be a key part of active experimentation, where refined knowledge and new strategies are enacted in professional contexts.

Journalling promotes self-reflection and is a powerful means by which supervisees can gain a deeper self-awareness between sessions (Collins et al., 2025). It facilitates experiential learning. In fact, Davys and Beddoe (2009) suggest taking experiential learning to the next stage where they see reflection as the primary method for learning and development. Reflection through journalling aligns with many of the models of supervision, including Proctor's (1986) three-factor model and Milne et al'.s., (2008) model, and supervisors can use specific prompts to facilitate journalling and self-reflection, setting tasks for between sessions, e.g. 'Reflect on your most challenging client from this week focusing on what was happening for you emotionally'. Insights gained from these reflections through journalling can be used within sessions, providing rich content for learning.

For suggestions on how experiential learning can be incorporated into supervision by both supervisor and supervisee see Johnson (2017) who suggests application exercises within supervision following Milne's (2009) update to the Kolb learning cycle, where he proposes a cycle of five different modes: experiencing, reflecting, conceptualising, planning, and experimenting.

9.4 Providing and Receiving Feedback

This section covers how to give constructive feedback; it looks at both formative and summative feedback and how to ensure that the environment is psychologically safe for that feedback to be accepted, and how to navigate challenging feedback conversations.

Feedback is one of the critical components of supervision in sport and exercise practice (Poczwardowski et al., 2023). Effective feedback within supervision is multifaceted (Johnson, 2017) and used to clarify and deepen the modes of experiential learning mentioned above. Without effective feedback, supervision would struggle to facilitate the development of supervisees' applied competencies and professional judgements. Sport and exercise practitioners are unique in that they work within often high-pressure and quickly changing environments with not only athletes but also coaches and teams. Feedback becomes even more central to success here and needs to be delivered thoughtfully to support skill and practice development. Take time during contracting to establish feedback expectations of both parties, including the frequency of feedback, how feedback is viewed, and what aspects of practice supervisees most want feedback on. Normalising constructive feedback and enabling ongoing feedback allows supervisees to track what they are doing well and what areas require improvement (McCarthy et al., 2024). Following from this, feedback needs to be both formative and summative within supervision. It must provide opportunities for ongoing development of identified areas while also providing an evaluative or outcome-based function.

9.4.1 Formative and Summative Feedback

Formative feedback should be interwoven throughout supervision so that it forms a continuous cycle that shapes learning. In sport psychology supervision, this could include timely, specific feedback in session that is rooted in observation and encourages self-reflection and the adjustment of behaviours. It can appear informal and should form a cornerstone of the supervisory process. Within supervision, the way formative feedback functions will depend on the stage of the supervisee, with novice supervisees perhaps learning more from directive feedback and experienced practitioners learning more effectively from a more collaborative feedback style. Summative feedback tends to be more evaluative and occurs at agreed points in supervision to assess progress against the goals that were set for supervision. Its evaluative components allow both the supervisor and the supervisee to understand how competencies are developing and what stage of professional development the supervisee is at. Summative or evaluative feedback should build on documented formative feedback, allowing supervisees to see how their ongoing development has contributed to the overall evaluation of their practice.

9.4.2 Feedback Techniques

Key techniques and strategies for providing feedback should be considered. For example, it is useful to start with an identification of strengths and then move into growth areas. It is also useful to ask the supervisee how they feel their progress is allowing a comparison of their own view with that of the supervisor. Basing feedback on specific examples is also a key consideration, for example identifying a clear situation (e.g., 'In the role play we undertook where you were working with a client who was frustrated'), linking that to behaviour (e.g., 'you appeared to be quite defensive in your questioning'), and explaining the impact of that behaviour (e.g., 'and the impact was that the conversation seemed to shut down'). This ensures feedback can be given in a non-judgemental way, sharing conversations that lead to development and growth, and checking in with the supervisee to see if their reflections match.

9.4.3 Psychologically Safe Feedback

Hutter et al. (2015) concluded that supervision in sport psychology serves many functions including increasing the supervisee's ability to cope with service delivery demands, aiding reflective practice, and providing support and guidance. Without feedback, these functions would be impossible to enact. We also refer you back to Chapter 8, where establishing a psychologically safe space for supervision was discussed. The psychological safety of the supervisory alliance provides a bedrock for honest and open feedback. Without that, no matter how well-intentioned the feedback is, it might not be accepted and instead could be perceived as threatening and punitive.

9.4.4 Managing Challenging Feedback Conversations

It is not uncommon in supervision for challenging feedback conversations to arise. Both supervisor and supervisee need to see the necessity for these to occur and be confident that they can occur without a rupture in the supervisory alliance during this key middle phase of supervision. These challenging conversations might centre on performance concerns, ethical issues, or even interpersonal behaviour. They are necessary as supervision is viewed as the gatekeeper of the profession, protecting clients and the profession (Poczwardowski et al., 2023).

Although necessary, they can, if not prepared for and managed well, disrupt the supervisory working alliance (Willians et al., 2016). Key to managing challenging conversations in feedback is the consideration of how supervisees prefer to get feedback, and that should be considered during the early stage of supervision. Having agreed feedback processes in place reduces confusion and can also buffer against the supervisee feeling that the feedback was harsh or personal rather than developmental and aligned with supervisory goals. When a difficult conversation is needed, the supervisor can highlight the shared expectations that were set, which can allow the conversation to proceed based on a professional collaborative agreement and not be taken as subjective judgement. It can also be a good idea to allow supervisees themselves to reflect on the area the supervisor has identified as needing to be addressed, for example, by offering, 'What areas do you feel were challenging for you in this situation?'. Supervisors can then offer differences between their own perspective and the self-appraisal of the supervisee so that these can be explored jointly, steering the conversation away from being perceived as judgemental. Using a process like the one identified for general feedback above can also help here. For example, offer a specific situation, the behaviour of interest and the impact of that so that the supervisee's sense of professional identity is protected via non-judgemental, clear language that signposts a clear direction for improvement. Framing challenging conversations around accountability can also be useful, acknowledging that the feedback will be uncomfortable to hear but that it's important to support practitioner development and improve the overall service provision offered by the supervisee.

Managing challenging feedback conversations is a necessary function of supervision, and one that requires preparation, understanding, and alignment with developing competencies. Avoiding such challenging conversations will have ongoing negative outcomes for the individuals involved and the profession.

9.4.5 Feedback: A Final Word

A final note for feedback is that it should be based on competencies and skills that the trainee needs to develop and which have been identified early in the supervisory relationship. It should be a balance between being supportive and reinforcing development and being a critique. Corrective feedback is important, but it should be specific to behaviours and offered in a timely fashion. Finally, feedback should not be framed as a test that supervisees either pass or fail, but as a process of development with no aim towards 'perfection' (McCarthy et al., 2024).

9.5 Addressing Plateaus and Regression

This segment examines common patterns of stalled progress or backward movement. It explores theoretical frameworks for understanding these patterns and provides approaches to intervention that reinvigorate development.

Progress and development within supervision are rarely linear. There will be times when progress seems to stall or even move backwards, and recognising when this is happening and responding to it is a responsibility of the supervisor to promote professional growth and ensure that the supervisee is practising competently. Theoretical perspectives on supervision can enable a better understanding of this; for example, taking a developmental model perspective such as that of Stoltenberg and McNeill (2010) we can see how supervisees might plateau or regress in their movement through stages of dependence to autonomy if they face a new challenge or a specific performance pressure in their practice environment. Similarly, if we take a reflective or experiential framework, we can see that a plateau or stall in development could easily be related to an ethical dilemma, a developing identity, or even a disruption in the supervisory working alliance. It is also possible that a stall is because of resistance (Johnson, 2017) which can manifest following evaluation that the supervisee failed to incorporate successfully into their development plan. To reintroduce momentum, we need a psychologically safe space where these challenges can be recognised and addressed.

Supervisors can share their working hypotheses with supervisees to foster insight, for example, 'I've noticed some caution and uncertainty in sessions and wondered if you're feeling a loss of confidence following the feedback you received from a client recently?' This can lead to conversations about perceived barriers to progress and development, which can help reinvigorate supervision through revisiting goals, expectations, and competency development. If a plateau is related to a loss of confidence, then a slight shift into emphasising strengths and reviewing progress can help to re-engage the supervisee with their development. Changing the supervisory methods used can also be beneficial at times of regression to avoid stagnation. For example, using live observation, role play or simulated case discussions may offer broader perspectives and assist supervisees to reorient to their development objectives.

Whatever the underlying cause of a stall in momentum, recognising it is occurring and framing it as a normal part of professional development can re-start progress towards goals.

9.6 Revising Goals and Approaches in the Middle Phase

This subsection addresses the ongoing adjustment of the supervision focus based on emerging needs and progress. It explores processes for collaborative review and modification of learning objectives and supervision methods as the relationship evolves.

As you will have seen by now, supervision in sport and exercise practice is a complex, nonlinear process. It needs to develop, to evolve as the supervisory working alliance develops and as the supervisee's competencies develop. Supervision cannot be static but must adapt to the emerging needs of the supervisee, and part of this is about altering the focus of the supervision based on emerging needs and progress. This alteration needs to be collaborative and can form part of the overall scaffolding of the supervisory process provided by the supervisor. For example, supervisees might not be ready to set goals around particularly complex skills or interventions early in the supervisory process but an initial goal in working towards a more complex skill could be set, then when reached a higher order goal could emerge through collaborative discussions in supervision (Milne & Reiser, 2017).

This ongoing adjustment of focus can be seen as a response to the emerging needs of the supervisee as they progress from being focused more on skill acquisition to being more autonomous and reflective regarding their practice. If we do not enable this type of recalibration, supervision can become stagnant and fail to be challenging and supportive.

As covered in Chapters 7 and 8, in the initial phase of supervision, goals will be set collaboratively, informed by relevant competency frameworks and organisational and contextual requirements as well as alignment with the supervisee's experience. This is not a one-off tick box exercise, though, and expectations should be laid out that these will be revisited and seen as living documents requiring updates and alterations. This can form part of the cycle of feedback, identifying progress and emerging needs. It can also run alongside the supervisor, transitioning from a more directive approach early in the relationship to one that promotes autonomy.

9.7 Summary

This chapter has focused on the key elements that contribute to effective supervision during the middle phases of the supervisory process. This is the longest phase of supervision, and the key focus is on the translation of goals into progress, whilst managing and maintaining momentum. We talked about the need for a balance between novelty and consistency and the importance of signposting to maintain this. We also covered the need for experiential learning to be embedded within supervision to help supervisees manage uncertainty and for the process to shift gradually from one led more by the supervisor to one where the supervisor has a more balanced, facilitative role. The importance of feedback, both formative and summative, and how to conduct challenging conversations around this was discussed before we considered how to address plateaus and regression and how to ensure supervision continues to provide challenge and development opportunities through revising goals and approaches.

Exercise 9.1: Detecting and Managing Supervision Plateaus

Reflect on a period (real or hypothetical) when your development plateaued.

1. Identify signs of stagnation.
2. Identify potential underlying causes (anxiety, blind spots, role conflict, avoidance).
3. Describe two supervisory interventions that would help re-establish momentum.
4. Describe what *you* (as supervisee or supervisor) must contribute.

10 Endings – Terminating the Supervisory Relationship Effectively

10.1 Introduction: The Importance of Planned Endings

Just as the initial phase of supervision is critical for establishing a strong foundation for the supervisory relationship, the conclusion of that relationship also demands careful planning and attention to detail. Endings in supervision, much like in therapy, can be uncomfortable and provoke feelings of loss, separation, and anxiety (Rabinowitz et al., 2025). Because of this, it can seem tempting to rush through or try to avoid this phase. However, endings can also elicit feelings of achievement, accomplishment, and gratitude. Honouring this termination process is not only a professional responsibility for both supervisor and supervisee but is also the final step in learning. It consolidates the progress that has occurred and prepares both parties for what lies ahead.

This chapter approaches endings from the perspective that they are just as important as the initial and middle phases of supervision. They require preparation and thoughtful execution for learning to be effectively integrated. Without a well-considered ending, the supervision may feel incomplete, leaving the supervisee uncertain about their achievements and unclear on their next steps. Endings can be seen as both science and art, and creating a safe, considered, and planned-for ending can influence the supervisee's overall beliefs about supervision. If we use the literature on therapeutic endings here as a proxy then Webb et al. (2018) have shown that poorly managed and executed endings left clients with negative emotions including loss and resentment, but endings that were well planned and executed tended to result in clients feeling a sense of accomplishment, pride and readiness to move on.

In this chapter, we will touch briefly on supervisee outcome evaluation, then explore in more depth how to evaluate the supervisory relationship during this ending phase using both informal and formal methods, considering tools available to enhance this. We will then consider how to prepare for the transition that is inherent in endings and how to discuss the next steps for the supervisee. We will explore strategies for recognising and

DOI: 10.4324/9781003485667-10

celebrating growth and achievement, consider appropriate boundaries for ongoing professional relationships, and conclude with an examination of supervisor reflection, focusing on systematic approaches to reviewing completed supervision from the supervisor's perspective.

10.2 Evaluating Supervisee Outcomes

Formal review is important and should be aligned with the goals that were collaboratively set during the initial phase of supervision (as well as those which have developed during the middle phase). Using the contract and collaboratively created goals based on competencies, the supervisor and supervisee can consider progress against each objective on the ILP. This can be done systematically by taking each and assessing development against clear criteria, offering specific examples of how the goal or objective has been achieved.

For sport and exercise supervision, both process and content indicators should be assessed (Pocwardowski et al., 2023). Process indicators are concerned with the 'how' or the quality of the work and allow for real-time adjustment to practice. They include the supervisory alliance, professional practice, reflective practice, and ethical competence, amongst others. Engagement with supervision can also be considered a process indicator. Outcome indicators are concerned with the impact of practice, so are more results oriented. They include elements such as skills assessment outcomes, athlete, coach or team feedback, and any intervention evaluations that have occurred. We need both within the complexity of sport and exercise practice, as we need to know whether change is occurring, what the reasons for that change are, and whether they lie within the practitioner or externally.

This final phase provides the opportunity for both the supervisor and the supervisee to reflect on the process and the progress that has been made. This reflection can be both formal and informal, encompassing multiple facets of the supervision that has been undertaken. This is not just an administrative task or something that requires a set input from both parties but is a powerful means by which learning can be highlighted, challenges and their conclusions reflected on, and a process of consolidation alongside a clear sense of progress can be gained.

10.3 Evaluating the Supervisory Relationship

Besides establishing evaluation criteria and focusing on the impact supervision has had on supervisees' practice and on specific athletes, coaches, teams, and systems, we can look at satisfaction with the supervisory relationship itself. Supervisory outcomes are complex, and defining outcomes or satisfaction with the supervisory relationship is also a complex consideration.

10.3.1 *Formal and Informal Evaluation*

The complexity of the supervisory relationship can make it difficult to define (Beinart & Clohessy, 2017) but it is generally agreed that it comprises goals, tasks, and bond (Bordin, 1983). It is a multifaceted relationship between the supervisee and supervisor, which extends to teams, coaches, and organisations within unique applied practice contexts (Poczwardowski et al., 2023; Beinart & Clohessy, 2017). These complexities make it even more important to formally and informally evaluate supervision and the supervisory relationship.

Informal evaluations and reviews constitute an integral mechanism for appraising the supervisory relationship, ensuring that its quality aligns with established standards of practice. These informal check-ins allow both the supervisor and supervisee to offer their reflections on the relationship alongside their honest feedback. This helps to normalise the evaluative aspect of supervision for the supervisee, helps with the supervisor's professional development, and can strengthen the supervisory alliance. These check-ins could happen at set intervals and can be tentatively introduced by the supervisor through questions such as 'Have you felt as though our goals are aligned or have there been any times when you felt our relationship was strained?' or 'Before we continue what elements of our relationship and process do you think we might adjust to allow you to maximise the benefit you gain from supervision?'. This aligns not only with a social constructionist perspective of supervision (see for example, Philp et al., 2007) where both supervisor and supervisee help create meaning but also with a more traditional educational model of supervision (Carroll, 1999). Importantly, this type of discussion enables real-time adjustments to be made to the supervisory working alliance and the goals of supervision, increasing the probability of successful outcomes.

10.3.2 *Using Recognised Assessment Tools*

Empirical research indicates that the quality of the supervisory relationship significantly influences a range of positive outcomes; consequently, practitioners should adopt a critical and reflective stance towards this relationship, actively engaging in efforts to conceptualise and operationalise its measurement. Standardised instruments and approaches for measuring supervision processes and outcomes can also be used besides the more informal check-ins. Employing them at preset times (for example, near the midpoint of supervision and again near the end) provides quantifiable data to inform both parties' understanding of the quality and satisfaction with the supervisory relationship. For reviews of a range of measures that exist, we refer you to Tangen and Borders (2016) and Beinart and Clohessy

(2017) and within this chapter, we will describe a selection of potential assessment tools that you can incorporate.

The first measure that can be used is developed from Bordin's (1983) concept of the supervisory working alliance. Developed by Bahrick (1989) the Working Alliance Inventory/Supervision (WAI/S) has both supervisor and supervisee formats and was adapted from Horvath and Greenberg's working alliance inventory for therapists (Horvath & Greenberg, 1989). This measure has sound psychometric properties and looks at three elements following Bordin's model: agreement of goals, tasks, and the bond between supervisee and supervisor.

A second tool is the Supervisory Relationship Questionnaire (SRQ) originally developed as part of a doctoral thesis by Palomo (2004) and then further developed and validated by Palomo et al. (2010). The SRQ is a 67-item measure comprising many of the core elements we have covered in this text as being key to the supervisory working alliance such as provision of a safe space (the 'safe base subscale' of the SRQ), structure, commitment, reflection, modelling, and formative feedback.

Considering the supervisory relationship effectiveness from a different perspective is a range of measures examining supervisory competence. See Gonsalvez (2021) for an overview. One of these, the Supervision Evaluation and Supervisory Competence (SE-SC) scale, assesses the competence of the supervisor from the supervisee's perspective across six subscales identifying specific competencies that predict overall evaluations of supervision (Gonsalvez et al., 2017). It provides a global measure of supervision satisfaction and supervision effectiveness in addition to containing 22 items that measure the six competencies (openness, caring and support; supervisors' knowledge and expertise; planning and management; goals directedness; restorative competencies and insight into the management of dynamics; and reflective practitioner competencies). There is also a short form of this measure, the SE-EC8 by Gonsalvez (2021) with one item for each competency and two items for overall satisfaction and effectiveness.

A final assessment tool to consider is the Leeds Alliance in Supervision Scale (LASS; Wainwright, 2010). This three-item measure is an effective tool in supervision for sport and exercise practitioners. Given its brevity, this measure can be administered at each session, providing a continuous assessment of the supervisory alliance. Furthermore, Lafferty et al. (2019) provide a supervisory perspective on the determinants of effective supervision in sport and exercise contexts.

Employing a combination of assessment tools is recommended to capture data from both supervisors and supervisees, enabling a dyadic analysis that integrates formal and informal measures for a comprehensive evaluation of the supervisory relationship. This also opens the possibility for a joint reflective discussion, which can feed into real-time modification and improve the quality of the supervisory relationship.

10.4 Preparing for Transition

This section highlights the fact that supervision is not a single event but a process. Ending a relationship and transitioning to the next phase is a skill that both the supervisor and supervisee need to acquire. This segment also addresses planned and unplanned changes in supervisory arrangements. It explores approaches to facilitating smooth transitions between supervisors and provides guidance for the proper transfer of responsibility and information.

10.4.1 Termination as a Skill

The effective termination of the supervisory relationship should be regarded as a professional competency. Although endings can be challenging, they require deliberate planning (Caspi & Reid, 2015). The supervisory relationship will differ depending on the stage that the supervisee is at; for example, supervisees who are in training will probably have shorter, more time-limited supervisory relationships, while more experienced supervisees may have supervisory relationships that span several years, necessitating different endings. Additional differences can occur for novice practitioners for whom the end of supervision may coincide with other important transitions, such as the end of placement and the move from being a trainee to a qualified practitioner entering the job market. This period can represent a significant transitional phase, which can impact the supervisee, and therefore careful management is required (Creaner, 2014).

Although the final point in supervision – the consideration of endings – should not be left until the last minute. We recommend planning for endings from the start of supervision, providing a clear time frame to work towards and introducing endings again around 4–6 weeks before the final supervision session (Caspi & Reid, 2015). Explicitly stating how many sessions are remaining allows both supervisor and supervisee to work towards that date and to use the remaining time to adjust the pace and scope of the work. Explicitly acknowledging this can be useful, for example, 'Looking at our schedule, we have four sessions remaining, so let's consider how we can best use that time to consolidate your learning so far and to plan for what comes next for you'.

10.4.2 Discussion of Next Steps

Core to the endings phase of supervision is ensuring that supervisees plan for their future, and here the supervisor can help them bridge the gap between the current and next professional step. Ryan and Deci's self-determination theory (SDT; Ryan & Deci, 2000) provides a framework within which we can consider the transfer of decision-making to the supervisee, ensuring the development of their autonomy. Sawatsky et al. (2022) outline the relationship between supervision and autonomy in clinical settings, and we can lean into this literature to view the relevance of this to the sport and exercise context. They highlight that supervisees can internalise the norms of their profession through supervision aligned with SDT and that this can motivate learning. Through an SDT lens, we can see that endings in supervision are a means by which supervisees can consolidate their learning, autonomy, and self-direction. Both parties play a role here, and the smooth unfolding of the process can be scaffolded through key supervisory questioning, for example asking what type of support the supervisee needs going forward (e.g., a new supervisor, or a peer supervision group) and where they could find that. Supervisors can also raise the question of how supervisees will continue their self-reflection and professional development, highlighting tools and techniques that have worked well to date.

A transition plan could be implemented collaboratively by the supervisor and supervisee, considering elements such as next steps, key strengths and achievements, new CPD or development opportunities, and recommended reading or resources. This could help the transition occur, providing valuable signposting and development needs while reinforcing the need for ongoing development and supervision (Poczwardowski et al., 2023).

The aim of this phase is to raise awareness that supervision is ending, to highlight the development towards autonomy and independence in the supervisee, and to signpost the supervisee towards independence within the context of professional growth being a long-term activity requiring support.

10.5 Celebrating Growth and Achievement

As mentioned above, at the end of supervision, we need to recognise growth and achievement. What we want to provide here is a recognition of growth and a sense of closure. There are different approaches that can be taken to marking the conclusion of supervision. Below we examine reflective exercises, celebration activities, and other methods for acknowledging accomplishments and facilitating healthy closure.

10.5.1 The Final Conversation

During the final conversation, we want to remain positive even if the supervisory relationship has been challenging or strained. The aim of this final conversation is to affirm the development that has occurred and the competence the supervisee now possesses. It is not a time to introduce any new feedback, just a time to summarise and recognise achievements. This recognition should focus on the supervisee's effort and self-determination, enabling internal validation. This can be done in different ways, for example:

- A Focus on Growth:

This final conversation can be viewed as a retrospective where growth from the beginning is summarised, facilitating an increase in the supervisee's confidence to move forward (Caspi & Reid, 2002) prompted by supervisory reflection. A supervisor might reference an example from the initial session and reflect on the development undertaken since, for example, 'In our first session I recall you expressed concern about your first interaction with the team, but over time you've developed into a confident practitioner capable of managing complex team dynamics'.

- A Recognition of Strengths:

The supervisor can reflect on and highlight the supervisee's strengths, offering specific examples such as, 'Your interpersonal skills are exemplary, allowing you to form strong connections with athletes, which they find authentic and developmental'. This approach aligns well with strengths-based supervision, which is particularly suited to the final conversation (see Wade & Jones, 2014 for more detail).

- A Final Positive Message:

Ending with a clear expression of support and encouragement is valuable. For example, 'I have thoroughly enjoyed working alongside you and being a witness to your professional development, and I'm sure you will continue to grow and be successful in your career'.

Alternatively, the final conversation could be structured around a review of data, notes, reflections and learning objectives that have been met. This could take the form of looking back at progress, looking forward to the next phase, and looking externally to how the supervisee will maintain competent practice and professional growth.

10.5.2 Other Closure Activities and Rituals

Supervisors and supervisees can have their own closure activities and rituals associated with the termination of supervision. Some of these might be informal, such as the giving and receiving of cards to acknowledge support and positive input. Sometimes, a more formal approach may be appropriate, such as asking supervisees to reflect on what they see as the key milestones in their development. This reinforces their own sense of agency and ownership of the process. Another option is to co-create a timeline of key developmental milestones, encouraging the supervisee to recognise their growth and development in areas that do not map directly to formal competencies but remain vital to professional development. This could include recognition of developments such as improved tolerance for ambiguity or the ability to manage organisational pressures – skills that can be critical in the unique contexts faced by sport and exercise practitioners. More creative activities can also be included, with many examples coming from the counselling literature, e.g. Hundley and Casado-kehoe's (2007) wisdom jar activity. These activities all require time, so introducing termination of supervision early is vital and allows for a range of emotional responses to be experienced and processed (Levendosky & Hopwood, 2017).

10.6 Follow-Up and Continued Professional Relationships

Within supervision, both parties should consider what they expect around post-supervision contact and relationship evolution. Clear boundaries for ongoing professional connections will need to be established, allowing a more consultative relationship to emerge. Ending a supervisory working alliance does not mean that all contact ceases; rather, it is an opportunity to reimagine the relationship in a way that supports consultation. In sport and exercise contexts, this transition needs the establishment of clear boundaries, roles, and expectations – like those defined during the initial phase of supervision. Both parties should have clarity on what communication and a continued professional relationship will look like. The field of sport and exercise psychology is relatively small, and both parties will likely encounter each other in future professional settings. Added to this, ongoing support is recommended for sport and exercise practitioners (Poczwardowski et al., 2023) so enabling a transition to a more consultative model where quarterly meetings occur or where sessions are scheduled to focus on specific complex issues can be professionally significant. In this emerging consultative model of an ongoing, continued professional relationship, the supervisor should adopt a more equal role alongside the supervisee, fostering a collaborative partnership rather than an evaluative dynamic.

10.7 Supervisor Reflection and Learning

This subsection addresses the supervisor's own learning process. It examines approaches to systematically reflecting on completed supervision to improve future practice and contribute to professional development as a supervisor.

As Contrastano (2020) shows, supervisors need to be open to learning and change because of their supervision. Effective supervisors need to enable, facilitate, and highlight professional growth in their supervisees, and they need to reflect on what they themselves have gained or learnt. This can be achieved through reflective practice combined with a critical examination of what was and was not effective, as well as consideration of their supervisory style and the tools, interventions, and approaches they used. Supervisors should themselves engage in supervision and maintain up-to-date knowledge of new and emerging literature and professional guidance. This commitment to development ensures the delivery of evidence-based supervision (Poczwardowski et al., 2023).

Recognised reflective models can facilitate learning from the supervisory experience. Gibbs' (1988) reflective cycle or Driscoll's (1994) model of reflection, for example, could provide a structured means of reflecting on what has been learned by the supervisor. This is vital because work by Cropley et al. (2007, 2020) has shown reflective practice can enhance service delivery and improve sport psychology support. They could demonstrate that reflective practice training led to enhancements in reflective practice and in practice.

Besides global reflections, supervisors can focus on specific elements of supervision, reflecting on effective interventions, ruptures in the supervisor working alliance and associated learning from that, or any evidence of parallel process. Supervisors can enhance their understanding of their growth edges through reflection on supervision, identifying areas for improvement such as cultural humility and consciousness, or remote supervision.

They can do this through self-reflective journalling, or peer supervision groups, and through enhancing reflective practice can model the type of honesty, planning and growth-focused thinking they would expect from supervisees.

10.8 Unplanned Endings

This chapter has highlighted the importance of planning for endings and managing them intentionally to achieve the best outcomes for all involved. However, there will be instances when the supervisory relationship ends unexpectedly, sooner or more abruptly than expected. These abrupt endings are arguably more likely to occur in sport and exercise psychology contexts where they can arise from factors such as financial cuts, organisational restructuring, a supervisee gaining a new role, or a personal or health emergency affecting either party. Abrupt endings can also occur in supervision within an academic or training route from staff or trainee illness or from a trainee unexpectedly having to place their studies on hold. These types of unexpected endings are often challenging for both supervisors and supervisees to navigate.

Returning to an earlier point, endings can elicit feelings of bereavement and loss (Webb et al. 2018) and can undermine professional identity development and confidence. Unexpected endings could be assumed to be more likely to result in these negative outcomes. We can look to the counselling literature for parallels and extrapolate from there; however, we need to be cautious of drawing parallels that may not exist. Fogaça et al., (2024) highlight the differences between sport psychology trainees and counselling trainees in their development and the issues they bring to supervision. So, while we hold the knowledge available to us from related literatures (for example, Dawson and Akhurst's, 2015 work on unplanned endings in counselling), we should also be cognisant of the specific domain of sport and exercise psychology and the unique pressure of applied practice within these contexts. Supervisees here are often balancing multiple roles, yet we have limited guidance on how to manage unexpected endings within complex applied practice settings (Tod et al., 2021). Given the lack of clear guidelines and the likelihood of abrupt endings in sport and exercise contexts, we need to take a proactive approach. We can do this by maintaining an awareness of the possibility and planning exit strategies from the outset. If such an abrupt termination occurs, we should aim to provide a final structured session to offer a sense of closure.

10.9 Summary

This chapter has considered endings or terminations of the supervisory relationship and the related evaluations, with a focus on the supervisory relationship. Planning is essential and should be considered at the initial stage of contracting, ensuring time is allocated for this vital phase. We considered how to evaluate the effectiveness of the supervisory relationship within a planned ending, incorporating both formal and informal methods and recognised assessment tools. Viewing termination as a skill; we emphasised that planning for the end is key to ensuring learning is carried forward. We also considered strategies for transitioning into a new, clearly defined consultative relationship. Finally, we underscored the importance of supervisory reflection and associated learning as a means by which to model the growth expectations and orientations supervisors seek to instil in their supervisees.

Exercise 10.1: Designing a Supervision Ending

You are preparing to end a 12-month supervision relationship. Write a two-part ending plan:

Part A – Supervisor focus:

- What feedback will you give?
- What evidence will you draw upon?
- How will you acknowledge growth and manage any unresolved issues?

Part B – Supervisee focus:

- What learning will you carry forward?
- What supports will you need next?
- What emotions arise, and how will you manage them?

11 Forms and Format of Supervision

11.1 Introduction

Applied sport psychology supervision has undergone considerable changes, now providing various structures to cater to the diverse requirements of professionals, their trainees, and the unique environments where they deliver their services. In this chapter, we will analyse the supervisory structures available to applied sport psychology professionals, ranging from conventional individual methods to modern, technologically advanced formats. Different supervisory forms and formats offer unique benefits, drawbacks, and uses in applied sport psychology. By understanding these different forms and formats, supervisors and supervisees can make well-informed decisions about which methods are most effective for their professional growth, considering real-world limitations and the requirements of working with athletes and sports organisations.

11.2 Individual Supervision

Individual supervision represents the traditional cornerstone of professional development in applied sport psychology. This one-to-one format creates a focused learning environment where a more experienced practitioner guides the development of a less experienced colleague through regular, dedicated meetings. The benefits of individual supervision in applied sport psychology are considerable because the format allows for (1) personalised attention to the supervisee's specific developmental needs, (2) space for in-depth exploration of complex cases and nuanced ethical dilemmas that frequently arise in sport contexts. The British Psychological Society's Division of Sport and Exercise Psychology (DSEP) emphasises individual supervision as a critical component of its qualification pathway, recognising its value in developing core competencies. Research shows that individual supervision creates a confidential environment in which supervisees can openly discuss difficulties specific to applied sport psychology practice, including navigating dual relationships in team settings or managing pressure from coaches

DOI: 10.4324/9781003485667-11

and organisations (Tod et al., 2009, 2011). Yet, individual supervision also presents several challenges. For instance, the resource-intensive nature of one-to-one supervision makes it a costly financial investment because the supervisee pays for the hourly services of a supervisor. Also, the limited perspective of a single supervisor may restrict the range of viewpoints and approaches to which the supervisee is exposed. As we have written in previous chapters, the effectiveness of individual supervision in applied sport psychology depends significantly on the quality of the supervisory relationship. When this relationship functions well, it provides a secure base from which supervisees can explore their professional identity and develop their practice. When it falters, however, the isolated nature of the format offers few alternative sources of support or perspective.

Case Vignette: Kelly and the Underachieving Golfer

Kelly, currently in training, is providing support to a regional golfer experiencing increased anxiety before competitions. She is feeling stressed because the golfer is demanding quick fixes. Kelly shared a comprehensive session transcript in her individual supervision. Her supervisor helps her examine the formulation, identify missed cues, and rehearse a grounding intervention she can use next session. In a one-on-one setting, it is possible to delve deeply into Kelly's confidence, technical abilities, and her fears of not measuring up, issues she would probably keep private in a group.

11.3 Group Supervision

Group supervision has gained prominence in applied sport psychology training as a valuable complement or alternative to individual approaches. This format brings together multiple supervisees under the guidance of one or more supervisors, creating a collaborative learning environment with unique dynamics and benefits (Henderson et al., 2014). The theoretical foundations for group supervision in applied sport psychology draw from group process theories and models of professional development. Proctor's (2008) functional model identifies three key purposes of supervision: normative (maintaining standards), formative (developing skills), and restorative (providing support), and facilitators can address these purposes effectively in group contexts. The social learning theory (Bandura, 1977) underpinning group supervision suggests that observing peers' work and receiving multiple perspectives enhances learning beyond what individual supervision alone can provide. In applied sport psychology, group supervision offers several advantages. For instance, the collaborative environment mirrors the team contexts in which various practitioners work, providing valuable parallels to navigate. The diversity of cases and approaches shared in groups exposes supervisees to a broader range of sport environments and intervention strategies than they might encounter in their own practice.

University training programmes typically involve group supervision to meet the education, training, and supervision needs of their trainees. These training programmes also provide individual supervision within a dyad (i.e., supervisor and supervisee). Supervisors of trainees in independent training routes (e.g., BPS Stage 2) also use group supervision. Group supervision, when appropriate conditions are met, presents several benefits, such as group dynamics, member relationships, feedback, and support that are not always available within a dyad. Within the supervision literature, however, group supervision is largely overlooked in theory and research. Not only is group supervision unheeded in the literature, but also those who undertake group supervision assume the principles and practices are the same as individual supervision (Riva & Smith, 2024).

11.3.1 What Is Group Supervision?

Some authors suggest that group supervision refers to more than one supervisee (Bernard & Goodyear, 2004). A group comprising two supervisees and one supervisor, however, is known as triadic supervision, a format that sits between individual and group supervision. Typically, when one considers a group and its functioning for group supervision, there ought to be sufficient supervisees to handle typical group dynamics like absences without a group being too large to cater to the individual needs of supervisees (Rowell, 2010). Our usual experience of supervision might be private – individual supervision – a supervisor and a supervisee. This hour of individual supervision is given to you generously as the supervisee. But other supervisees stimulate a new enterprise of collaboration, sharing, and debate. The exclusive role of the supervisor gives way to the collective knowledge, experience, and understanding of the group. Perhaps the mediated experience of peers working with athletes, coaches, and teams means the content and process of their work land more reassuringly than the 'word' of the experienced supervisor.

Successful group supervision depends on the members and the group facilitator in equal measure. The group creates its own energy and enthusiasm, though it needs course-plotting (Proctor, 2008). When a group facilitator has a strong grasp of group dynamics, it opens your eyes to the benefits of groups and, with the right skills, it leads to healthy outcomes. And like all forms of supervision, deep learning opportunities lie within, though there are drawbacks. People come to groups, perhaps without knowing that we all need to belong to a group. Lew and Bettner's model of the 'Crucial Cs' (1995) shows we need to feel we belong and *connect*. By taking responsibility, we empower ourselves and feel *capable*. We matter and can effect change; therefore, we *count*. Finally, *courage* allows us to confront difficult situations and push past fear (Henderson et al., 2014).

According to Lammers (1999), group supervisors ought to be familiar with the structure and process of working groups (Bion, 1961), the stages in the development of working groups (Lacousiere, 1980; Tuckman, 1965), and how parallel processes extend into a supervision group (Stoltenberg & Delworth, 1987). As a systemic exercise, group supervision offers a forum for trainees, for example, to meet regularly with peers and an experienced professional to discuss professional issues. The supervisory process comprises tasks and functions. For trainees at different stages of their training process, a supervisor and supervisee undertake various supervisory *tasks*. Holloway's Systems Approach to Supervision (SAS) model presented five supervisory tasks: counselling skills, case conceptualisation, professional role, emotional awareness, and self-evaluation. The functions of supervision are the activities undertaken to achieve monitoring/evaluating, instructing/advising, modelling, consulting, and supporting/sharing (Holloway & Carroll, 1999).

11.3.2 Structured Group Formats

Structured group supervision formats follow predetermined agendas and protocols to ensure systematic coverage of learning objectives. These approaches typically include *case presentation models* where supervisees present cases following a standardised format, with designated time for presentation, questions, feedback, and discussion. This structure ensures comprehensive case analysis and fair participation for all members. A second approach is the *competency-based format*, where sessions focus on developing specific competencies relevant to applied sport psychology practice, such as needs assessment, case conceptualisation, intervention planning, or ethical decision-making. Finally, we have *theme-centred groups* in which supervision sessions address predetermined themes relevant to applied sport psychology practice, such as working with teams, managing organisational stressors, or supporting athletes through injury. This approach ensures breadth of learning across critical domains. A blend of case presentation, competency-based or theme-centred groups works best to meet the needs of the group but in all cases the effectiveness of structured formats depends on clear guidelines, skilled facilitation, and flexibility to address emergent needs while maintaining focus on a curriculum especially for trainees. In our experience and the gathering research, early-career practitioners implore structured approaches because they benefit from explicit guidance and systematic skill development.

Case Vignette: The Academy Squad Rotation

Six trainees from a university meet in a structured group supervision session each week. Oliver presents a case involving a gymnastics team with strong perfectionistic tendencies. Within a standard case presentation structure, the group offers questions for clarification and introduces alternative perspectives. A fellow trainee, with experience in an artistic sport, has insights into organisational dynamics that Oliver had not considered. Following the session, the supervisor recaps the key themes and relates them to the competencies.

11.3.3 Process-Oriented Groups

Process-oriented group supervision emphasises interpersonal dynamics and emergent learning rather than predetermined content. This approach draws from group therapy traditions, focusing on the 'here and now' interactions within the supervision group as a vehicle for professional development. Though less common in applied sport psychology, process-oriented groups provide valuable opportunities to explore parallel processes between group dynamics and team sport environments (Jacobsen, 2007). These groups help practitioners to develop awareness of one's interpersonal influence and blind spots. These groups also build the capacity to manage complex relational dynamics common in sports settings and especially in team sports. They also enhance emotional intelligence and reflective capacity. Running these process-oriented groups, however, requires sophisticated skills in recognising and working with group dynamics (Proctor, 2008). The facilitator or supervisor must balance attention to individual learning needs with an awareness of group-level processes, using both to enhance supervisees' development. Research suggests that process-oriented approaches may be valuable for addressing countertransference issues in applied sport psychology practice, where practitioners' own athletic histories and sport-related values may unconsciously influence their work with athletes and teams.

Case Vignette: Tension in the Football Squad Discussion

While participating in process-oriented group supervision, Jamie repeatedly interjected during a discussion about a football team conflict involving another trainee. The supervisor stops the material and prompts the group to examine the current events (e.g., What is happening right now?). Jamie confesses to experiencing pressure to seem capable, and others note her interruptions echo the power dynamics outlined within her football squad. This introspective look helps us better grasp the parallels between group dynamics and team sports.

11.3.4 Peer Consultation Groups

Peer consultation groups represent a more egalitarian approach to group supervision, where members share responsibility for providing feedback and support without a designated supervisor (Borders, 2012). These groups may be entirely peer-led or include periodic input from a senior supervisor. Like other group-oriented models, peer consultation groups offer several advantages, including fostering professional autonomy and interdependence. The peer consultation group offers a sustainable support structure beyond formal training, which crucially reduces isolation for practitioners working in remote or specialised settings. Perhaps less visible are the opportunities to develop consultation and feedback skills, which are valuable for team interventions. One word of warning is that, despite their collaborative nature, effective peer consultation groups in applied sport psychology need clear structures and ground rules. With these frameworks and guidelines, the peer supervision group can likely stick to its meeting times, share the leading of discussions, create guidelines for case sharing, and supplement methods for ensuring actions are taken based on the information learned.

Case Vignette: Remote Consultants in Women's Football

Three individuals in the early stages of their careers in women's football engage in monthly peer consultations. The case Sarah is working on concerns a midfielder's dip in confidence following a change in coaching staff. In the absence of a senior supervisor, peers ask questions that delve into concepts, reflection, and practical applications. Another practitioner member has gone through a comparable process of adapting to coaching changes. Her peers recognise possible blind spots, such as organisational politics and identity threat. Sarah leaves with new ideas – and a sense of solidarity.

11.4 Dyad and Triad Supervision

Dyan and triad models represent intermediate formats between individual and group supervision, offering unique advantages for applied sport psychology training. These small-group approaches create opportunities for multiple roles and perspectives while maintaining focused attention on each participant's development. In the supervision triad, three participants rotate through the roles of supervisor, supervisee, and observer. Trainees will be familiar with triads and dyads in learning basic counselling skills. Within this structure, trainees, for example, acquire experience in multiple roles, which develops versatile skills applicable in various professional contexts. In the observer role, the trainee cultivates metacognitive awareness, objective analysis, and opportunities to offer feedback. The rotating roles mean that the format efficiently uses supervision time while providing multiple perspectives. Besides offering feedback, participants develop skills in receiving feedback non-defensively (Falender & Shafranske, 2021).

Dyad models pair supervisees who work together under a supervisor's guidance. Sometimes trainees work within the same organisation, and this approach means that supervisees could observe each other's sessions with athletes or teams. Together, they could collaborate on case conceptualisation and intervention planning, reflect on parallel cases, or complementary skill development. Feedback from each other would supplement supervisor input. Although research on triad and dyad models in applied sport psychology supervision remains limited, evidence from related fields suggests these formats effectively balance the depth of individual supervision with the diverse perspectives of group approaches. These models may be valuable for developing consultation skills relevant to applied sport psychology practice, where practitioners often work collaboratively with coaches, medical staff, and other support personnel.

Case Vignette: Dyadic Supervision: Paired Rugby Trainees

Lewis and Eve, who are trainees at the same rugby academy, are supervised jointly. Lewis presents a case about emotional regulation in a flanker; Eve, having observed similar behaviour in her own sessions, notices patterns Lewis missed. The supervisor facilitates a joint formulation and highlights the similarities and differences in their approaches. In this dyadic environment, collaborative learning occurs alongside individualised attention.

Case Vignette: Triadic Supervision: Rotating Roles in a Triadic Environment

During a triadic supervision session, Ava acts as the supervisee, Mark is the observer, and the supervisor guides the process. Ava recounts a story of a swimmer experiencing burnout. Mark's observations highlight subtle emotional signals Ava missed, like the athlete's vocal inflection when discussing parental expectations. Once the roles were switched, Mark found himself in the position of being supervised and learned how feedback from observers could enhance the analysis of cases.

11.5 Live Supervision

Live supervision involves direct observation of the supervisee's work with clients, allowing for immediate feedback and guidance. In applied sport psychology, this approach has relevance given the field's frequent emphasis on observation and intervention in natural performance environments. Several possibilities exist in this scenario for live supervision. Some trainees learn applied sport psychology by having a supervisor watch them work with an athlete or team, either in person or from behind a one-way mirror. By observing in real-time, this approach provides the ability to assess verbal and nonverbal exchanges without delay. Within these scenarios, supervisors can give instant direction using an earpiece or text communication during the session. With this technology, corrections can be made instantly, without disrupting the conversation with the athlete. Shadowing is also an option; this format allows the person being supervised to watch the supervisor work with athletes before slowly gaining more responsibility under supervision. This apprenticeship approach effectively builds practical abilities in intricate sports settings. In real-world sports settings like practices, competitions, or team meetings, the supervisor watches the supervisee at work. This method of observing in the field helps us understand how the person being supervised handles the complicated aspects of sports settings, going beyond standard office meetings. With this type of live supervision, the supervisor can evaluate actual skills in actual situations instead of just depending on what the person says about themselves and what happened. Providing instant feedback stops unhelpful habits from solidifying. Supervisors can use shadowing to show strategies for challenging situations, and field observation helps those being supervised feel at ease with being observed, like how athletes receive critiques in sports. There are always difficulties associated with live supervision. For instance, disrupting the relationship between the supervisee and athlete, difficulties in organising observations in sports environments, and the need for supervisees to handle performance anxiety when being observed. Successful execution of live observation hinges on having explicit agreements with everyone involved, careful planning, and thorough reviews to extract the most valuable lessons (Haggerty & Hilsenroth, 2011).

Case Vignette: Workshop Observation at a Football Academy

Molly, who is in training, is leading a resilience workshop for U15 football players. Her supervisor observes her session from the back of the room. Molly quickens her pace with an activity once the players get fidgety. While on a break, the supervisor privately advised her to manage her tempo and leverage the collective energy. Following the session, a review occurs, encompassing Molly's inner thoughts and the players' behavioural tendencies.

11.6 Distance and Technology-Mediated Supervision

Integrating technology has transformed supervision possibilities in applied sport psychology, creating new opportunities for connection across geographic boundaries and enhancing traditional approaches through digital tools. This evolution is relevant in sports contexts, where practitioners often travel with teams or work with athletes in diverse locations across a season. So, for example, seeking supervision from a supervisor in San Francisco while living in London is more accessible and manageable now than ever before.

11.6.1 Videoconference Supervision

Videoconference supervision enables real-time visual and audio connections between supervisors and supervisees, regardless of location. This approach has become increasingly sophisticated, with research showing its effectiveness compared to in-person supervision across multiple outcomes (Jordan & Shearer, 2019). For sport psychology practitioners, videoconference supervision offers several advantages. First, there is permanence of supervision despite travel schedules for competitions because the supervisee and supervisor do not need to be in the same room. Second, videoconferencing provides access to specialised supervisors with expertise in specific sports or issues across the globe (Rousmaniere et al., 2017). Third, there are reduced travel times and costs, particularly for practitioners in remote locations. Finally, there is an opportunity to connect supervision sessions with performance environments. To realise these advantages, however, we need to consider how we best implement videoconference supervision. For instance, we need to ensure adequate technology infrastructure, address confidentiality concerns, and develop protocols for managing technical difficulties. Research suggests that establishing rapport may require additional attention in videoconference formats, though this challenge diminishes with familiarity (Ratcliffe & Kaluzeviciute-Moreton, 2024). The COVID-19 pandemic accelerated the adoption of videoconference supervision in applied sport psychology, with many practitioners reporting unexpected benefits beyond convenience, including increased frequency of shorter check-ins and greater flexibility in scheduling around athletic competitions.

Case Vignette: Traveling with the National Team

A London-based supervisor is having a video conference with Priya, who is currently travelling with a national cricket team for their qualifying tournament. Priya details the emotional pain an athlete experiences after a disappointing deselection. Priya's session notes and diagrams of team role tensions are being reviewed by the supervisor via screen sharing. Even with time zone differences, videoconferencing ensures supervisors can still provide support during periods with a lot of travel.

11.6.2 Asynchronous Supervision Methods

Along with the usual synchronous supervision methods, asynchronous supervision methods involve time-shifted interaction between supervisors and supervisees, offering flexibility that accommodates the irregular schedules common in sport contexts and the opportunity for the supervisor to learn more about the practicum work undertaken by their supervisee. These approaches supplement synchronous supervision sessions and require time from the supervisor and supervisee beyond the typical supervision hours (Haggerty & Hilsenroth, 2011). One of the most valuable asynchronous supervision methods is the recorded session review. Supervisees submit audio (or video) recordings of their work with athletes for supervisor review and feedback. This method allows for detailed analysis of specific skills, interventions, and techniques. Most training programmes require structured reflection protocols where supervisees complete guided reflection templates following their work with athletes, which supervisors review and comment on. This approach develops reflective practice habits while providing supervision input at intervals across the supervisory relationship. Training programmes also seek written client-case studies as part of their assessment process. Written case consultations provide supervisees with opportunities to write case presentations and questions, receiving detailed written feedback from supervisors. This approach encourages thoughtful reflection and documentation of supervision. In group supervision, online discussion forums allow supervisees to post cases or questions for supervisor and peer input, establishing an ongoing dialogue that can be accessed at convenient times. This format combines individual feedback with the benefits of multiple perspectives. Research shows that asynchronous methods may enhance reflective depth by allowing supervisors and supervisees time to consider their responses rather than reacting immediately; however, these approaches require clear expectations regarding response timeframes and may be less effective for urgent situations requiring immediate guidance.

Case Vignette: Video Review for Skill Refinement

Hugo shared a 20-minute video of his session with a Paralympic table tennis player. His supervisor watches it later and adds comments with time stamps: ‘At 08:45, I noticed that your question stopped the athlete from speaking’ and ‘Consider using reflective summaries in this instance’. Hugo submits a written reflection before their upcoming live session. This approach accommodates his unpredictable competitive schedule.

11.6.3 Technology Platforms and Tools

The effectiveness of technology-mediated supervision depends significantly on the platforms, tools, and purpose. Applied sport psychology supervisors now have access to secure videoconferencing platforms, content management systems, session recording and analysis tools, virtual reality applications, and AI-enhanced feedback systems. Videoconferencing platforms and case management systems provide enhanced security and protect confidentiality for all users. Content management systems mean it is possible to schedule sessions, securely store case notes and assessments, and communicate with clients safely and confidentially. Supervisors and supervisees now have access to software that facilitates the recording, annotation, and review of sessions with clients. From a training perspective, VR applications mean supervisors can create immersive training environments for applied sport psychology skills development. And automated analysis tools can process large amounts of session data to identify patterns and areas for development.

Even with the various technologies available to supervisors and their supervisees, they must consider some factors. Security and confidentiality are paramount in all supervisory activities. Faced with technological progress, supervisors should find a balance between innovation and ethical standards, making sure digital tools bolster, not undermine, supervision quality in the realm of applied sport psychology. The dependability of various devices and internet connections creates a positive supervisory experience, which keeps things interesting. Mostly, these technologies are easy to use; however, most still require some training. Finally, the cost of these technologies means they are not always accessible to all parties.

11.7 Interprofessional and Team Supervision

The multidisciplinary nature of sport performance support creates unique opportunities for interprofessional supervision in applied sport psychology. This approach brings together professionals from different disciplines to provide comprehensive supervision that reflects the integrated team environments in which many applied sport psychologists work. At its broadest reach, interprofessional supervision could include input from clinical or counselling psychologists, performance directors and sports coaches, strength and conditioning specialists, sports medicine physicians and physiotherapists, nutritionists, and other health professionals. For sport psychology practitioners, this field offers advantages like honing teamwork skills for comprehensive support teams, understanding how psychological methods fit with other aspects of athlete care, encountering varied professional viewpoints, and preparing for the complex environments of high-performance sports.

Despite the benefits of interprofessional teams, they, like any team, need basic rules and efficient ways of operating, so that each role is clearly defined and there is mutual respect for all professional perspectives. With these fundamentals in place, skilfully incorporating different perspectives becomes achievable. It is challenging to deal with diverse professional terminologies, handle the potential for power imbalances in different areas, and set clear expectations for using specialised skills.

Case Vignette: High-Performance Team Meeting

At a top-tier triathlon facility, a team comprising a psychologist, physiologist, nutritionist, and strength and conditioning coach collaboratively oversees a trainee who is working with an athlete experiencing overtraining symptoms. Each discipline contributes a perspective: the physiologist notes recovery markers; the S&C coach highlights load patterns; the psychologist explores motivation. The trainee learns how psychological input fits within an integrated support system.

11.8 Consultation versus Supervision

In professional development within applied sport psychology, the difference between supervision, consultation, and mentoring is an important aspect to consider. Although these processes have some similarities, they are different in key aspects that influence how they are conducted and what results they produce. Under supervision, we see a structured, official relationship with specific duties, a clear chain of command with assessments, emphasis on professional growth in various skills, accountability for the supervisee's work from a legal and ethical standpoint, and frequent, planned meetings with a set agenda. Consultation and mentoring often involve short-term interactions centred on specific problems, a cooperative dynamic between colleagues, a more focused approach to individual cases or difficulties, the consultant offering support without taking charge of the client's care, and a format that adapts to the supervisee's requirements.

Sport psychology might not always clearly define the different processes. An experienced professional could, for instance, mentor a co-worker, offering a mix of guidance and advice. Setting clear expectations is crucial when building supervisory or consultative relationships in sport psychology. One could address the following questions:

- What is the most important goal we hope to achieve together?
- What duties do we each hold?
- How will this procedure be organised and recorded?

- Are there any evaluation components included?
- How will we handle keeping things private and sharing information?

By recognising these differences, applied sports psychology professionals can better choose the right type of professional help for their individual requirements and level of development.

11.9 Matching Format to Context and Need

Determining the most effective supervision style means a thorough assessment of different aspects concerning the context, the supervisee's needs, and any existing real-world limitations. Considering the wide range of settings where practitioners operate, this decision becomes especially intricate within applied sport psychology. We normally consider four key factors: developmental stage, practice context, learning objectives, and practical constraints. Research shows that the supervision needs of professionals change as they gain experience: beginners typically thrive with frequent individual supervision; those with moderate experience may benefit from a combination of individual and group formats; and advanced practitioners might find consultation or peer models more effective. In applied sport psychology, the practice environment is a significant factor. Group supervision that reflects team dynamics could be advantageous in team sports, while individual sports might emphasise one-on-one supervision, and high-performance settings may need supervisory methods that adapt to travel and competition schedules. Learning objectives are a key element for all those who are supervised. Live supervision or structured methods could be most helpful for learning skills, while professional identity might grow through process groups, and specialised expertise might need remote supervision from experts (Goldberg et al., 2016). Like all supervisory dynamics, we must address real-world challenges. These include distance, which may require using technology; budget limitations, which may influence whether we meet individually or in groups; and time availability, which may dictate if we use real-time or self-paced methods.

11.10 Hybrid Models of Supervision

Hybrid supervision models use various formats, aiming to capitalise on the advantages of different methods and lessen their drawbacks. Applied sport psychologists increasingly favour these combined models, as they understand that a single supervision style cannot meet every developmental need. Supervisors and their team members can choose from many hybrid supervision approaches. Several university programmes use a teaching style that blends individual and group work, switching between personal supervision for thorough case study analysis and group discussions to get different viewpoints. Supervision may be enhanced with technology based on the agreement between the supervisor and supervisee, which involves adding digital tools to in-person supervision for continuous support outside of meetings. Options might include secure messaging services for rapid consultations; alongside shared digital environments designed for resource sharing. Some university programmes use developmental progression models, enabling a systematic shift in supervision styles as training professionals grow, possibly starting with highly structured individual supervision and slowly introducing peer consultation as they gain independence. Supervisors and those they supervise might use context-dependent frameworks during supervision, emphasising specific needs based on the sport calendar phases, potentially using more intensive methods during the off-season and more adaptable, technology-driven methods during competition. The ongoing development of hybrid supervision models in applied sport psychology provides potentially beneficial methods for supporting the complex and multifaceted needs of professionals in diverse sporting environments. Like other techniques, hybrid models are most successful when there is transparent communication about the objectives and methods of each supervisory aspect. While combining formats might seem easy, the most effective approach involves thoughtful integration; regular assessment of the model's performance; and a willingness to adapt, ensuring continuity and efficient information exchange between different supervision aspects aids this process.

Case Vignette: Blending Formats in a Taught Doctorate

A trainee receives:

- weekly individual supervision for case formulation
- weekly group supervision for competency development
- live observations during youth academy sessions
- asynchronous feedback on process notes

For example, the supervisor observes a live session, provides immediate feedback, and later in the week the trainee presents a more reflective version in the group setting. The hybrid model ensures depth (individual work) and breadth (peer learning) (Table 11.1).

11.11 Conclusion

Supervision's varied styles and structures also mirror applied sport psychology because they consider the intricate settings in which professionals operate. Supervision structures range from conventional one-on-one

Table 11.1 Comparison of Supervision Formats

Supervision format	*Description*	*Strengths*	*Limitations/risks*	*Best used when*
Individual supervision	One-to-one supervision between a supervisor and a supervisee.	• Highly personalised guidance • Depth of case exploration • Strong supervisory alliance • Confidential and safe environment	• Resource-intensive • Limited breadth of perspectives • Quality depends heavily on one supervisor	• Early-career trainees • Complex or sensitive cases • When intensive skill development is required
Group supervision (structured)	Multiple supervisees with a supervisor; structured agendas (case presentations, competencies, themes).	• Exposure to diverse cases • Peer learning • Efficient use of the supervisor's time • Mirrors team dynamics in sports	• Risk of unequal participation • Requires skilled facilitation • Confidentiality more complex	• University cohorts • Early-career stage needing structure • Training programmes with broad competency coverage
Group supervision (process-oriented)	Focus on the group dynamics and relational processes occurring in the present moment.	• Develops emotional intelligence • Helps identify parallel processes • Strong reflective development	• Can feel abstract • Requires advanced facilitator skills • Not ideal for beginners	• Advanced trainees • Practitioners dealing with relational/team issues • When interpersonal patterns need exploration
Peer consultation groups	Peer-led or semi-structured groups without a designated supervisor.	• Promotes autonomy • Reduces isolation in independent practice • Encourages collaborative problem-solving	• Risk of blind spots • No evaluative gatekeeping • Requires clear ground rules	• Post-qualification practitioners • Consultants working remotely or solo • Ongoing peer support

Supervision format	*Description*	*Strengths*	*Limitations/risks*	*Best used when*
Dyadic supervision	Two supervisees share supervision with one supervisor.	• Peer support • Shared learning • Efficient for similar caseloads/settings	• Risk of comparison/competition • Less individual attention	• Paired trainees within same organisation • Cases benefiting from shared perspectives
Triadic supervision	Three participants rotate through roles (supervisor, supervisee, observer).	• Develops metacognitive and observation skills • Efficient use of time • Multiple perspectives	• Observer role may feel passive • Requires clear role definition	• Skill acquisition settings (e.g., counselling skills labs) • Early- to mid-stage trainees
Live supervision (in-room, field, shadowing)	Supervisor observes supervisee in real time; may use earpiece or immediate feedback.	• Immediate correction/prevention • Deep learning through observation • Real-world performance environment capture	• Logistical challenges • May disrupt supervisee–client rapport • Can trigger performance anxiety	• High-stakes environments • Skills requiring behavioural precision • Early-stage practitioners learning technique
Videoconference supervision	Remote real-time supervision via digital platforms.	• Accessible regardless of geography • Consistent supervision through travel seasons • Access to specialist supervisors	• Technical issues • Rapport building may be slower • Confidentiality/security concerns	• Consultants with national/international caseloads • Sport contexts involving extensive travel

(*Continued*)

Table 11.1 (Continued)

Supervision format	*Description*	*Strengths*	*Limitations/risks*	*Best used when*
Asynchronous digital supervision (recorded sessions, written feedback)	Time-shifted supervision using recordings, written case reflections, online forums.	• Allows deep analysis • Encourages reflective practice • Flexible for irregular schedules	• Delayed feedback • Less effective for urgent issues • Requires strong writing/analysis skills	• Time-poor supervisees • Supervision of detailed technique (video review) • Training programmes with assessment components
Interprofessional supervision	Supervision across disciplines (e.g., psychology + coaching + medical).	• Broad perspectives • Mirrors interdisciplinary sports teams • Enhances role clarity within systems	• Power imbalances likely • Conflicting professional standards • Requires strong facilitation and clear boundaries	• High-performance teams • Complex athlete cases requiring multidisciplinary input
Hybrid supervision models	Combination of formats (e.g., individual + group; live + asynchronous; remote + in-person).	• Highly adaptable • Optimises the strengths of multiple approaches • Supports developmental progression	• Requires planning/ coordination • Risk of inconsistency if poorly integrated	• Long-term training pathways • Supervisors managing varied caseloads • Programmes seeking comprehensive competency coverage

methods to novel tech-based formats and combined hybrid models, each presenting its own strengths and weaknesses. The success of supervision relies not on following one ideal method, but on carefully choosing methods that fit individual development, practical settings, and learning goals. The field of applied sport psychology is progressing, and as it does, the way we supervise practitioners will probably change to keep pace with shifts in sports, new technology, and our knowledge of how practising professionals grow. We might see virtual reality and artificial intelligence tools become more integrated, along with more advanced hybrid models. Also, we could see a stronger focus on interprofessional methods that acknowledge the multidisciplinary nature of modern support for sports performance. Regardless of the supervision form and format, the primary aim is consistent: to cultivate sport psychology professionals who are thoughtful, moral, and successful in their practice, and who can successfully manage the intricate challenges of aiding athletes and sports groups. When supervisors and those they oversee understand different supervision options and make good choices about how to use them, it helps people learn and benefits the profession.

Exercise 11.1: Choosing the Right Supervision Format

Given four contexts:

1. A trainee working with a national team that travels constantly.
2. Two practitioners embedded in the same youth academy system.
3. A remote private practitioner without local colleagues.
4. A high-performance environment with an interprofessional team.

For each context:

1. Choose the most appropriate supervision format (individual, group, triadic, live, tech-mediated, interprofessional, hybrid).
2. Justify your selection.
3. Identify the limitations of the chosen format.
4. Suggest one complementary supervision method to address limitations.

12 Trainee Development, Difference, and Diversity

12.1 Introduction

Supervision is a primary catalyst for trainee development, providing the opportunity to explore our own experiences, learn and grow. Here, we will focus on identifying trainees' needs on practicum placements and how trainees can support themselves through the supervision process. We shall also explore why an understanding of diversity and difference matters in the helping professions and wider social context. Our practice does not occur in a silo. We bring with us our own biases and experiences of difference and diversity. Supervision offers a platform to explore these histories and assumptions and how they might interact or show up in our professional practice. This crucial support allows us to work with a range of client issues, while recognising and, where necessary, addressing power, prejudice, oppression, inequality, disability, class, sexism and ageism, amongst others, in both society and helping relationships.

12.1.1 Trainee Development

Despite the individualistic nature of trainee development, several routes, pathways, and trajectories have been proposed. Two consistent components of trainee development are: appropriate opportunities and the capacity to self-support (McEwan & Tod, 2015; Verner et al., 2021). The quality of an output is in part determined by the quality of the input. Trainee development is no different. The quality, appropriateness, support, and challenge available within trainee placements are therefore key and something we shall explore. It is a trainee's responsibility to facilitate their own growth; supervision is a vehicle for which trainees most often hold the role of the driver.

12.2 Sourcing and Creating Development Opportunities

A commonly cited challenge for trainee sport psychologists is accruing the required applied practice opportunities (McEwan & Tod, 2015). In other

DOI: 10.4324/9781003485667-12

applied psychology settings, 'ready-made' placements are often available (Woods et al., 2015). This discrepancy can frustrate some, with trainees often craving supervisors or institutions to provide clients or placement opportunities (McEwan & Tod, 2023). However, the experience of creating suitable practicum placements can empower the trainee, supporting the development of the skills necessary for navigating the post-training world. Further, getting experience is one thing. Getting the *right* experiences can be something entirely different. Trainees should try to view their practicum experiences (and time in training collectively) as an opportunity to explore as many environments as possible, seeking experiences that are enriching and educational. Explorations suggest that over two-thirds of practicum placements cite the capacity to provide additional hours, or no/low-cost support as a motive for running placements, highlighting the transactional component of placements that does not necessarily align with trainee development (Hatcher et al., 2012). Supervision is a space in which trainees can explore placement ideas and concepts, seeking to create a development plan that provides opportunities that align with their long-term goals and careers. By discussing these concepts early, trainees can proactively seek beneficial learning opportunities that provide both comfort and challenge.

12.3 Identifying Needs and Using Supervision Effectively

To identify your needs, you need to know where you are trying to get to – and how does one know what they do not know? Effectively identifying your needs and supporting yourself through supervision therefore begins with cultivating curiosity – about practice, about relationships, about the self. A useful framework for supporting the process of need development and exploration is the Johari Window (Luft & Ingham, 1955). Luft and Ingham's (1955) 2 × 2 matrix explores the degree of knowledge or awareness known to self (known and not known) alongside the degree of knowledge or awareness known by others, to generate four domains:

1. The Open Area or Arena: This section is formed by the intersection between information known both to the self (trainee) and other (supervisor). Arguably the easiest section, this may constitute the need to develop content knowledge (e.g., understanding of therapeutic modalities or intervention types) or aligned personal development goals (e.g., capacity to interact with specific client groups or presentations). Themes that emerge in this area may align with those observed in typical developmental trajectories, marking the points trainees and supervisors both *expect* to attend to (Fogaca et al., 2024).
2. The Blind Area: Here, information and awareness about a trainee is unknown to the trainee, but known or understood by the supervisor.

Here it is the trainee's responsibility to enter supervision with intrigue and openness, while the supervisor brings avenues for further exploration. This might include feedback on a trainee's way of being or highlighting gaps in awareness and understanding. Trainees are encouraged to be inquisitive here, using session notes, recordings, or intervention plans to ask supervisors: *what do you see, hear, think?*

3. The Hidden Area or Facade: When the trainee holds knowledge of the self, but the supervisor does not hold access to it, the result is termed the hidden area or façade. The development and maintenance of facades are predominantly because of feelings of vulnerability. Here trainees should endeavour to bring authenticity and transparency to the supervisory relationship to facilitate growth and development. A question you might ask yourself to see if you are spending too much time here might be: are there themes that I avoid bringing to supervision or that I recognise repeating in my practice?
4. The Unknown Area: Arguably the most complex domain, the unknown reflects an interpersonal space where both the trainee and supervisor lack the conscious awareness of relevant information. Development in this area may be best captured by creativity, where the trainee and supervisor collaborate to explore new ideas, solutions, or areas of development. A key question might be: does this feel inquisitive or exploratory?

The Johari Window offers a practical way to consider how you can identify needs in supervision, but how might you practically resource yourself? At regular intervals, it is helpful to pause and reflect on your own development, the supervision you receive, and what you expect for the future.

12.4 Difference and Diversity in Applied Practice and Supervision

Trainee development exists in a social context, so too does applied practice. Effective practice in the helping professions therefore requires the capacity to recognise and explore difference and diversity. In applied sport and exercise psychology contexts, difference and diversity appear in numerous ways. At a global level, this might explore the broader organisational structure or context and representation within it (Lago et al., 2023; Spaaij et al., 2020). This may trickle down into our own experiences operating in such contexts. Previous research has narrated the challenges of applied psychologists entering sporting environments based on characteristics such as gender (Curvey et al., 2023; Goldman & Gervis, 2021), race (Carter & Davila, 2017; Yu et al., 2016), alongside the profession more broadly (Bejar et al., 2022; McCarver et al., 2019). Despite organisations framing inclusion as important, literature consistently suggests that the intention is not represented in meaningful change (Gardner et al., 2023) often rendering the psychologist, by choice or necessity, as the voice of change. At a more micro-level, inclusion is an important consideration for our interactions with clients, considering how our clients' stories shape their interactions and behaviours (Kelly et al., 2024; Kontos & Breland-Noble, 2002; Martin et al., 2020).

12.4.1 Understanding the Self

A first step might be to explore your own experiences of difference and diversity. Our own experiences, biases, and assumptions influence the way we interact with the world and our practice. Trainees from minoritised backgrounds may experience additional pressures in their training, including heightened scrutiny, perceived tokenism, or access limitations. Proactive consideration (both personally and in supervision) is therefore required not only for professional growth, but as these experiences/biases/assumptions may metaphorically trip us up if inadequately addressed. For example, a trainee from a low socioeconomic status background may attribute feedback around their appearance to experiences of discrimination and not simply the appropriateness of their attire to the environment, while a trainee with previous experiences of racism may question if questioning their impact in the environment reflects them personally, rather than the field more broadly. These scenarios are intentionally murky, as ascertaining discrimination often is. While individuals do occasionally intentionally discriminate or marginalise, much is unintentional, intertwined heavily with the perceptions of both parties. Here are some prompts to explore your own experiences of difference and diversity:

1. What have my experiences been in relation to difference and diversity?
2. What aspects of my identity have been most salient across my life, education, and sport?
3. Have I experienced marginalisation or exclusion previously? How have these experiences shaped my worldview and sense of belonging?
4. What exposure have I had to difference? How might this shape my confidence in interacting with others?
5. Do I notice myself making assumptions about athletes, coaches, or organisations?
6. Are there any client groups, identities, or presentations that elicit discomfort or overconfidence?

12.5 Understanding the Client in Context

Ethical and effective practice begins with the development of a therapeutic alliance. To do so, applied practitioners are required to enter the client's frame of reference, understanding how an individual's characteristics influence how they view the world. The UK's Equalities Act (2010) denotes nine protected characteristics: age, disability, gender, marriage, pregnancy and maternity, race, religion or beliefs, sex, and sexual orientation, intended to systemically address inequalities that are prevalent within sport and society (Dwight & Biscomb, 2018). Although not an exhaustive list, this can be a useful place to explore how our clients' experiences shape their identities, coping strategies, relationships, and ability to engage with sport psychology practitioners.

When recognising and actively working with diversity and difference, practitioners are better positioned to understand the meaning clients are attributing to certain situations and select effective interventions. For example, male athletes may be less able or willing to express emotions verbally, shaped by gendered expectations in the environment; here, using colour or actions to represent emotional states may be more beneficial while developing psychological safety and expression skills. Holding an awareness of difference can also influence how clients' presentations are conceptualised. Psychological presentations are not rarely individual deficits or personal challenges and can often be contextualised by the systemic barriers, exclusion, or experiences of the client. Understanding not just what is happening, but why it is happening within the broader context can help us avoid pathologising adaptive responses to challenging situations and environments.

12.5.1 Case Example: Lucy

Craig (pseudonym), the team coach, had approached me before a session early in the season. As the new psychologist, I was still familiarising myself with the players, coaching staff, and environment. 'Lucy is such a talented athlete, sees the game so well, great athlete; it's just a shame she's so disorganised and disinterested in team meetings – do you think you could help?' I was filled with curiosity. Shortly after, the players appeared on the pitch wearing red tops, white skorts, and red socks. Except for Lucy, who appeared in the contrasting kit of a white top, red skort, and white socks. I observed what could be described as jovial banter, as teammates and staff joked about, 'How could Lucy get it wrong again?!' As the session started, Craig asked if everyone had gone through the playbook to a crowd of nods. I had skimmed through the team's 32-page playbook before the session, hoping to have some semblance of what was going on. As the session unfolded, the challenges Craig described emerged. In free-play scenarios, Lucy was everywhere and central to her team's success. In set plays, she would often find herself lost or making errors, much to the dismay of both Craig and her teammates.

As I was new to the squad, I had arranged informal 10–15-minute catch-ups with each of the athletes with a simple objective – build some rapport and introduce services. After that session was my first one-on-one encounter with Lucy. After the general formalities/procedures, I asked Lucy if she could tell me a little about herself. During this time, she disclosed an intellectual disability that rendered her unable to read. Her inability to turn up in the right kit, or in-act plays, was not through disinterest, but an inability to access the information as provided. I asked if she had disclosed this before with the team or coaches. She had, sort of, but was embarrassed and wanted to find a way to muddle through. After some discussion, I questioned if it might be possible for us to discuss this with Craig. He had made it clear he wanted to support Lucy and wanted the best for her. Lucy agreed, and we arranged a meeting before the next session. As Lucy shared her experience, Craig was aghast. While he was aware of Lucy's disability, he had not taken the time to grasp the extent to which it interacted with her ability to function. A conscientious coach, Craig's behaviour changed. The kit for the day was posted in a colour picture (alongside the text), playbooks were not only discussed and written down, but played out over lunch using a variety of condiments to represent players. The perception of Lucy changed from one of being 'disorganised and disinterested' to 'a diligent leader' almost overnight.

12.6 Cultural Competence and Transcultural Effectiveness

The fact that cultural competence is listed as a core competency of applied sport psychologists highlights that, contrary to idealistic beliefs that those seeking to work in helping professions inherently possess the capacity to be culturally competent, it is indeed a skill that requires development (Benuto et al., 2019; Quartiroli, et al., 2020). Derived from the work of Bennett (1993), Van Weerdenburg (1996) created a six-stage developmental model of intercultural sensitivity, indicating markers towards transcultural effectiveness that run parallel to the developmental path of supervisees and supervisors respectively (Hawkins & Shohet, 2012). The six stages are:

1. Denial: the capacity to only see one's own culture and experience as real or true.
2. Defence: the positioning of one's own culture as 'right' or 'good' compared to other cultures.
3. Minimisation: the expression of elements of one's own cultural worldview as universally experienced truths.
4. Acceptance: the recognition that there are multiple equally complex and valuable worldviews, of which one's own culture is a small piece.
5. Cognitive adaptation: the ability to appreciate and view the world from alternative perspectives or 'different eyes'.
6. Behavioural adaptation: the capability to adapt behaviour to suit different cultural relationships, situations, and demands.

Stages one and two have been posited as culturally insensitive and unethical psychologist positions (Hawkins & Shohet, 2012). Despite being a core competency, few sport psychology practitioners attest to deliberately considering or centring cultural competence (or the exploration of diversity and difference more broadly) in their practice, or developmental journeys (Quartiroli et al., 2022; Ryba et al., 2025). Competence, and indeed cultural competence, does not develop by itself (Brinkmann & van Weedenburg, 2014). The requirement for conscious developmental attention, and the reported lack of it, likely serves as an explanation for the high prevalence of culturally insensitive reports of practice in sport psychology contexts (Gupta & Divekar, 2022; Lafferty et al., 2022). It is therefore posited that trainee and qualified practitioners alike regularly question: *how am I addressing diversity and difference within my practice (and supervision)?*

12.6.1 Case Examples: Learning through Mistakes

Sport, like most things, is global. Our lives, experiences, and exposures may not be. A career in sport psychology can provide the fortune of working with individuals from a range of backgrounds, all while exploring the world. This privilege can, though, bring challenges. Growing up in the southeast of England, in a conservative British household with limited exposure to travel or education, my exposure to difference and diversity was, at best, limited. On entering the profession, I was cognisant of this, but perceived that my training, general propensity towards curiosity and politeness, built upon the rhetoric of 'manners are free', would support me in navigating this shortcoming. Below are some examples of, on the face of it, small acts that got me into bother.

- Moving to shake hands when introducing myself to a coach from a culture where shaking hands is perceived as an act of aggression.
- Having office sweets that were taken by a Muslim athlete, only to realise they contained gelatine and were therefore not Halal.
- Wishing an athlete a 'Merry Christmas' from a culture that did not celebrate it.
- Using the phrase 'not too shabby' in a nation where 'shabby' sounds similar to vulgar terminology in the native language.
- Leaving a slightly too long silence after an athlete disclosed I could likely tell their sexuality based on their appearance as I endeavoured to respond.

These transgressions should highlight that errors happen. Clients do not, overall, at least, expect us to have all the answers. They do, though, expect us, and indeed it is our role too, to endeavour to be there with them. A key aspect of trainee development is therefore not necessarily needing to know every facet of difference and diversity but being able to take ownership and be transparent about that gap. Supervision provides us with an opportunity to explore how and why these errors happen. At a surface level, these errors can occur because of a lack of awareness or ignorance that could have been eased with a simple 'could you tell me more about' or the selection of more neutral language 'enjoy the festive period'. At a deeper level, supervision is a platform to explore whether these comments reflect deeper-held biases or assumptions about the world and how we navigate it.

12.7 Summary

In this chapter, we have explored some facets of trainee development and difference and diversity. Trainee development in the helping professions is a dynamic, socially situated process that extends beyond skill acquisition to include self-awareness, reflexivity, and ethical responsibility. Supervision plays a central role in this journey, offering a structured space in which trainees can identify developmental needs, navigate power dynamics, and critically reflect on their practice. Actively engaging with supervision enables trainees to source meaningful learning opportunities, support themselves through uncertainty, and integrate feedback in purposeful ways. Crucially, effective practice cannot be separated from considerations of difference and diversity. Understanding how identity, culture, and social context shape both practitioner and client experiences enhances relational depth and intervention effectiveness. By embedding these considerations throughout supervision and applied work, trainees are better equipped to work responsively, inclusively, and competently within complex sporting and social environments.

Exercise 12.1: Questions to Support Exploring Practicum Opportunities in Supervision

1. Do you want to be in an environment that already has psychology services? (e.g., under another psychologist).
2. Are there specific types of populations you are interested in working with? (e.g., exercise settings, youth athletes, high-performance sport).
3. Are there any sports you are particularly interested in? (e.g., team sports, extreme sports).
4. Do you want or need to be model-specific (e.g., cognitive behavioural practice) and how might this influence the environments that are suitable?
5. Are you getting exposure to a range of different experiences and environments?

6. What barriers might exist for you seeking to gain placements in different environments? (e.g., own experience in that sport).
7. What practical constraints exist around gaining different experiences? (e.g., finances, time, availability).
8. Do you feel your placement is providing you with what you need? (e.g., appropriate support, opportunities, flexibility, exposure, time).

13 The Good, the Bad, and the Ugly of Supervision

13.1 Introduction

Having made it this far in the book, we do not feel the need to reiterate the importance of supervision for supervisee development and practice; however, stating that supervision is always a positive or facilitative process would be misleading. As with any form of service delivery (including applied sport psychology), the interpersonal propensity of supervision creates the potential for experiences that are profoundly positive, or conversely, have a pernicious impact (Ramos-Sanchez et al., 2002). Researchers have broadly prioritised exploring the characteristics of effective supervision in which enriching and supportive experiences are shared (Foltz et al., 2015; Kilminster & Jolly, 2000). Attention has though increasingly turned to the uncomfortable reality that poorly facilitated supervision exists, and can be harmful or abusive, eliciting adverse consequences for either the supervisee or supervisor (Ellis, 2017; Hutman et al., 2023). Recognising this continuum – from facilitative to harmful supervision – is therefore essential.

In this chapter, we will explore said continuum, providing indicators of good and bad supervisory practice alongside practical examples and tasks designed to support the reader in not only understanding but recognising features of effective and ineffective supervision. To support this process, we will utilise the unified framework for understanding and assessing supervision practice presented and tested by Ellis (2001; Ellis et al., 2014, 2015), categorising supervision as exceptional (the good), inadequate (the bad), and harmful (the ugly). We begin by exploring what facilitates good supervision, followed by exploring power and anxiety in supervision that compromises bad and harmful practice. Before beginning this exploration, an important caveat is that the boundaries between exceptional, inadequate, and harmful supervision warrant attention and consideration, as they are not concretely demarcated.

DOI: 10.4324/9781003485667-13

13.2 The Good: Characteristics of Effective and Exceptional Supervision

Efforts to identify the components and practices facilitative of effective applied psychology supervision, alongside the mechanisms to achieve it, are extensive – but what does that mean? (Borders, 2014; Foo Kune & Rodolfa, 2013; Simpson-Southward et al., 2017). In Ellis et al'.s (2015) conceptualisation good supervision begins with what they term 'minimally adequate supervision' – here, the supervisory standards and requirements delineated by the relevant regulatory body are adhered to (e.g., facilitates minimum required contact time and ensures content aligns with regulatory requirements). On fulfilling this prerequisite, the potential to co-create exceptional supervision occurs; supervision that is powerful, profound, or inspirational. Exceptional supervision is said to comprise: (a) a supervisory relationship that clearly exceeds criteria for minimally adequate supervision; (b) implements best practices for clinical supervision consistently; (c) is characterised by the development and maintenance of a collaborative, professional supervisory relationship held with appropriate professional boundaries; and (d) embodies a deep trust and respect for both parties' identities, promoting empowerment, insight and professional development.

13.2.1 Competent Supervision and Supervision Best Practices

In relation to criterion (a) minimum requirements or markers of competent supervision are already explored throughout the text (examples). We would encourage readers to use regulatory body guidelines as a checklist of sorts, ensuring supervision meets the said requirements. We have coupled points (a) and (b) because of their complementary nature. Markers of competent supervision are predominantly competence-based, in that they stipulate the required declarative knowledge for supervision to be conducted. Conversely, best practice guidelines describe (evidence-informed) ways in which knowledge can be implemented. Extensive best practice guidelines have been created within clinical settings (see ACES, 2011; Falender et al., 2014; or O'Donovan, 2011 for exploration). For example, Borders (2014) delineates the twelve sections of the *Best Practices in Clinical Supervision* document (ACES, 2011) that explore the phases and processes in conducting supervision, required supervisor skills and characteristics, and competent supervisory behaviours. Best practice statements are often built within the relevant professional context. While the guidelines are deemed relevant to sport psychology practitioners, it is worth noting the novelties and distinctions of applied sport contexts. For example, one discipline-based difference may include communication within the supervisory dyad. Clinical practice and supervision typically occur in structured, regimented settings where supervisory access is readily available (e.g., in clinic) enabling the application of rigid communication guidelines (e.g., supervisory contact during 9–5 working hours). Conversely, the unpredictability, chaos, and loose structure of applied sport practice, combined with practitioners often working in silos, may present a requirement for more flexible supervisory access (Quartiroli et al., 2025). Limited evidence as to the efficacy of best practice guidelines is currently available, particularly in sporting domains, requiring caution and further exploration (Tugendrajch et al., 2021).

13.2.2 Supervisory Relationship

Good sport psychology practice begins with the relationship. Supervision is no different, with the supervisory alliance embraced as 'the very heart and soul of supervision' (Watkins, 2014). Managed appropriately, the supervisory alliance produces a sense of safety and security facilitative of learning and exploration, in which professional vulnerabilities can be openly shared and explored (Lafferty et al., 2019). Because of the importance, various researchers have endeavoured to model the qualities of effective supervisory relationships. We depict some of these determinants within Table 13.1, highlighting shared themes (Beinart, 2002; Weaks, 2002; Palomo et al., 2010; Pearce et al., 2013; McMahon, 2014). Across all explorations, the importance of relational empowerment and safety is emphasised. In good supervision, the relationship is used as a vehicle for empowerment, validating experience and providing a platform for collaborative discussion and criticism. Establishing clear boundaries from the outset of the supervisory relationship (alongside successfully maintaining them) also consistently promotes positive supervisory outcomes. As a supervisee continues to gain professional competence, their developmental needs adapt; in healthy alliances, supervisors and supervisees respond to their needs, proactively addressing concerns or exploring further avenues for growth and development. In dyadic relationships, both parties can seek the same quality from one another exhibited somewhat differently. For example, supervisees report effective supervisory alliances when they perceive their supervisor to be both invested and committed to their development, shown through responsiveness, planning or intrigue. Similarly, supervisors express increased enthusiasm when supervisees demonstrate investment in their own learning and development, taking initiative and proactively contributing to service delivery (Clohessy, 2008).

13.2.3 The Realist: Addressing Conflict, Discomfort, and Mistakes

Mistakes happen. Across the duration of a supervisory relationship, there is an inevitability of errors in communication, judgement, or action, even where both parties hold the best intentions. The marker of 'good' supervision is not then that these errors occur, but how the supervisor

Table 13.1 Critical Determinants of Supervisory Relationships

Beinart (2002)	*Weaks (2002)*	*Palomo et al., (2010)*	*Pearce et al., (2013)*	*McMahon (2014)*
Nine categories of the effective supervisory relationship	Qualities of effective supervisory relationships	Six factors of the Supervisory Relationship Questionnaire (SRQ)	Five factors in the Supervisory Relationship Measure (SRM)	Four guiding principles for the supervisory relationship
Boundaried	Equality	Safe base	Safe Base	Offering emotional presence and sensitivity
Supportive	Challenge	Structure	Supervisor commitment	Valuing vulnerability and competence
Open Relationship	Safety	Commitment	Trainee contribution	Offering knowledge and experience with humility
Respectful		Role model	External influences	Supporting continued personal and professional growth
Committed		Reflective education	Supervisor investment	
Sensitive to needs		Formative feedback		
Collaborative				
Educative				
Evaluative				

and supervisee work to repair the supervisory alliance, paralleling the rupture-repair process between psychologist and client (Watkins, 2024). An acceptance of the realism of alliance ruptures is thoughtfully portrayed in Pearlstein and Soyster's (2019) reflexive account of the supervisory experiences of trainees with disabilities, highlighting the restorative qualities of transparency, humility, and flexibility. Owning these moments can elicit further benefits for both the supervisee and supervisor, as while not only a prerequisite to continue working together effectively, successfully repairing tensions and ruptures has been observed to strengthen the supervisory relationship (beyond pre-rupture states) and positively contribute to clinical process and outcomes (Falnder et al., 2014; Safran et al., 2011).

13.2.4 Case Example: Zoe

The following excerpt is from my reflective diary. In the lead-up to this supervision meeting, I was experiencing tummy-turning levels of anxiety. My uncertainty, stemming from a concoction of ongoing contextual demands (e.g., safeguarding issues, programme requirements), personal and/or professional development challenges (e.g., exploration of therapeutic modalities) and supervisory apprehension (e.g., what was going on?) was obstructing my capacity to engage meaningfully with my supervisor. Until this point, I had been plagued by experiential avoidance, concerned over the ramifications of challenging superiority.

> It's strange; psychologists don't have to look very far before someone emphasises the importance of 'the relationship'. Today, the relationship felt make or break. Supervision this year has been bumpy at times, do *I trust my supervisor? Why do I feel this way? Is that acceptable? How transparent should I be? How transparent is he being? What standards do I expect*? Ultimately, fuelled by frustration and a kick up the butt from the boyfriend, I had a '**** it' moment. I'm always upfront, maybe a little less brutal, and yet, I am glad I was. To strip back the glitz and say I'm upset (time) or confused ('good'?!) provided a space for healing and understanding. In those moments of authenticity lies a power because the relationship was strong enough, I felt comfortable (eventually), to share those sentiments. As psychologists' it is easy to talk about 'managing the power-imbalance' or 'letting the client take the lead', ultimately a real strength of relationship can be observed when the 'client' is able to vocalise negative emotions – this is something I endeavour to strive for in future practice and supervision.

In actively addressing my concerns, several areas of personal and professional development emerged. From a supervisory alliance perspective, my supervisor's capacity and willingness to meet me with vulnerability and compassion enabled an enhanced shared perspective of how I (and we) can do this better. Opportunities to engage with varied literature on power, authenticity, and therapeutic relationships emerged, with my drive for knowledge and improvement stimulated. My lived experience of successful rupture resolution provided a benchmark and tangible representation of true success within therapeutic relationships and alliances, alongside modelling effective practitioner behaviours. Finally, having raised issues of discontent, a behaviour typically demonised in sporting contexts, and not only survived but thrived, my willingness to be vulnerable and motivation to engage was enthusiastically reinstated.

13.2.5 Development and Enhancement

In what is intended to be a learning relationship, it should be no surprise that exceptional supervision contains both perceived (e.g., *I feel like I am developing contextual awareness/understanding')* and tangible (e.g., '*I can now confidently develop a client intervention for choking grounded in cognitive-behavioural therapy*) changes in development. Learning experiences that are relevant, appropriate, and helpful should be advocated for and explicitly or implicitly linked with the supervisee's stage of development (Hutter et al., 2015). For sport psychologists, supervision may focus more acutely on developing the contextual skills required to operate in the environment, particularly for those seeking to practise in high performance. The complexities of high-performance sport environments and how to work effectively in them are seldom reported, with supervision being recommended as a platform for exploring these necessary skills (Eubank et al., 2014). Well-timed and appropriate supervisor self-disclosure may feature here, with supervisors' experiences bringing to life and contextualising supervisees' learning, particularly early-trainee psychologists whose present experience may largely be academic (Mehr & Daltry, 2022).

Challenges in effective knowledge translation are regularly observed in sports performance environments (Bartlett & Drust, 2020). Knowledge-translation difficulties are further complicated by how the recipient, in this case the supervisee, perceives the supervisor's actions. To help bridge this gap, Table 13.2 explores some effective supervisor behaviours alongside supervisee responses, or consequential behaviours. The fluidity in this table should support a supervisee in recognising potential positive responses (e.g., perceived increased self-confidence) back to supervisor behaviours (e.g., the provision of autonomy in intervention decision-making and exploration) or forwards to their own behaviours (e.g., improved capacity to demonstrate context-relevant behaviours). While these examples

Table 13.2 Examples of Effective Supervision Behaviours and Potential Impacts on the Bad and the Harmful: When Supervision Fails

Effective supervision behaviours (*things you might see/hear*)	*Potential supervisee responses* (*things you may feel*)	*Potential supervisee outcomes* (*things you may do*)
Endeavours to provide autonomy and empowerment (including support/encouragement)	Increased motivation	Enhanced willingness and capacity to self-disclose
Constructive feedback framed in developmental orientation	Increased self-confidence	Improved therapeutic outcomes and clinical decision making
Invitations for reflection and exploration of competence and development	Emotionally safe and secure	Increased engagement in both content and process
Collaborative and integrated ways of working (goals, assessment, feedback)	Warmth, genuineness, empathy	Adaptations to ways of working and style of delivery
Active pursuit to understand context and experiencing	Valued and supported	Increased attunement to functional aspects of therapeutic alliances
Purposeful formation of supervisory alliance addressing concepts with transparency and clarity	Enlightened/insightful	Active pursuit of skill or knowledge acquisition and development
Managed disclosure and self-disclosure of the supervisor and supervisee	Listened to and understood	Recognise continued development of professional identity
Demonstrations of clinical, practical and ethical knowledge and skills	Appropriately challenged and stimulated	Increased context-relevant behaviours and approaches
Responsivity to supervise needs, shifting session content as relevant	Reassurance	
Provide solutions (or space to explore solutions) relative to the context		

highlight supervision done well, unfortunately, supervision experiences are not always 'good'.

To our knowledge, the phenomenon of supervision 'going badly' is not readily represented in the applied sport psychology literature; however, working under the premise that applied sport psychology often mirrors, or represents allied health professions suggests addressing bad supervisory practice is pertinent. Literature in clinical and counselling psychology indicates that up to 93% of supervisees experience inadequate supervision and over half of supervisees report being recipients of harmful supervision across their journey in applied practice (Chircop Coleiro et al., 2022; Ellis et al., 2014). Ellis et al'.s (2014) conceptualisation of poor practice differentiates between inadequate and harmful experiences. Inadequate supervision is defined as:

> When the supervisor is unable or unwilling to enhance the professional functioning of the supervisee, monitor the quality of the professional services offered to the supervisee's clients, serves as a gatekeeper to the profession, or fails to provide the minimal level of supervisory care as established by the discipline or profession.
>
> (Ellis et al., 2014, p. 440)

Conversely, harmful supervision reflects:

> Supervisory practices that result in psychological, emotional, and/or physical harm or trauma to the supervisee...The two essential components of harmful supervision are: (a) that the supervisee was genuinely harmed in some way by the supervisors' behaviours or (b) the supervisor's behaviour is known to cause harm, even though the supervisee may not identify the behaviours as harmful.
>
> (Ellis et al., 2014, p. 440)

The line between inadequate and harmful supervision can often be blurry, creeping up surreptitiously or unbeknownst to the supervisee or supervisor. For example, in relation to applied practice oversight, bad practice may include insufficient monitoring of supervisee activities and practice (e.g., limited observation and case discussion). A lack of oversight could though become harmful, or ugly practice based on factors including frequency, duration or nature (e.g., no case discussion for a significant period, supervisor unable to gain applied practice oversight when working close to limits of competence) that could leave the supervisee or client at risk and constitute a neglect of professional responsibilities (Hutman et al., 2023). We will therefore explore these two proponents together, focusing on power, anxiety, and developmental needs.

13.2.6 Power

Power exists in all relationships, including in supervision because of the natural hierarchical structure (Andersen, 1994). The existence of power in supervision is not fundamentally problematic. Supervisees report instances where the power differential between themselves and their supervisor is used positively (e.g., sharing knowledge and expertise, providing constructive and directed feedback; Murphy & Wright, 2005). It is therefore not the existence of power in the supervisory relationship that is cause for concern, or a marker of poor supervisory practice, but a failure to attend to power dynamics and the potential vulnerability for the supervisee. This creates an interesting conundrum for supervisors to consider: when and how do their supervisees perceive power as being problematic versus being beneficial (Cook et al., 2018)? Challenges are enhanced because of the fluidity of power dynamics. This moves the needle from an early acknowledgement of power in the supervisory relationship, to a sustained, committed effort to understanding one another, accounting for socio-political and psychological factors, in which the unequal distribution of power and authority is acknowledged and negotiated.

So, what does this look like in practice? Indicators (knowingly or unknowingly) of the misuse or abuse of power in supervision include:

- Supervisee/supervisor challenges and vulnerabilities are diminished, overlooked or minimised.
- The presence of a 'surveillance mentality' in which difficulties are addressed in a manner that leaves little room for growth, learning, or reflection.
- Expertise or knowledge is used to create dominance, with the supervisor positioned as 'all-knowing' and the supervisee as 'incompetent' – with little space for the supervisee to own their own experiences.
- The compromising of boundaries (e.g., dual roles, inappropriate relationships).
- Seeking personal gain or exploitative relationships.
- Using authority to create dependency and force adherence.
- Making macro- and microaggressions towards the supervisee (e.g., blatant racism, homophobia, ableism).
- An overemphasis on the 'self' of the supervisor, including ego-endorsing outcomes.

Additional powerful questions for readers to consider are: Where do individuals perceive the power lying between supervisor and supervisee to reside? Particularly regarding certain aspects of supervision (e.g., goal development) and what biases may influence how supervision is conducted? Power dynamics play out uniquely, and our perceptions of their manifestation, while highly individualised, may also be influenced by relevant characteristics. In relation to culture and race, Hernández and McDowell (2010) noted the salience of addressing race, cultural identities, and social norms because of their interplay with privilege. In explorations of supervisory power and gender, female supervisees have been observed to perceive less power in relation to clinical goals and discourse around power than their male counterparts (Wind et al., 2021). An investigation on supervisory behaviours in a group supervision context indicated that when supervised by a male supervisor, female supervisees were given more direction and requested their opinion half as often as male supervisees in the group (Granello et al., 1997; Stefano et al., 2017). In this example, the misuse of power is not particularly overt. These subtle discretions of supervisors, though, act to silence and dismiss the voice of the supervisee, quietly eroding confidence and belief.

13.2.7 Anxiety

The presence of supervisee and supervisor anxiety is typical, with the narcissistic dangers of the learning process and the requirement for vulnerability evident (Mollon, 1989). Sources of supervisee anxiety are often self or other-oriented and have been attributed to factors including: the evaluative nature of supervisory interactions and related approval anxiety, a lack of clarity regarding expectations, roles and responsibilities, conflicting roles and challenges in applied practice (Ellis et al., 2015; Kocyigit, 2024). Meanwhile, supervisors reported anxiety commonly relates to self or context-oriented factors such as difficulties in navigating their own personal characteristics, navigating their role as an evaluator, concerns over supervision quality, or organisational culture/demand issues (Kuo et al., 2016).

As for our clients, anxiety is not by nature harmful, or a marker of poor supervision. The first question both parties might seek to ask is: *Is the degree of experienced anxiety influencing either party's capacity to function effectively?* Elevated anxiety can negatively influence the effectiveness of both supervision and the supervisees' applied performance (Ladany et al., 2013). Performance decrements can include a reduced willingness to disclose, decreased engagement in content, and induced supervisee defensiveness (Ellis et al., 2015). For a supervisee, this shift in their locus of attention towards their internal voice can act as a precursor to ethical violations, further perpetuating feelings of anxiety. On considering whether there is an effect, the next space of exploration is: *Is the anxiety a consequence of the supervisor's or supervisee's behaviour?* Inadequate or harmful supervision, anxiety is a product of action and not merely the process of supervision itself. Examples might include receiving overly negative feedback that is disparaging, inconsistent, or belittling; an inappropriate pathologisation of behaviour; or stigmas, bias, or discrimination (Cartwright, 2020; Hutman et al., 2023). For the supervisory alliance to function effectively, an investment in the reduction of anxiety should be apparent – in bad supervision, its presence is barely acknowledged and acts as a strong indicator of the supervisory alliance gone wrong.

13.2.8 Developmental Needs

Another area in which supervision can become bad or harmful is when the supervisee's developmental or in-the-moment needs are inadequately or poorly attended to (Hutman et al., 2023). Developmental needs may not be addressed because of contextual challenges or a deficit in delivery-based skills; for example, the provision of inadequate time or attention to attend to needs or inattentiveness in exploring the supervisees' developmental needs, such as holding unrealistic expectations or being overly task-focused (Poczwardowski et al., 2023). Alternatively, the supervisor may lack the clinical expertise required to facilitate the supervisee's development (Barrett et al., 2020). This may include an inability to understand the supervisee's or client's presentation, an under-exploration of clinical knowledge and skills, or the provision of inadequate guidance and direction (Ladany et al., 2013). At best, failing to address the development of sport psychologists may lead to stagnation. Stagnation is common in the development of any professional, with periods of stagnation arguably required to allow the practitioner to recover and reset for growth (Carlsson, 2016); however, continued stagnation can lead to burnout and apathy, with ethical questions posed regarding why the supervisor continues to provide a supervision service (and presumably some form of payment) if the service is not providing benefit. Poor attention to developmental needs can also result in unethical practice that is harmful to the supervisee and the client if they cannot develop the skills or receive the support to provide the service.

13.3 Case Example: Finding the Right Fit

Navigating the ethical, competence-based, and ever-changing tightrope of balancing mental health versus performance-based intervention is a key talking point for applied sport psychology and therefore trickles into supervision (McHenry et al., 2022). To enhance mental health or clinical competency, sport psychology practitioners can benefit extensively from seeking interprofessional (e.g., from clinical psychologists) supervision. Finding a supervisor who aligns with my developmental needs is something I have at times found challenging. For example, when approaching some sport psychologist supervisors, the overarching focus on 'content' and 'performance' has felt incompatible with my values and beliefs.

Conversely, when approaching some clinical psychology supervisors, the focus has been so tightly held to the 'context' of applied sport psychology (and the chaos that occurs within) that I have felt time was wasted or process-related needs were inadequately explored. This example should highlight the importance of (a) articulating developmental needs, but (b) finding the right fit in attending to your developmental needs. Supervisors bring their own biases, experiences, expectations, and fears into supervision (Nelson et al., 2008). Finding one that can challenge but also sit comfortably with their own positioning is therefore a priority.

13.4 Recognising and Addressing Poor Supervision

The capacity to recognise and address inadequate or harmful supervision is an important skill to develop. Bad supervision has immediate impacts on both the supervisor and supervisee, increasing anxiety and non-disclosure rates, alongside negatively influencing mental health in both personal and professional contexts (Cartwright, 2020; Ellis, 2017). Critically, the negative impacts on learning potential and professional development are sustained long beyond the termination of that supervisory relationship. Supervisees' career-path choices, developmental and career trajectories, therapeutic competence and self-esteem continue to be affected, impacting both the practitioner and the clients they serve (Beddoe, 2017; Hutman et al., 2023; McNamara et al., 2017). Harmful supervision rarely occurs in isolation, with features of inadequate or bad supervision often presenting far sooner (Grant et al., 2012). On this basis, we recommend that 'bad' supervision is proactively attended to. The following questions are designed to support the reader in identifying and addressing bad supervision.

- What are the difficulties that I am experiencing? Am I able to name them?
- What do these difficulties concern?
  - Are they relational, e.g., how heard do you feel by the supervisee/supervisor?
  - Are they structural, e.g., how accessible/responsive are they?
  - Are they need-based, e.g., do they relate to meeting developmental needs?
- What intervention/action have you taken to address these concerns?
  - Have you reflected on the 'I'? Sought external counsel or perspective?
  - Have you raised the concern? If so, was this met with compassion and curiosity?
  - Have you remained mindful of or monitored for changes in this difficulty?

- Is it time to consider an ending? What are the practicalities surrounding different supervision sources?
    - Is reporting required/necessary e.g., in instances of abusive supervision.

The quiet pervasiveness of inadequate and abusive supervision can create a sense of hopelessness in the supervisee. Shame and embarrassment are feelings woven throughout accounts of harmful supervision, with self-criticism for a lack of recognition or behaving in a manner to please their supervisor rife (Ellis, 2017; Reiser & Milne, 2017). We would encourage supervisees concerned by the supervision they are receiving to be proactive – you deserve better, and it exists.

13.5 Summary

In this chapter, we have explored some behaviours and consequences of supervision that are good, bad, or ugly. The examples provided are not intended to be exhaustive but hopefully provide a navigational tool to explore the effectiveness and health of supervisory relationships. Much of the research on supervision quality and effectiveness is oriented from the perspective of the supervisor – addressing the effect of their skills, qualities, and behaviours on supervisees. It is important, though, not to negate the responsibilities of the supervisee or their capacity to create good, bad, or ugly experiences for their supervisor. It is helpful, therefore, for both parties to question: *Is this working for me? If not, why not? And what might be done to address it?* We are mindful that research on the topic is predominantly oriented towards clinical populations, requiring us to extrapolate information into sporting populations, incorporating anecdotal evidence and experience. Future research exploring supervision effectiveness and practices in sporting environments from the perspective of the supervisor and supervisee would be beneficial.

Exercise 13.1: Reflective Questions to Explore the Supervisory Alliance

Supervisees are encouraged to explore their experiences in the supervisory alliance to ensure that it is at a minimum functional. The following questions stimulate intrigue into how one finds a supervisory relationship.

1. What challenges do you experience in forming working alliances?
2. What previous experiences (both positive and negative) have you had in supervisory or learning environments?

3. How might personal demographic or sociocultural factors (e.g., gender, race, socioeconomic status) influence how you engage in supervision, or the most appropriate supervisor for you?
4. What contextual factors (e.g., supervisor as marker) exist that may impede your ability to interact in supervision? How willing are you to raise these?
5. How invested do you feel you (as supervisee or supervisor) are in this relationship and the development of the other party?
6. What shows up for you (i.e., thoughts or feelings) when interacting with your supervisor?

14 Professional Considerations in Supervision

14.1 Introduction

The current professional status of applied sport psychology still garners significant debate (Winter & Collins, 2016). Increased prominence of sport psychology is clear in academic and applied contexts, as well as in the media and general societal discourse (Portenga et al., 2017). This growth has led to an exponential increase in those pursuing careers in the field worldwide. Naturally, this has resulted in an increased need for and utilisation of supervision services. Applied practitioners and academics alike have documented the evolution of professionalism in 'applied sport psychology', highlighting some illusions and challenges that exist in the space (Martin, 2019; Wagstaff & Quartiroli, 2020). In this final chapter, we shall explore some of the professional considerations inherent in supervision and where it may sit within the broader landscape of applied psychology. We shall address fitness to practise, professional requirements for supervision, and the role of supervision in the professionalisation of applied sport psychology.

14.2 Fitness to Practise

Over recent decades, international recognition of the requirement for the assessment and monitoring of psychologists' fitness to practise is evident (Sofronoff et al., 2011). While subtle nuances emerge in expressions of fitness to practise, organisations (e.g., British Psychological Society's (2022) fitness to practise framework, UK; Association for Applied Sport Psychology's (2024) Ethics code of principles and standards, USA) posit fitness to practise around three core categories: knowledge and competence, character and conduct, and health and well-being. Applied practitioners are required to show they have sufficient knowledge and skills to satisfy fundamental standards of safety and quality for practice, that they show strong moral character, behaving in a manner congruent with regulations and environmental expectations, and that they hold an appropriate

DOI: 10.4324/9781003485667-14

psychological state to conduct work ethically and effectively. We will briefly explore some examples of how components of fitness to practise may emerge in supervision.

14.3 Knowledge and Competence

Much of this book has explored how supervision contributes to the development of knowledge and competence. In relation to fitness to practise, supervision is a failsafe to pause or re-direct focus and attention if significant or potentially dangerous gaps in knowledge or competence emerge. The BPS states: 'members should not provide professional services that are outside their areas of knowledge, skill, training and experience' (BPS, 2017, p. 6). However, difficulties uncovering what this looks like in practice appear, with reports of insufficient adaptations to ethical guidelines for functioning in sporting environments and a lack of consensus regarding boundaries of competence (Prior et al., 2025; Watson et al., 2017). What constitutes 'within knowledge and competence' should continually evolve as the supervisee pursues their development.

A common example of where applied sport psychologists may inadvertently be exposed to knowledge and competence-based violations is in the murky waters of performance versus mental health. A supervisee may begin consultation with a client with a performance-oriented presentation (i.e., self-confidence). However, as the therapeutic relationship develops, the client may disclose clinically oriented presentations (i.e., eating disorders). Depending on the practitioner's knowledge and competence, continuing practice *may* present a risk of negligence and harm to the client, practitioner, or organisation (Moore, 2003). Occurrences such as these can present surreptitiously, leaving the supervisee exposed. Supervision allows the supervisee to discuss the situation and consider ethical action steps. Depending on the circumstances, this might include a continuation of practice or referral. The supervisee should continuously seek to answer: *Am I working within my knowledge and competence? If not, how am I going to acquire the required knowledge/competence or appropriately redirect services.* Meanwhile, their supervisor may ask: *Is the supervisee demonstrating/holding the prerequisite skills? If not, how will I support or intervene?* This intervention may be pertinent to novice practitioners who have not yet developed the level of self-awareness necessary to truly understand their limits of knowledge and competence. One cannot truly know they are competent until they have attempted to use their competence.

For example, when discussing issues of role clarity and boundaries in sporting contexts, a novice practitioner is initially reliant on developing their knowledge of the problem (e.g., what are practical skills to manage role clarity). It is then hoped that knowledge of a situation will transfer into competent action or behaviour (e.g., I know it is important to establish clear working hours, and I will establish these expectations in initial meetings). However, knowledge of does not necessarily mean the practitioner is ready or confident enough in their skills to utilise them effectively, with the extent of the challenge not necessarily available or known to the practitioner until they are waist deep (e.g., experiencing boundary violations at an event). An experienced supervisor may identify or perceive challenges ahead of time or help raise and address these with their supervisee.

14.4 Character and Professional Conduct

The dominance of the therapeutic relationship as the conduit for change has resulted in waves of research exploring the characteristics and behaviours (conduct) of sport psychologists (Sharp et al., 2015). Understanding the characteristics and behaviours that constitute 'good' character and conduct is essential because of the ethical requirement to maintain them. Differentiations have been observed amongst those who can operate successfully in the environment, implying that the process of obtaining qualification and applied practice opportunities acts as a self-filter. This emphasises the practical need for good character and conduct, as individuals with these qualities are more likely to achieve successful and enduring careers (Lubker et al., 2008; Woolway & Harwood, 2020). An assumption may then be made that those able to function in the environment 'do' act with moral character and conduct. However, anecdotal evidence and continuous scandal highlight that some sport psychology practitioners do demonstrate poor moral character and conduct (i.e., in relation to abuse; Kerr & Stirling, 2019). This problem was highlighted by Johnson & Campbell (2002) who argued that while maintaining good moral conduct is required and implicitly understood, the lack of explicit measurement and evaluation is problematic for the field. The authors posit that psychological professions could adopt character assessments akin to those in legal settings (e.g., admission to the US Bar) to ensure appropriate moral character and conduct. While a process so formal and restrictive is likely inappropriate, the fact any process ceases to exist is of interest. Perhaps supervision provides a relevant space to ensure behaviour is congruent with the standards of good character and conduct.

14.5 Health and Well-Being

Several occupational and systemic factors that risk compromising the health and well-being of those operating in applied psychology contexts exist, including organisational stress (Fletcher et al., 2011), compassion or emotional labour fatigue (Stevens & Al-Abbadey, 2024) and burnout (Magdaleno & Meyer, 2023). Applied sport psychology research has also highlighted novel stressors, including the perennial threat to quality of life (because of hours of working, flexibility, time away from home) and cognitive fatigue from working in ever-changing, unstable work environments (Mercer et al., 2025; Quartrioli et al., 2022). Experiencing challenges to health and well-being does not automatically constitute a breach of fitness to practise. However, the cumulative strain experienced can compromise or impair ethical and competent service delivery if inadequately addressed. Supervision here serves as a platform for proactively recognising and considering any threats to health and well-being. If/when supervisees are experiencing situations that pose a risk to practitioner health and well-being, they are expected to raise these with their supervisor. Collaboratively reflecting on these concerns can create direction for the supervisee to develop effective self-care strategies or behaviours that maintain or restore well-being (Haugen & Hoff, 2024). For example, Hings et al. (2020) exploration of the emotional labour training gap in sport psychologists highlighted the value of supervision in supporting novice and experienced practitioners to develop the self-awareness and resources to manage emotional labour demands effectively. It is also worth noting that sometimes suitability to continue applied practice is sufficiently compromised that supervision may lead to recognition of the need to temporarily or permanently suspend applied practice until health and well-being concerns are sufficiently addressed.

14.6 Case Study: Zoe

1. Personal Reflection: 'I'm so *expletive* frustrated and lost, I feel like I'm drifting. Standing by in silence is not doing nothing; it's being compliant. There's so much good work happening (I think…) which, granted, is reflected in feedback (players/coaches) and outcomes, but it just doesn't feel enough. The gaps are too big, and I just quite know how to fill them, or, that I want to? I don't know what to do next. Definitely something to discuss in supervision'.

2. Supervision: "That was exactly what I needed. Reassured that I am doing okay. Curious about exploring some questions that came up – in particular, how does/did the organisational context compromise me/us from the beginning? These explorations have left me questioning my capacity to create organisational change, alongside re-considering how I judge myself and my effectiveness in the environment. In stripping things back to 'what are the core dilemmas' – how do you maintain service quality? – I feel slightly more able to separate the wood from the trees. The next step is to action these thoughts – what do I do differently?!"

The above extracts are from my (Zoe's) reflections on an applied sport psychology role and subsequent supervision session. My reflections highlight that because of the working environment and my personal/professional resourcing - I was experiencing a degree of burnout that was beginning to influence my behaviours (e.g., decreased motivation / withdrawal, and apathy towards pursuing solutions). Supervision provided an opportunity to discuss, understand, explore, and label my experiences. Having achieved a greater degree of understanding, supervision provided a space to evaluate any direct or indirect impacts on my practice and what proactive solutions (self-care, personal therapy, and leaving the organisation) I was going to create. Supervision also fostered the opportunity to explore areas of success and productivity (e.g., exploring case studies). Fortunately, in this situation, my fitness to practise was not compromised. However, I am mindful that should I have continued in that environment, it may well have been. This reflection should highlight the value of supervision in both identifying potential fitness to practise violations, alongside facilitating interventions before that point is reached.

14.7 Supervision as a Catching and Safeguarding Mechanism

Supervision is often the mechanism responsible for assessing fitness to practise, and in which concerns regarding fitness to practise being compromised are highlighted or identified. However, the role of the supervisor may vary significantly based on the context within which supervision is occurring. In tertiary education environments, programmes must typically be approved by regulatory bodies to deliver courses. For example, in the UK, universities must demonstrate that they satisfy several standards of education and training to gain HCPC approval. One such standard (3.16) requires that 'there must be thorough and effective processes in place for ensuring the ongoing suitability of learners' conduct, character and health' (Finch & Corrie, 2024). In these environments, supervisors may be better protected or offered greater guidance regarding the nature, duration, frequency, and content of fitness to practise assessments. Conversely, less rigid guidance is available for providing supervision in independent training contexts or to post-qualification practitioners. Supervisors in these environments may then be tasked with devising their own fitness to practise assessments and considering their timely application.

The process of delivering fitness to practise assessments or reporting violations of fitness to practise is reported as a source of tension for supervisors (Birkett et al., 2025). Supervisors can perceive an incongruence between their responsibility to develop (e.g., to nurture, facilitate supervisee growth and provide relevant support) and their responsibility to evaluate (e.g., to monitor development, ensure competence and gatekeep the profession). Finch and Tedam (2023) termed this tension 'failure to fail', highlighting a range of factors likely to impede one's capacity to do so successfully (see exercise 15.1). Despite this reluctance, impediments to fitness to practise are identified in both clinical training programmes (Oliver et al., 2004) and for practising professionals (Maben et al., 2021). Supervisors are therefore responsible for preparing themselves for supervisees whose fitness to practise presents as impaired and proactively contemplating the best course of action.

This tension can be exacerbated by the transactional element of supervision and the supervisor's own desire for feelings of competence. Supervision is a revenue stream for supervisors. Financial ties and security may compromise a supervisor's willingness to raise issues of fitness to practise, if raising these concerns impacts their own income (mirroring the poor practice that can occur between an applied practitioner and client).

14.8 Professional and Regulatory Requirements for Supervision

Despite the abundance of literature emphasising the importance of supervision, little focus has been placed upon, nor consensus exists as to the degree of supervision engagement that is professionally required (Foltz et al., 2015; Jooste et al., 2016). Much of the literature around supervision requirements is directed towards those in educational or vocational programmes aimed at acquiring certification. Large variations are observed in the requirements for supervision based on nationality, culture, adopted training route, and regulatory body regarding minimum time requirements, structure (i.e., formal versus informal) and frequency (Poczwardowski et al., 2023). For example, in the UK, three training routes to securing registered status as a sport psychologist are available: (1) CASES SEPAR route, (2) BPS Stage 2 Independent Route, (3) Professional Doctorates, each of which varies regarding supervision requirements (see Table 14.1). Hours engaged in supervision are not indicative of effective supervision or effective psychologist development but can show how valued supervision is by organisational systems.

The supervision requirements for applied sport psychologists are generally significantly below those mandated for allied psychology professions (i.e., counselling/clinical). In a comparison of trainee clinical and sport and exercise psychologists' professional development, McEwan and Tod (2023) additionally reported that clinical trainees received greater access to direct supervision of their practice, supervision contact (with access to multiple supervisors), and collaboration/observation directly in the environment. *But why does this matter?* Inconsistency both within sport and exercise psychology and compared to relevant psychological domains (e.g., clinical) raises intriguing questions about the professionalisation of the field.

Table 14.1 Differences in Supervision Requirements Based on the UK Professional Training Route

	Minimum hours of supervision	*Frequency requirements*	*Supervision format*
CASES SEPAR	50	Individually 1 × Per Month	Individual or group supervision can be predominant style
		1 × Quarterly Review	Agreement negotiated between supervisor and supervisee
BPS QSEP Stage 2	8	1 × Quarterly Meeting	Individual or group supervision can be predominant style Agreement negotiated between supervisor and supervisee
UK Professional Doctorate	60	Year 1: 1 hour per 6 client hours	Individual supervision is the dominant delivery approach.
		Year 2/3: 1 hour per 8 client hours	Programme requirements in-part dictate delivery.

High variation in supervision volume and quality of contact may alter the developmental course of trainee practitioners and result in inconsistencies in the output of qualified sport and exercise psychologists (Quartiroli et al., 2023). While the prominence of sport psychology is growing, uncertainty remains amongst sport governing bodies around the integration and application of sport psychology services. This uncertainty can elicit recurrent questions about the cost-benefit of employing sport and exercise psychologists, encouraging caution in their recruitment. If supervision acts as a quality control measure for practitioner development, how is the field holding itself back through inconsistent professional requirements?

Learning and engagement in supervision should be considered a lifelong process. Although an ethical responsibility, discrepancies in supervision engagement are only exacerbated post-qualification. Experienced practitioners have stated the importance of supervision in competently navigating ethical challenges and maintaining good practice (Sharp et al., 2021). Mixed findings are observed in the literature regarding sport psychologists' engagement in supervision, perhaps because of reporting biases. Some research (e.g., Sharp et al., 2021) demonstrates promising continued engagement in supervision; however, alarmingly, a complete lack of engagement post-qualification has also been observed (e.g., McEwan &

Tod, 2015; Shapiro & Poczwardowski, 2020). One reason attributed to a lack of engagement is that there are currently no mandates (that we are aware of) that currently exist requiring engagement. This contrasts with colleagues in counselling, for example, who are required to undertake a minimum of 1.5 hours of clinical supervision monthly throughout the course of their career (BACP, 2008) or clinical psychology where lifelong engagement is a requirement to practise (Jones, 2011).

This awareness-action gap may be a cause for alarm. Barriers to engagement such as cost, time, and difficulties in locating/sourcing an appropriate supervisor exist (Fogaca et al., 2024). However, the lack of continued supervision may generate further challenges in the field's professionalisation. Applied practitioners suggest that other avenues of continued professional development (e.g., pursuits of academic publishing, peer support, or educational programmes) are equivalent to engagement in supervision or elicit greater career security and trajectories warranting further investment. A varied continued personal development profile is of course helpful; however, negating supervision may stifle innovation and development. When only seeking counsel from peers or those within one's own environment, practitioners are more likely to experience confirmation bias, where individuals hold similar experiential views or perceive a more limited capacity to show independent and critical thinking.

To navigate this, the profession of sport psychology should consider ways to increase post-qualification supervision engagement. Increased regulatory requirements in other domains, while effective, have not been received favourably by applied practitioners (Nicholas & Goodyear, 2020). Another question for exploration may be how well the field sets up the foundational importance of supervision during training routes. If supervision is infrequently and inconsistently delivered or perceived to be insufficient or inadequate for the practitioner's development, what motivation will they hold to overcome subsequent barriers to engagement when it is no longer necessitated? In addition, supervisors may question how successfully they are modelling the importance of supervision.

14.9 Role of Supervision in Professionalisation

With exponential growth in those seeking to become applied sport psychology practitioners comes an exponential growth in supervision. As a field, there is a requirement to consider how appropriately trained supervisors are to deliver the service, if the product they are offering is fit for purpose, and how this is contributing to the further professionalisation of the field. In exploring the professionalisation of fields, Howard (1998) distinguished between the high and low road to professionalisation. The high road results in the development and provision of genuinely effective and proven services. The low road leads to the creation of an illusion of effective service to satisfy latent consumer demand. Howard further argues that particularly those in helping professions should seek to professionalise with integrity. Gray's (2010) exploration of professionalisation in coaches posits that while supervision has the potential to facilitate a field taking the 'high road', its presence necessitates the exploration of several questions. These include:

- ***Are supervisors appropriately trained to deliver supervision?***

Extensive focus is placed on the training of applied sport psychology practitioners. Counterintuitively, the same cannot be said for supervisors or those delivering the said training. Expert opinion on the need for supervisor training is unanimous across the field, often forcefully, with the concomitant neglect of supervisor training raising international cause for concern (Borders et al., 2023; Gonsalvez & Milne, 2010). Requirements to become a supervisor are often postulated around: (1) a designated period post-qualification, and (2) engagement in some form of training programme. In relation to postulate 1, a dangerous assumption is being made that the duration of time post-qualification corresponds with applied experience and development, and that those who are capable of 'doing' are also capable of 'supervising'. The recruitment of those who can 'do' into roles of 'teaching' is commonly observed in sport (i.e., player to coach transitions) and is often accompanied by criticism regarding the lack of professionalism involved (i.e., lack of appropriate skills). Applied sport psychology therefore risks falling into the same trap. In relation to postulate 2, some regulatory bodies only require a basic supervision course to practise as a supervisor. Wheeler (2004) notes that supervisors perceive basic courses to not adequately prepare them to deliver supervision competently and that supervision training should be continuous and staggered over a significant period. An important caveat here is that despite present requirements for 'supervision training', a grandfather clause exists where those who began providing supervision pre-regulation are often still allowed to do so. This is reflected in statistics around supervision training engagement, where up to 75.9 per cent of those offering supervision services have had little to no training in supervision delivery (Watson et al., 2004). If supervision is considered so essential to ethical and effective practice, the profession must consider further how successfully we are establishing the provision?

- ***Are supervisors providing a high-quality service?***

To support the professionalisation of field supervision, which leads to conversations regarding service quality and the development of

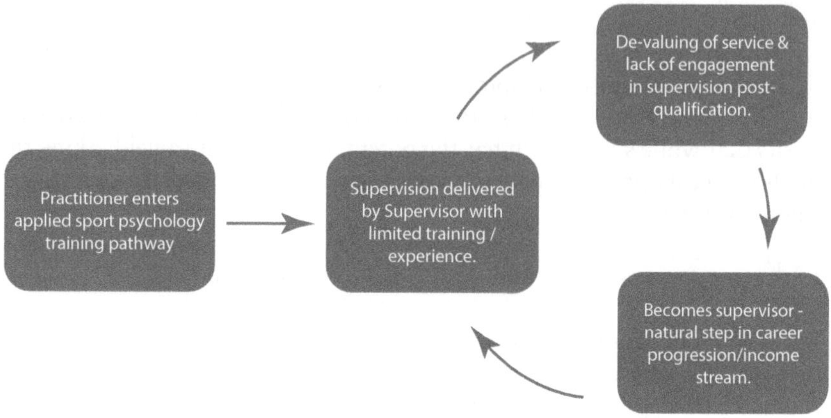

Figure 14.1 Cycle pertaining to issues of value and engagement in supervision.

promotable outcomes (i.e., sport psychology elicits x benefits) is arguably required. If we start from the foundation that competent supervision results in supervisee development, we must ask: Are supervisors delivering competent, let alone high-quality services? Anecdotally, an increased number of 'group'-based supervision programmes are being offered. While undoubtedly beneficial, supervisors must question whether this service provision is appropriate for the needs of those they supervise. This is particularly evident for trainee practitioners, who may be more conscious of financial and time costs, or cannot understand the value of individual supervision. Perhaps the lack of post-qualification professionals engaging in supervision reflects a perceived lack of benefit and low-quality supervision experiences, creating a vicious cycle (Figure 14.1). Finding ways to break this cycle should be of high concern to the field. One solution to this challenge is centred on increased regulation. Risks with increased regulation may emerge, for example, access, bureaucratic processing and cost. The unattractiveness and potential push-back from practitioners around increased regulation may be too dominant for such change to occur. If this is the case, increased education and awareness around what 'good' supervision looks like and why it is of career-long importance is required – as how does one know what they do not know? Supervisors are likely to practise in alignment or distinct contrast to their own experiences in supervision and without the knowledge of other options, or what excellence looks like, how can they be expected to perform differently?

- ***How is supervision contributing (or not) to the professional representation of the field?***

How much responsibility do supervisors have for allowing low-quality practice or ensuring supervisees adequately represent themselves and the profession? The following quote is from a high-performance sports coach, Luke (pseudonym).

> One experience I had was particularly negative. I turned up to watch a young player compete. Another spectator struck up a conversation with me, and it turned out he was a sport psychologist working with a player who was in the process of moving to our club. I was astounded that a sport psychologist would disclose their client's identity to a person they had only met minutes before. The whole thing unsettled me massively. It felt like he was using the child to get an 'in' into our programme. If I had not had previous positive experiences with professional and experienced sport psychologists, it would have put me off the field completely. This opinion was shared by another coach who was with me who said he was sceptical of the way sport psychologists worked and interacted.

Without endeavouring to read too much into one situation, this quote should highlight the unprofessional and unethical behaviour that still occurs within the field and the consequences it has on how the field is perceived by prospective colleagues and employers. While it is hoped that issues of confidentiality and anonymity have been raised within this practitioner's training and applied experiences, it is possible that this has not been sufficient to impact this practitioner's behaviour, or that the transactional component of working in this space (e.g., trying to secure work or employment) leads to individuals' standards being compromised. Behaviour such as this perpetuates the stigma and caution that surrounds sport and exercise psychology practice. Supervisors should consider how clearly they are discussing issues that pose a risk to the continued professionalisation of the field and what behaviours they are engaging in as required.

While these questions are in no means designed to be exhaustive, it is hoped that they prompt the reader to consider the broader role of supervision in the field's professionalisation. Changes in discourse in any profession, including the health professions, are challenging, and the sport/sport psychology context is no different. In instrumentally shaping those who enter the profession, greater attention to the various facets of supervision may enhance the quality and value of the profession.

14.10 Summary

In this chapter, we have explored the role of supervision in the professionalisation of applied sport and exercise psychologists. Avenues for future research on the utility of supervision are provided alongside questions regarding supervision's place in driving quality and opportunity in the field.

It is hoped the reader may consider their own use of supervision and how the quality of supervision received may impact continued engagement. We have tentatively questioned the requirement for more stringent supervision requirements. If as a field we regard supervision so highly, what are we doing to ensure high-standard delivery and consistent engagement?

Exercise 14.1: Considering Factors Likely to Result in 'Failure to Fail'

1. Role Strain: *How do my own demands influence my ability to accurately assess practice/provide supervision?*
2. Role Conflict: *How do I perceive my role between supervisor/teacher and examiner/gatekeeper? Are there any other shared roles with this supervisee or the organisation that may present a conflict of interest?*
3. Fear of Litigation: *What consequences do I perceive from raising fitness to practise concerns?*
4. The Role of Optimism: *Do I perceive these concerns will resolve themselves with time? Is this reflection accurate? How does my perception of individuals' capacity to change influence the way I interact?*
5. Misplaced Belief of Self-Addressing: *What responsibility am I placing on the supervisee? Is self-addressing (e.g., agreed behaviour change) sufficient to address the issue?*

References

Abbey, D. S., Hunt, D. E., & Weiser, J. C. (1985). Variations on a theme by Kolb: A new perspective for understanding counseling and supervision. *The Counseling Psychologist*, *13*(3), 477–501. https://doi.org/10.1177/0011000085133016

Abdulrahman, K. A. B., & Alzayed, A. A. (2025). Mastering time management in the context. In Bin AbdulrahmanK. A. & H. Darami (Eds.), *Essential learning skills for health professions students*. Springer Nature.

Adams, M. (2024). *The myth of the untroubled therapist: Private life, professional practice*. Taylor & Francis.

Amaro, C. M., Mitchell, T. B., Cordts, K. M. P., Borner, K. B., Frazer, A. L., Garcia, A. M., & Roberts, M. C. (2020). Clarifying supervision expectations: Construction of a clinical supervision contract as a didactic exercise for advanced graduate students. *Training and Education in Professional Psychology*, *14*(3), 235–241. https://doi.org/10.1037/tep0000273

Andersen, M. B. (1994). Ethical considerations in the supervision of applied sport psychology graduate students. *Journal of Applied Sport Psychology*, *6*(2), 152–167.

Andersen, M. B. (2005). Coming full circle: From practice to research. In M. B. Andersen (Ed.), *Sport psychology in practice* (pp. 287–298). Human Kinetics.

Andersen, M. B. (2012). Supervision and mindfulness in sport and performance psychology. In S. M. Murphy (Ed.), *The Oxford handbook of sport and performance psychology* (pp. 725–737). Oxford University Press.

Andersen, M. B. (2021). *Doing sport psychology: 21st anniversary edition with original authors' reflections*. Amazon Kindle Direct Publishing.

Andersen, M. B., Barney, S. T., & Waterson, A. K. (2016). Mindfully dynamic meta-supervision: The case of AW and M. In J. G. Cremades & L. S. Tashman (Eds.), *Global practices and training in applied sport, exercise, and performance psychology: A case study approach* (pp. 330–342). Taylor & Francis.

Andersen, M. B., Van Raalte, J. L., & Brewer, B. W. (1994). Assessing the skills of sport psychology supervisors. *The Sport Psychologist*, *8*, 238–247.

Andersen, M. B., Van Raalte, J. L., & Brewer, B. W. (2001). Sport psychology service delivery: Staying ethical while keeping loose. *Professional Psychology: Research and Practice*, 32(1), 12–18. https://doi.org/10.1037/0735-7028.32.1.12

Andersen, M. B., Van Raalte, J. L., & Harris, G. (2000). Supervision II: A case study. In M. B. Andersen (Ed.), *Doing sport psychology* (pp. 167–179). Human Kinetics.

Andersen, T. (1991). *The reflecting team: Dialogues and dialogues about the dialogues*. Norton.

Anderson, A. G., Miles, A., Mahoney, C., & Robinson, P. (2002). Evaluating the effectiveness of applied sport psychology practice: Making the case for a case study approach. *The Sport Psychologist*, *16*(4), 432–453.

Association for Applied Sport Psychology. (2024). *Association for applied sport psychology ethical principles and standards*. https://appliedsportpsych.org/about-the-association-for-applied-sport-psychology/ethics/

Association for Counselor Education and Supervision Taskforce on Best Practices in Clinical Supervision. (2011, April). *Best practices in clinical supervision*. www.acesonline.net/wp-content/uploads/2011/10/ACES-Best-Practices-inclinical-supervision-document-FINAL.pdf

Avent, J. R., Wahesh, E., Purgason, L. L., Borders, L. D., & Mobley, A. K. (2015). A content analysis of peer feedback in triadic supervision. *Counselor Education and Supervision*, *54*, 68–80. https://doi.org/10.1002/j.1556-6978.2015.00071.x

Bandura, A. (1977). *Social learning theory* (Vol. 1, pp. 141–154). Prentice Hall.

Bahrick, A. S. (1989). *Role induction for counselor trainees: Effects on the supervisory working alliance* [Doctoral dissertation, ProQuest Dissertations & Theses].

Bejar, M. P., Shigeno, T. C., Larsen, L. K., & Lee, S. M. (2022). The state of diversity in the Association of Applied Sport Psychology: Gaining momentum or still swimming upstream? *Journal of Applied Sport Psychology*, *34*, 1372–1386

Barney, S. T., & Andersen, M. B. (2014). Meta-supervision: Training practitioners to help others on their paths. In J. G. Cremades & L. S. Tashman (Eds.), *Becoming a sport, exercise, and performance psychology professional: A global perspective* (pp. 339–346). Psychology Press.

Barney, S. T., Andersen, M. B., & Riggs, C. A. (1996). Supervision in sport psychology: Some recommendations for practicum training. *Journal of applied sport psychology*, *8*(2), 200–217.

Bartlett, J. D., & Drust, B. (2020). A framework for effective knowledge translation and performance delivery of sport scientists in professional sport. *European journal of sport science*, *21*(11), 1579–1587.

Barrett, J. D., Gonsalvez, C. J., & Shires, A. (2020). Evidence-based practice within supervision during psychology practitioner training: A systematic review. *Clinical Psychologist*, *24*(1), 3–17.

Batten, S. V., & Santanello, A. P. (2009). A contextual behavioral approach to the role of emotion in psychotherapy supervision. *Training and Education in Professional Psychology*, *3*(3), 148–156. https://psycnet.apa.org/doi/10.1037/1931-3918.a0014801

Beddoe, L. (2017). Harmful supervision: A commentary. *The Clinical Supervisor*, *36*(1), 88–101.

Beinart, H. (2002). *An exploration of the factors which predict the quality of the relationship in clinical supervision* [Unpublished D.Clin.Psych. thesis]. Open University/British Psychological Society.

Beinart, H. (2012). Models of supervision and the supervisory relationship. In L. Steen & I. Fleming (Eds.), *Supervision and clinical psychology* (2nd ed., pp. 47–62). Routledge. https://doi.org/10.4324/9780203805817-5

Beinart, H. (2014). Building and sustaining the supervisory relationship. In D. L. Milne & C. E. Watkins (Eds.), *The Wiley international handbook of clinical supervision* (pp. 255–281). Wiley. https://doi.org/10.1002/9781118846360.ch11

Beinart, H., & Clohessy, S. (2017). *The effective supervisory relationship: Best evidence and practice*. Wiley Blackwell.
Bell, H., Hagedorn, W., & Robinson, E. (2016). An exploration of supervisory and therapeutic relationships and client outcomes. *Counselor Education and Supervision*, *55*(3), 182–197.
Benuto, L. T., Singler, K., Newlands, R. T., & Casas, J. B. (2019). Training culturally competent psychologists: Where are we and where do we need to go? *Training and Education in Professional Psychology*, *13*(1), 56–63.
Bennett, M. J. (1993). Towards ethnorelativism: A developmental model of intercultural sensitivity. In R. M. Paige (Ed.), *Education for the intercultural experience* (pp. 21–71). Intercultural Press.
Bennett, S., & Deal, K. H. (2009). Beginnings and endings in social work supervision: The interaction between attachment and developmental processes. *Journal of Teaching in Social Work*, *29*, 101–117. https://doi.org/10.1080/08841230802238179
Berger, S. S., & Buchholz, E. S. (1993). On becoming a supervisee: Preperation for learning in a supervisory relationship. *Psychotherapy: Theory, Research, Practice, Training*, *30*(1), 86–92.
Bernard, J. M., & Goodyear, R. K. (2004). *Fundamentals of clinical supervision* (3rd ed.). Allyn & Bacon.
Bernard, J. M., & Goodyear, R. K. (2014). *Fundamentals of clinical supervision* (5th ed.). Pearson.
Bernard, J. M., & Goodyear, R. K. (2018). *Fundamentals of clinical supervision*. Pearson Education.
Bernard, J. M., & Goodyear, R. K. (2019). *Fundamentals of clinical supervision* (6th ed.). Pearson.
Bion, W. F. (1961). *Experiences in groups*. Basic Books.
Bird, M. D., Swann, C., & Jackman, P. C. (2024). The what, why, and how of goal setting: A review of the goal-setting process in applied sport psychology practice. *Journal of Applied Sport Psychology*, *36*(1), 75–97.
Birkett, L., Hagan, A. J., & Verity, S. J. (2025). Well, or well enough? An exploration of the need for guidance addressing clinician wellbeing and fitness to practice in UK clinical psychologists. medRxiv. https://doi.org/10.1101/2025.02.03.25321570
Borders, L. D. (2012). Dyadic, triadic, and group models of peer supervision/consultation: What are their components, and is there evidence of their effectiveness? *Clinical Psychologist*, *16*(2), 59–71. https://doi.org/10.1111/j.1742-9552.2012.00046.x
Borders, L. D. (2014). Best practices in clinical supervision: Another step in delineating effective supervision practice. *American Journal of Psychotherapy*, *68*, 151–162.
Borders, L. D., & Brown, L. L. (2022). *The new handbook of counselling supervision*. Routledge.
Borders, L. D., Dianna, A. J., & McKibben, B. W. (2023). Clinical supervisor training: A ten-year scoping review across counselling, psychology, and social work. *The Clinical Supervisor*, *42*(1), 164–212.
Borders, L. D., Glosoff, H. L., Welfare, L. E., Hays, D. G., DeKruyf, L., Fernando, D. M., & Page, B. (2014). Best practices in clinical supervision: Evolution of a counseling specialty. *The Clinical Supervisor*, *33*(1), 26–44. https://doi.org/10.1080/07325223.2014.905225
Bordin, E. S. (1983). A working alliance-based model of supervision. *The Counseling Psychologist*, *11*(1), 35–42.

Bowlby, J. (1988). During the first third of this century there were two great proponents of developmental psychiatry–Adolf Meyer and Sigmund Freud. Both believed that. *The American Journal of Psychiatry*, *145*, 1–10.
Boyd, J. (1978). *Counselor supervision: Approaches, preparation, practices.* Accelerated Development.
Brinkmann, U., & van Weerdenburg, O. (2014). Why we need intercultural competences. In *Intercultural readiness: Four competences for working across cultures* (pp. 19–34). Palgrave Macmillan.
British Association for Counselling & Psychotherapy. (2008). *How much superivsion should I have? Information sheet S1.* British Association for Counselling & Psychotherapy.
British Association of Sport and Exercise Sciences. (2018). *Supervision guidelines for sport and exercise psychology professionals.*
British Psychological Society. (2017). *Standards for the accreditation of applied psychology training programmes.* https://www.bps.org.uk/accreditation
British Psychological Society. (2021). *Code of ethics and conduct.*
British Psychological Society. (2024). *Supervision guidance for psychologists.*
Bucky, S. F., Marques, S., Daly, J., Alley, J., & Karp, A. (2010). Supervision characteristics related to the supervisory working alliance as rated by doctoral-level supervisees. *The Clinical Supervisor*, *29*(2), 149–163.
Callahan, J. L., Almstrom, C. M., Swift, J. K., Borja, S. E., & Heath, C. J. (2009). Exploring the contribution of supervisors to intervention outcomes. *Training and Education in Professional Psychology*, *3*(2), 72–77. https://doi.org/10.1037/a0014294
Callahan, J. L., Love, P. K., & Watkins, C. E., Jr. (2019). Supervisee perspectives on supervision processes: An introduction to the special issue. *Training and Education in Professional Psychology*, *13*(3), 153–159. https://doi.org/10.1037/tep0000275
Cameron, S., & Turtle-Song, I. (2002). Learning to write case notes using the SOAP format. *Journal of Counseling and Development*, *80*(3), 286–292.
Caplan, G. (1970). *The theory and practice of mental health consultation.* Basic Books.
Carlsson, J. (2016). The developing practitioner – growth and stagnation of therapists and counsellors. *Psychotherapy Research*, *26*(2), 258–259.
Carroll, M. (1996). *Counselling supervision: Theory, skills and practice.* Cassell.
Carroll, M. (1999). Training in the task of supervision. In E. Holloway & M. Carroll (Eds.), *Training counsellor supervisors* (pp. 45–66). SAGE Publications.
Carroll, M. (2014). *Effective supervision for the helping professions.* SAGE Publications.
Carter, L., & Davila, C. (2017). Is it because I'm black? Microaggressive experiences against Black professionals in sport and exercise psychology. *Professional Psychology: Research and Practice*, *48*(5), 287–293.
Cartwright, D. (2020). Relational processes and the emergence of harmful supervision events: A narrative analysis of a single case. *Counselling & Psychotherapy Research*, *20*(2), 344–354.
Casement, P. (1985). *On learning from the patient.* Tavistock.
Casement, P. (1990). *Further learning from the patient: The analytic space and process.* Tavistock.
Caspi, J., & Reid, W. J. (2002). *Educational supervision in social work: A taskcentered model for field instruction and staff development.* Columbia University Press.

Caspi, J., & Reid, W. J. (2015). Preparing for supervision beginnings and endings. In J. Caspi & W. J. Reid (Eds.), *Educational supervision in social work* (pp. 156–171). Columbia University Press. https://doi.org/10.7312/casp10852-006

Chandler, C., Eubank, M. R., Nesti, M. S., & Tod, D. (2016). Personal qualities of effective sport psychologists: Coping with organisational demands in high performance sport. *International Journal of Sport Psychology*, *47*(4), 297–317.

Cheon, H. S., Blumer, M. L. C., Shih, A. T., Murphy, M. J., & Sato, M. (2009). The influence of supervisor and supervisee matching, role conflict and supervisory relationship on supervisee satisfaction. *Contemporary Family Therapy*, *31*, 52–57.

Chidiac, M. A., Denham-Vaughan, J., & Osborne, L. (2018). The relational matrix model of supervision: Context, framing and inter-connection. *Gestalt Journal of Australia and New Zealand*, *14*(2), 45–64.

Chircop Coleiro, A., Creaner, M., & Timulak, L. (2023). The good, the bad, and the less than ideal in clinical supervision: A qualitative meta-analysis of supervisee experiences. *Counselling Psychology Quarterly*, *36*(2), 189–210. https://doi.org/10.1080/09515070.2021.2023098

Cliffe, T., Beinart, H., & Cooper, M. (2016). Development and validation of a short version of the supervisory relationship questionnaire. *Clinical Psychology and Psychotherapy*, *23*(1), 77–86. https://doi.org/10.1002/cpp.1935

Clevinger, K., Albert, E., & Raiche, E. (2019). Supervisor self-disclosure: Supervisees' perceptions of positive supervision experiences. *Training and Education in Professional Psychology*, *13*(3), 222–226.

Clohessy, S. (2008). Supervisors perspectives on their supervisory relationships: A qualitative analysis [Doctoral dissertation, University of Hull].

Collins, C. R., Sauce, H., Wafer, A., & Guzman, E. (2025). Using reflective journaling in supervision as a means of promoting self-care practices. *Social Work*, *70*(3), 225–232. https://doi.org/10.1093/sw/swaf019

Constable, C., Delaney, C., Clutterham, A., & Markiewicz, A. (2022). The development of the Reflecting Team Utterances Framework: Process, reflections and applications. *Journal of Family Therapy*, *44*(2), 193–204. https://doi.org/10.1111/1467-6427.12360

Contrastano, C. M. (2020). Trainee's perspective of reciprocal vulnerability and boundaries in supervision. *Journal of Psychotherapy Integration*, *30*(1), 44.

Cook, R. M., McKibben, W. B., & Wind, S. A. (2018). Supervisee perception of power in clinical supervision: The power dynamics in supervision scale. *Training and Education in Professional Psychology*, *12*(3), 188–195.

Corey, G., Corey, M. S., & Callanan, P. (1998). *Issues and ethics in the helping professions* (5th ed.). Brooks/Cole.

Corey, G., Haynes, R. H., Moulton, P., & Muratori, M. (2020). *Clinical supervision in the helping professions: A practical guide*. John Wiley & Sons.e the Paragraph Text

Corrie, S., & Lane, D. (2015). *CBT supervision*. SAGE Publications.

Creaner, M. (2014). *Getting the best out of supervision in counselling and psychotherapy: A guide for the supervisee*. SAGE Publications.

Cropley, B., Hanton, S., Miles, A., Niven, A., & Dohme, L.-C. (2020). Developing the effectiveness of applied sport psychology service delivery: A reflective practice intervention. *Sport & Exercise Psychology Review*, *16*(1), 38–60. https://doi.org/10.53841/bpssepr.2020.16.1.38

Cropley, B., Miles, A., Hanton, S., & Niven, A. (2007). Improving the delivery of applied sport psychology support through reflective practice. *The Sport Psychologist*, *21*(4), 475–494. https://doi.org/10.1123/tsp.21.4.475

Cropley, B., & Neil, R. (2014). The neophyte supervisor: What did I get myself into? In CremadesJ. G. & L. S. Tashman (Eds.), *Becoming a sport, exercise, and performance psychology professional: A global perspective* (pp. 219–227). Routledge.

Cropley, B., & Neil, R. (2016). The neophyte supervisor: Navigating the swampy lowlands through collaborative approaches to supervision. In J. G. Cremades & L. S. Tashman (Eds.), *Global practices and training in applied sport, exercise, and performance psychology: A case study approach* (pp. 221–229). Taylor & Francis.

Curvey, R. M. G., White, S. C., Hargons, C. N., Englis, M. T., Jensen, K. C., Bosco, M. K., Thompson, M. E., Leavens, S., & Murphy, A. M. (2023). "Can you work with athletes as a female?": Career experiences of female sport psychology practitioners. *Women in Sport and Physical Activity Journal*, *31*(2), 73–81.

Cushion, C., Nelson, L., Armour, K., Lyle, J., Jones, R., Sandford, R., & O'Callaghan, C. (2010). *Coach learning and development: A review of literature*. Sports Coach UK.

Davys, A. M., & Beddoe, L. (2009). The reflective learning model: Supervision of social work students. *Social Work Education*, *28*(8), 919–933. https://doi.org/10.1080/02615470902748662

Dawson, D., & Akhurst, J. (2015). "I wouldn't dream of ending with a client in the way he did to me": An exploration of supervisees' experiences of an unplanned ending to the supervisory relationship. *Counselling and Psychotherapy Research*, *15*(1), 21–30.

DeRoma, V. M., Hickey, D. A., & Stanek, K. M. (2007). Methods of supervision in marriage and family therapist training: A brief report. *North American Journal of Psychology*, *9*(3), 415–422.

De Stefano, J., Hutman, H., & Gazzola, N. (2017). Putting on the face: A qualitative study of power dynamics in clinical supervision. *The Clinical Supervisor*, *36*(2), 223–240.

Driscoll, J. (1994). Reflective practice for practice. *Senior Nurse*, *14*(1), 47–50.

Driscoll, J. (2007). Supported reflective learning: the essence of clinical supervision. In *Practising clinical supervision: A reflective approach for healthcare professionals* (pp. 27–50). Baillière Tindall.

Dwight, A., & Biscomb, K. (2018). Ten years of the UK's equality standard for sport. *European Journal for Sport and Society*, *15*(2), 171–188.

Edmondson, A. C. (2018). *The fearless organization: Creating psychological safety in the workplace for learning, innovation, and growth* (1st ed.). Wiley.

Ellis, M. V. (2001). Harmful supervision: A cause for alarm. *Journal of Counseling Psychology*, *48*, 401–406.

Ellis, M. V. (2017). Clinical supervision contract and consent statement and supervisee rights and responsibilities. *The Clinical Supervisor*, *36*(1), 45–159. https://doi.org/10.1080/07325223.2017.1321885

Ellis, M. V., Ayala, E. E., Kotary, B., Berger, L., & Hanus, A. (2015). *Exceptional clinical supervision: Testing a taxonomy and assessing occurrence*. Paper presented at the 123rd Annual Convention of the American Psychological Association.

Ellis, M. V., Berger, L., Hanus, A. E., Ayala, E. E., Swords, B. A., & Siembor, M. (2014). Inadequate and harmful clinical supervision: Testing a revised framework and assessing occurrence. *The Counseling Psychologist*, *42*, 434–472.

Ellis, M. V., Hutman, H., & Chapin, J. (2015). Reducing supervisee anxiety: Effects of a role induction intervention for clinical supervision. *Journal of Counseling Psychology*, *62*(4), 608–620.

Enlow, P. T., McWhorter, L. G., Genuario, K., & Davis, A. (2019). Supervisor–supervisee interactions: The importance of the supervisory working alliance. *Training and Education in Professional Psychology*, *13*(3), 206–214.

Eubank, M., Nesti, M., & Cruickshank, A. (2014). Understanding high-performance sport environments: Impact for the professional training and supervision of sport psychologists. *Sport and Exercise Psychology Review*, *10*(2), 30–37.

Fagernäs, S., Spännargård, Å., & Alfonsson, S. (2024). The development of the psychotherapists' supervision preferences questionnaire—derived from the proctor model. *Counselling and Psychotherapy Research*, *24*(4), 1191–1205. https://doi.org/10.1002/capr.12726

Falender, C. A. (2014). Clinical supervision in a competency-based era. *South African Journal of Psychology*, *44*(1), 6–17. https://doi.org/10.1177/0081246313516260

Falender, C. A. (2018). Clinical supervision—the missing ingredient. *American Psychologist*, *73*(9), 1240–1250. https://doi.org/10.1037/amp0000385

Falender, C. A., & Shafranske, E. P. (2012). *Getting the most out of clinical training and supervision: A guide for practicum students and interns*. American Psychological Association.

Falender, C. A., & Shafranske, E. P. (2021). *Clinical supervision: A competency-based approach*. American Psychological Association.

Falnder, C. A., Shafranske, E. P., & Ofek, A. (2014). Competent clinical supervision: Emerging effective practices. *Counselling Psychology Quarterly*, *27*(4), 393–408.

Finch, J., & Corrie, S. (2024). Student fitness to practice procedures on accredited and regulatory programmes: A narrative review of the literature. *Practice*, *6*(2–3), 161–174.

Finch, J., & Tedam, P. (2024). Failure to fail or fast tracking to failure: A critical exploration of social work placements. *Social Work Education*, *43*(7), 2024–2039.

Finlay, L. (2022). *The therapeutic use of self incounselling & psychotherapy*. SAGE Publications.

Fitzpatrick, S. J., Monda, S. J., & Butters Wooding, C. (2016). Great expectations: Career planning and training experiences of graduate students in sport and exercise psychology. *Journal of Applied Sport Psychology*, *38*(1), 14–27.

Fleming, I., & Steen, L. (Eds.). (2012). *Supervision and clinical psychology: Theory, practice and perspectives* (2nd ed.). Routledge.

Fletcher, D., Rumbold, J. L., Tester, R., & Coombes, M. S. (2011). Sport psychologists' experiences of organizational stressors. *The Sport Psychologist*, *25*(3), 363–381.

Fogaça, J. L., Quartiroli, A., & Wagstaff, C. R. (2024). Professional development of sport psychology practitioners: From systematic review to a model of development. *Psychology of Sport and Exercise*, *70*, Article 102550.

Fogaça, J. L., Watson, J. C., & Zizzi, S. J. (2020). The journey of service delivery competence in applied sport psychology: The arc of development for new professionals. *Journal of Clinical Sport Psychology*, *14*(2), 109–126.

Fogaca, J. L., Zizzi, S. J., & Andersen, M. B. (2018). Walking multiple paths of supervision in American sport psychology: A qualitative tale of novice supervisees' development. *The Sport Psychologist*, *32*(2), 156–165.

Foltz, B. D., Fisher, A. R., Denton, L. K., Campbell, W. L., Speight, Q. L., Steinfeldt, J., & Latorre, C. (2015). Applied sport psychology supervision experience: A qualitative analysis. *Journal of Applied Sport Psychology*, *27*(4), 449–463.

Foo Kune, N. M., & Rodolfa, E. R. (2013). Putting the benchmarks into practice: Multiculturally competent supervisors—effective supervision. *The Counseling Psychologist*, *41*(1), 121–130.

Friedlander, M. L., Siegel, S. M., & Brenock, K. (1989). Parallel processes in counseling and supervision: A case study. *Journal of counseling psychology*, *36*(2), 149.

Friedlander, M. L., & Ward, L. G. (1984). Development and validation of the Supervisory Styles Inventory. *Journal of Counseling Psychology*, *31*(4), 541.

Gaete, J., & Strong, T. (2017). Facilitating supervisees' developing competence through supervisory conversation. *Counselling Psychology Quarterly*, *30*(2), 166–187. https://doi.org/10.1080/09515070.2016.1167013

Gardner, A., Love, A., & Waller, S. (2023). How do elite sport organizations frame diversity and inclusion? A critical race analysis. *Sport Management Review*, *26*(3), 339–360.

Gibbs, G. (1988). *Learning by doing: A guide to teaching and learning methods*. Oxford Further Education Unit.

Gibson, A. S., Ellis, M. V., & Friedlander, M. L. (2019). Toward a nuanced understanding of nondisclosure in psychotherapy supervision. *Journal of Counseling Psychology*, *66*(1), 114–121.

Goldberg, S. B., Rousmaniere, T., Miller, S. D., Whipple, J., Nielsen, S. L., Hoyt, W. T., & Wampold, B. E. (2016). Do psychotherapists improve with time and experience? A longitudinal analysis of outcomes in a clinical setting. *Journal of Counseling Psychology*, *63*(1), 1–11. https://doi.org/10.1037/cou0000131

Goldman, A., & Gervis, M. (2021). Women are cancer, you shouldn't be working in sport: Sport psychologists' lived experiences of sexism in sport. *The Sport Psychologist*, *35*(2), 85–96.

Gonsalvez, C. J. (2014). Establishing supervision goals and formalizing a supervision agreement. In C. E. Watkins & D. L. Milne (Eds.), *The Wiley international handbook of clinical supervision*. Wiley.

Gonsalvez, C. J. (2021). A short scale to evaluate supervision and supervisor competence (SE-SC8). *Clinical Psychology and Psychotherapy*, *28*(2), 452–461. https://doi.org/10.1002/cpp.2510

Gonsalvez, C. J., Calvert, F. L. (2014). Competency-based models of supervision: Principles and applications, promises and challenges. *Australian Psychologist*, *49*(4), 200–208.

Gonsalvez, C. J., Hamid, G., Savage, N. M., & Livni, D. (2017). The supervision evaluation and supervisory competence scale: Psychometric validation. *Australian Psychologist*, *52*(2), 94–103. https://doi.org/10.1111/ap.12269

Gonsalvez, C. J., & Milne, D. L. (2010). Clinical supervisor training in Australia: A review of current problems and possible solutions. *Australian Psychologist*, *45*(4), 233–242.

Granello, D. H., Beamish, P. M., & Davis, T. E. (1997). Supervisee empowerment: Does gender make a difference? *Counselor Education and Supervision*, *36*(4), 305–317.

Grant, J., Schofield, M. J., & Crawford, S. (2012). Managing difficulties in supervision: Supervisors' perspectives. *Journal of Counseling Psychology*, *59*(4), 528–541.

Gray, D. E. (2010). Journeys towards the professionalisation of coaching: Dilemmas, dialogues and decisions among the global pathway. *Coaching: An International Journal of Theory, Research and Practice*, *4*(1), 4–19.

Guggenbuhl-Craig, A. (1971). *Power in the helping professions*. Spring Publications.

Gunn, J. E., & Pistole, M. C. (2012). Trainee supervisor attachment: Explaining the alliance and disclosure in supervision. *Training and Education in Professional Psychology*, 6(4), 229–237.

Gupta, S., & Divekar, S. (2022). A symmetry or asymmetry: Reflecting upon realities of cultural practice in sport psychology. *Sport & Exercise Psychology Review*, 17(1).

Haggerty, G., & Hilsenroth, M. J. (2011). The use of video in psychotherapy supervision. *British Journal of Psychotherapy*, 27(2), 193–210.

Haluch, P., Radcliffe, J., & Rowley, C. (2022). The quest for professional self-understanding: Sensemaking and the interpersonal nature of applied sport psychology practice. *Journal of Applied Sport Psychology*. Advance online publication. https://doi.org/10.1080/10413200.2021.1914772

Hatcher, R. L., Wise, E. H., Grus, C. L., Mangione, L., & Emmons, L. (2012). Inside the practicum in professional psychology: A survey of practicum site coordinators. *Training and Education in Professional Psychology*, 6(4), 220–228.

Haugen, E. N. J., & Hoff, K. (2024). Self-care and emotional competence in supervision: Helping sport psychology trainees foster professional well-being. *Journal of Clinical Sport Psychology*, 1–14.

Hawkins, P., & McMahon, A. (2020). *Supervision in the helping professions* (5th ed.). McGraw–Hill Education.

Hawkins, P., & Shohet, R. (1989). *Supervision in the helping professions*. Open University Press.

Hawkins, P., & Shohet, R. (2000). *Supervision in the helping professions: An individual, group and organizational approach*. Open University Press.

Hawkins, P., & Shohet, R. (2012). *Supervision in the helping professions* (4th ed.). Open University Press.

Hawkins, P., & Smith, N. (2013). *Coaching, mentoring and organizational consultancy: Supervision and development* (2nd ed.). Open University Press/McGraw-Hill.

HCPC. (2025a). *Supervision, leadership and culture*. The HCPC. https://www.hcpc-uk.org/standards/meeting-our-standards/supervision-leadership-and-culture/

HCPC. (2025b). *Supervision templates*. The HCPC. https://www.hcpc-uk.org/standards/meeting-our-standards/supervision-leadership-and-culture/supervision/supervision-case-studies-and-templates/supervision-templates/

Heckman-Stone, C. (2004). Trainee preferences for feedback and evaluation in clinical supervision. *The Clinical Supervisor*, 22(1), 21–33.

Henderson, P., Millar, A., & Holloway, J. (2014). *Practical supervision: How to become a supervisor for the helping professions*. Jessica Kingsley Publishers.

Hernández, P., & McDowell, T. (2010). Intersectionality, power, and relational safety in context: Key concepts in clinical supervision. *Training and Education in Professional Psychology*, 4(1), 29–35.

Hewson, J. (1999). Training supervisors to contract in supervision. In E. Holloway & M. Carroll (Eds.), *Training supervisors to contract in supervision* (pp. 67–91). SAGE Publications. https://doi.org/10.4135/9781446218044.n4

Hill, H. R. M., Crowe, T. P., & Gonsalvez, C. J. (2016). Reflective dialogue in clinical supervision: A pilot study involving collaborative review of supervision videos. *Psychotherapy Research*, 26(3), 263–278. https://doi.org/10.1080/10503307.2014.996795

Hindes, Y. L., & Andrews, J. J. W. (2011). Influence of gender on the supervisory relationship: A review of empirical research from 1996 to 2010. *Canadian Journal of Counselling and Psychotherapy*, *45*(3).

Hings, R. F., Wagstaff, C. R., Anderson, V., Gilmore, S., & Thelwell, R. C. (2020). Better preparing sports psychologists for the demands of applied practice: The emotional labor training gap. *Journal of Applied Sport Psychology*, *32*(4), 335–356.

Holloway, E. L. (1995). *Clinical supervision: A systems approach*. SAGE Publications.

Holloway, E., & Carroll, M. (1999). *Training counselling supervisors: Strategies, methods and techniques*. SAGE Publications.

Horvath, A. O., & Greenberg, L. S. (1989). Development and validation of the Working Alliance Inventory. *Journal of Counseling Psychology*, *36*(2), 223–233. https://doi.org/10.1037/0022-0167.36.2.223

Howard, A. (1998). Roads to professionalisation: Dare we travel the 'integrity route'?. *British Journal of Guidance and Counselling*, *26*(2), 303–309.

Hundley, G., & Casado-Kehoe, M. (2007). The wisdom jar: A creative metaphor for terminating counseling supervision. *Journal of Creativity in Mental Health*, *2*(2), 33–38. https://doi.org/10.1300/J456v02n02_04

Hutman, H., Ellis, M. V., Moore, J. A., Roberson, K. L., McNamara, M. L., Peterson, L. P., ... & Zhou, S. (2023). Supervisees' perspectives of inadequate, harmful, and exceptional clinical supervision: Are we listening? *The Counseling Psychologist*, *51*(5), 719–755.

Hutter, R. I., Oldenhof-Veldman, T., & Oudejans, R. R. D. (2015). What trainee sport psychologists want to learn in supervision. *Psychology of Sport and Exercise*, *16*(1), 101–109. https://doi.org/10.1016/j.psychsport.2014.08.003

Ilgen, J. S., de Bruin, A. B., Teunissen, P. W., Sherbino, J., & Regehr, G. (2021). Supported independence: The role of supervision to help trainees manage uncertainty. *Academic Medicine*, *96*(11S), S81–S86.

Inskipp, F. (1999). Training supervisees to use supervision. In E. Holloway & M. Carroll (Eds.), *Training counselling supervisors: Strategies, methods and techniques* (pp. 184–210). SAGE Publications. https://doi.org/10.4135/9781446218044.n9

Jacobsen, C. H. (2007). A qualitative single case study of parallel processes. *Counselling & Psychotherapy Research*, *7*(1), 26–33. https://doi.org/10.1080/14733140601140410

James, I. A., Milne, D., Marie-Blackburn, I., & Armstrong, P. (2007). Conducting successful supervision: Novel elements towards an integrative approach. *Behavioural and Cognitive Psychotherapy*, *35*(2), 191–200. https://doi.org/10.1017/S1352465806003407

Johnson, E. A. (2017). *Working together in clinical supervision: A guide for supervisors and supervisees* (1st ed.). Momentum Press.

Johnson, W. B., & Campbell, C. D. (2002). Character and fitness requirements for professional psychologists: Are there any?. *Professional Psychology: Research and Practice*, *33*(1), 46.

Jordan, S. E., & Shearer, E. M. (2019). An exploration of supervision delivered via Clinical Video Telehealth (CVT). *Training and Education in Professional Psychology*, *13*(4), 323–330. https://doi.org/10.1037/tep0000245

Jones, F. (2011). Clinical psychology: Training and development. In G. Davey (Ed.), *Applied psychology* (pp. 111–126). Wiley.

Jones, L., Evans, L., & Mullen, R. (2007). Multiple roles in an applied setting: Trainee sport psychologist, coach and researcher. *The Sport Psychologist*, *21*, 210–226.

Jooste, J., Kruger, A., Steyn, B. J. M., & Edwards, D. J. (2016). Essential competencies in contemporary applied sport psychology: Comparative perspectives from South Africa and the United Kingdom. *African Journal for Physical and Health Sciences*, *22*(1), 1–32.

Kadushin, A. (1976). *Supervision in social work*. Columbia University Press.

Kagan, H. K., & Kagan, N. I. (1997). Interpersonal process recall: Influencing human interaction. In C. E. Watkins (Ed.), *Handbook of psychotherapy supervision*. Wiley.

Kelly, A. L., Williams, C. A., Jackson, D. R., Turnnidge, J., Reeves, M. J., Dugdale, J. H., & Wilson, M. R. (2024). Exploring the role of socioeconomic status and psychological characteristics on talent development in an English soccer academy. *Science and Medicine in Football*, *8*(3), 251–259.

Kennerley, H., & Clohessy, S. (2010). Becoming a supervisor. In M. Mueller, et al. (Eds.), *Oxford guide to surviving as a CBT therapist*. Oxford Guides to Cognitive Behavioural Therapy. Oxford University Press. https://doi.org/10.1093/med:psych/9780199561308.003.0016

Kennerley, H., Kirk, J., & Westbrook, D. (2017). *An introduction to cognitive behaviour therapy: Skills and applications*. SAGE Publications.

Kerr, G., & Stirling, A. (2019). Where is safeguarding in sport psychology research and practice? *Journal of Applied Sport Psychology*, *31*(4), 367–384.

Kilminster, S. M., & Jolly, B. C. (2000). Effective supervision in clinical practice settings: A literature review. *Medical Education*, *34*(10), 827–840.

Knox, S., Edwards, L. M., Hess, S. A., & Hill, C. E. (2011). Supervisor self-disclosure: Supervisees' experiences and perspectives. *Psychotherapy*, *48*(4), 336–341. https://doi.org/10.1037/a0022067

Kocyigit, M. (2024). Novice supervisees' anxiety in counselling supervision: A phenomenological study. *Studies in Continuing Education*, *46*(1), 65–81.

Kolb, D. A. (2014). *Experiential learning: Experience as the source of learning and development* (2nd ed.). Pearson Education.

Kontos, A. P., & Breland-Noble, A. M. (2002). Racial/ethnic diversity in applied sport psychology: A multicultural introduction to working with athletes of color. *The Sport Psychologist*, *16*(3), 296–315.

Knowles, Z., Gilbourne, D., Tomlinson, V., & Anderson, A. G. (2007). Reflections on the application of reflective practice for supervision in applied sport psychology. *The Sport Psychologist*, *21*(1), 109–122. https://doi.org/10.1123/tsp.21.1.109

Kumari, N. (2011). Personal therapy as a mandatory requirement for counselling psychologists in training: A qualitative study of the impact of therapy on trainees' personal and professional development. *Counselling Psychology Quarterly*, *24*(3), 211–232.

Kuo, H.-J., Landon, T. J., Connor, A., & Chen, R. K. (2016). Managing anxiety in clinical supervision. *The Journal of Rehabilitation*, *82*(3), 18.

Lacoursiere, R. (1980). *Life cycles of groups*. Human Sciences Press.

Ladany, N., Mori, Y., & Mehr, K. E. (2013). Effective and ineffective supervision. The *Counseling Psychologist*, *41*(1), 28–47. https://doi.org/10.1177/0011000012442648

Lafferty, M. E., Coyle, M., Prince, H. R., & Szabadics, A. (2022). "It's not just a man's world"–Helping female sport psychologists to thrive not just survive. Lessons for supervisors, trainees, practitioners and mentors. *Sport & Exercise Psychology Review*, *17*(2).

Lafferty, M. E., Hemmings, B., Katz, J., Cunliffe, M., & Eubank, M. (2019). Many roads can lead to Rome—Supervisors' perspectives on successful supervision and its challenges. *Sport & Exercise Psychology Review*, *15*(2), 14–20. https://doi.org/10.53841/bpssepr.2019.15.2.14

Lago, I., LagoPeñas, C., & LagoPeñas, S. (2023). Work group diversity in professional football: An individual-level approach to the effects of diversity in organizations. *Social Science Quarterly*, *104*(4), 927–942.

Lammers, W. (1999). Training in group and team supervision. In E. Holloway and M. Carroll (Eds.), *Training counselling supervisors: Strategies, methods and techniques* (pp. 91–105). SAGE Publications.

Lee, E. H., Pitts, S., Pignataro, S., Newman, L. R., & D'Angelo, E. J. (2022). Establishing psychological safety in clinical supervision: Multi-professional perspectives. *The Clinical Teacher*, *19*(2), 71–78. https://doi.org/10.1111/tct.13451

Levendosky, A. A., & Hopwood, C. J. (2017). Terminating supervision. *Psychotherapy*, *54*(1), 37–46. https://doi.org/10.1037/pst0000096

Lew, A., & Bettner, B. L. (1995). *A parent's guide to understanding and motivating children.* Connexions Press.

Litherland, G., Schulthes, G., Cowles, C., & Ewe, E. (2023). The proctor model of clinical supervision: An introduction for professional counselors. *The Journal of Counselor Preparation and Supervision*, *17*(5), 4.

Liu, W., Zhang, P., Liao, J., Hao, P., & Mao, J. (2016). Abusive supervision and employee creativity: The mediating role of psychological safety and organizational identification. *Management Decision*, *54*(1), 130–143. https://doi.org/10.1108/MD-09-2013-0443

Lochner, B. T., & Melchart, T. P. (1997). Relationship of cognitive style and theoretical orientation to psychology interns' preferences for supervision. *Journal of Counseling Psychology*, *44*(2), 256–260.

Loganbill, C., Hardy, E., & Delworth, U. (1982). Supervision: A conceptual model. The *Counseling Psychologist*, *10*(1), 3–42.

Lubker, J. R., Visek, A. J., Geer, J. R., & Watson II, J. C. (2008). Characteristics of an effective sport psychology consultant: Perspectives from athletes and consultants. *Journal of Sport Behavior*, *31*(2), 147–165.

Luft, J., & Ingham, H. (1955). The Johariwindow, a graphic model of interpersonalawareness. *Proceedings of the Western Training Laboratory in Group Development*. University of California.

Maaß, U., Kühne, F., Poltz, N., Lorenz, A., Ay-Bryson, D. S., & Weck, F. (2022). Live supervision in psychotherapy training—A systematic review. *Training and Education in Professional Psychology*, *16*(2), 130–143.

Maben, J., Hoinbille, L., Querstret, D., Taylor, C., Zadasa, M., & Abrams, R. (2021). Living in limbo: Experiences of healthcare professionals during the HCPC fitness to practice investigation process in the UK. *BMC Health Services Research*, *21*(1), 839.

Magdaleno, A., & Meyer, B. B. (2023). Identifying predictors of burnout and health of certified mental performance consultants. *The Sport Psychologist*, *37*(4), 297–305.

Martin, J. (2019). Is the profession of sport psychology an illusion? *Kinesiology Review*, *9*(2), 92–103.

Martin, J., Guerrero, M., & Snapp, E. (2020). Disability and sport psychology. In G. T. Tenenbaum & R. C. Eklund (Eds.), *Handbook of sport psychology* (4th ed.). Wiley.

Maurya, R. K. (2023). A qualitative content analysis of ChatGPT's client simulation role play for practicing counseling skills. *Counselling and Psychotherapy Research*, 1–17. https://doi.org/10.1002/capr.12699

Maurya, R. K., & DeDiego, A. C. (2025). Artificial intelligence integration in counsellor education and supervision: A roadmap for future directions and research inquiries. *Counselling and Psychotherapy Research*, *25*(1). https://doi.org/10.1002/capr.12727

McCarver, Z., Anderson, S., Vosloo, J., & Harenberg, S. (2019). Diversity characteristics and experiences of discrimination in certified mental performance consultants. *The Sport Psychologist*, *33*(3), 228–231.

McCarthy, P., Gupta, S., & Burns, L. (2023). *Cognitive behaviour therapy in sport and performance: An applied practice guide*. Routledge.

McCarthy, P. J., Gupta, S., Burns, L., & McCann, B. (2024). *Training and supervision in sport and exercise psychology*. Routledge. https://doi.org/10.4324/9781003367208

McEwan, H. E., & Tod, D. (2015). Learning experiences contributing to service-delivery competence in applied psychologists: Lessons for sport psychologists. *Journal of Applied Sport Psychology*, *27*(1), 79–93. https://doi.org/10.1080/10413200.2014.952460

McEwan, H. E., & Tod, D. (2023). Trainee clinical and sport and exercise psychologists' experiences of professional development: A longitudinal study. *Psychology of Sport and Exercise*, *64*, 102343.

McEwan, H. E., Tod, D., & Eubank, M. (2019). The rocky road to individuation: Sport psychologists' perspectives on professional development. *Psychology of Sport and Exercise*, *45*, Article 101542. https://doi.org/10.1016/j.psychsport.2019.101542

McHenry, L. K., Beasley, L., Zakrajsek, R. A., & Hardin, R. (2022). Mental performance and mental health services in sport: A call for interprofessional competence and collaboration. *Journal of Interprofessional Care*, *36*(4), 520–528.

McLeod, J., & McLeod, J. (2014). *Personal and professional development for counsellors, psychotherapists and mental health practitioners*. Open University Press.

McMahon, A. (2014). Four guiding principles for the supervisory relationship. *Reflective Practice*, *15*(3), 333–346.

McNamara, M. L., Kangos, K. A., Corp, D. A., Ellis, M. V., & Taylor, E. J. (2017). Narratives of harmful clinical supervision: Synthesis and recommendations. *The Clinical Supervisor*, *36*(1), 124–144.

Mehr, K. E., & Daltry, R. M. (2022). Supervisor self-disclosure, the supervisory alliance, and trainee willingness to disclose. *Professional Psychology: Research and Practice*, *53*(3), 313.

Meijen, C., & Manley, A. (2010). The supervision process through the eyes of the supervisor. *Sport & Exercise Psychology Review*, *6*(2), 43–46. https://doi.org/10.53841/bpssepr.2010.6.2.43

Mendoza, D. W. (1993). A review of Gerald Caplan's theory and practice of mental health consultation. *Journal of Counseling and Development*, *71*(6), 629–635.

Mercer, R. A. J., Russell, J. L., Strack, D. S., Coutts, A. J., & McLean, B. D. (2025). Work demands, responses, and coping strategies for staff in high-performance sport: A scoping review. *Sports Medicine*.

Milne, D. (2009). *Evidence-based clinical supervision: Principles and practice*. Wiley.

Milne, D., Aylott, H., Fitzpatrick, H., & Ellis, M. V. (2008). How does clinical supervision work? Using a "best evidence synthesis" approach to construct a basic model of supervision. *The Clinical Supervisor*, *27*(2), 170–190. https://doi.org/10.1080/07325220802487915

Milne, D., & Reiser, R. P. (2017). *A manual for evidence-based CBT supervision.* Wiley Blackwell. https://doi.org/10.1002/9781119030799

Mollon, P. (1989). Anxiety, supervision and a space for thinking: Some narcissistic perils for clinical psychologists in learning psychotherapy. *British Journal of Medical Psychology*, *62*(2), 113–122.

Mollon, P. (1997). Supervision as a space for thinking. In G. Shipton (Ed.), *Supervision of psychotherapy and counselling.* Open University.

Moore, Z. E. (2003). Ethical dilemmas in sport psychology: Discussions and recommendations for practice. *Professional Psychology: Research and Practice*, *34*(6), 601–610.

Murphy, M. J., & Wright, D. W. (2005). Supervisees' perspectives of power use in supervision. *Journal of Marital and Family Therapy*, *31*(3), 283–295.

Muse, K., & McManus, F. (2013). A systematic review of methods for assessing competence in cognitive–behavioural therapy. *Clinical Psychology Review*, *33*(3), 484–499. https://doi.org/10.1016/j.cpr.2013.01.010

Muse, K., McManus, F., Rakovshik, S., & Thwaites, R. (2016). Development and psychometric evaluation of the Assessment of Core CBT Skills (ACCS): An observation-based tool for assessing cognitive behavioural therapy competence. *Psychological Assessment*, 1–14. https://doi.org/10.1037/pas0000372

Nottingham, S. L. (2018). Perceptions of clinical supervision with and without bug-in-ear technology. *International Journal of Athletic Therapy and Training*, *23*(6), 239–245.

Neenan, M., & Dryden, W. (2021). *Cognitive behaviour therapy: 100 key points and techniques.* Taylor & Francis.

Nelson, M. L., Barnes, K. L., Evans, A. T., & Triggiano, P. J. (2008). Working with conflict in clinical supervision: Wise supervisors' perspectives. *Journal of Counseling Psychology*, *55*(2), 172–184.

Nicholas, H., & Goodyear, R. (2020). Supervision of a sample of clinical and counselling psychologists in the UK: A descriptive study of their practices, processes and perceived benefits. *The European Journal of Counselling Psychology*, *9*(1), 41–50.

Norcross, J. C. (Ed.). (2011). *Psychotherapy relationships that work: Evidence-based responsiveness* (2nd ed.). Oxford University Press.

Norcross, J. C., & Guy, J. D. (2007). *Leaving it at the office: A guide to psychotherapist self-care.* Guilford Press.

Norcross, J. C., & Rogan, J. D. (2013). Psychologists conducting psychotherapy in 2012: Current practices and historical trends among division 29 members. *Psychotherapy*, *50*, 490–495. https://doi.org/10.1037/a0033512

Norcross, J. C., & Wampold, B. E. (2011). What works for who? Tailoring psychotherapy to the person. *Journal of Clinical Psychology*, *67*(2), 127–132.

Oddli, H. W., Heinonen, E., Hau, S., Nielsen, J., Esterhazy, R., Hillestad Hodd, C., & Strømme, H. (2021). Learning processes and acquisition of knowledge and skills in training and supervision of psychotherapy and counselling: A study protocol for a scoping review. *Frontiers in Psychology*, *12*. https://doi.org/10.3389/fpsyg.2021.718314

O'Donovan, A., Halford, W. K., & Walters, B. (2011). Towards best practice supervision of clinical psychology trainees. *Australian Psychologist*, *46*, 101–112.

Oliver, M. N., Bernstein, J. H., Anderson, K. G., Blashfield, R. K., & Roberts, M. C. (2004). An exploratory examination of student attitudes toward "impaired" peers in clinical psychology training programmes. *Professional Psychology: Research and Practice*, *35*(2), 141–147.

Ooijen, E., & Spencer, L. (2017). Practitioners' perspectives on how supervision training has impacted their practice. *Counselling & Psychotherapy Research*, *17*(4), 283–290. https://doi.org/10.1002/capr.12128

Palomo, M. (2004). *Development and validation of a questionnaire measure of the supervisory relationship* [Unpublished doctoral thesis]. University of Oxford.

Palomo, M., Beinart, H., & Cooper, M. (2010). Development and validation of the Supervisory Relationship Questionnaire (SRQ) in UK trainee clinical psychologists. *British Journal of Clinical Psychology*, *49*(2), 131–149. https://doi.org/10.1348/014466509X441033

Pawar, M., & Anscombe, A. W. (2022). Models of professional supervision in social work. In M. Pawar & A .W. Anscombe (Eds.), *Enlightening professional supervision in social work* (pp. 71–97). Springer. https://doi.org/10.1007/978-3-031-18541-0_4

Pearce, N., Beinart, H., Clohessy, S., & Cooper, M. (2013). Development and validation of the supervisory relationship measure: A self-report questionnaire for use with supervisors. *British Journal of Clinical Psychology*, *52*, 249–268.

Pearlstein, J. G., & Soyster, P. D. (2019). Supervisory experiences of trainees with disabilities: The good, the bad, and the realistic. *Training and Education in Professional Psychology*, *13*(3), 194–199.

Philp, K., Guy, G., & Lowe, R. (2007). Social constructionist supervision or supervision as social construction? Some dilemmas. *Journal of Systemic Therapies*, *26*(1), 51–62. https://doi.org/10.1521/jsyt.2007.26.1.51

Poczwardowski, A., Andersen, M. B., Van Raalte, J. L., Harwood, C., Si, G., Tshube, T., & Noce, F. (2023). ISSP position stand: Competent supervision in sport psychology. *International Journal of Sport and Exercise Psychology*, *21*(6), 931–950. https://doi.org/10.1080/1612197X.2023.2229342

Poczwardowski, A., Sherman, C., & Ravizza, K. (2004). Professional philosophy in the sport psychology service delivery: Building on theory and practice. *The Sport Psychologist*, *18*, 445–463.

Portenga, S. T., Aoyagi, M. W., & Cohen, A. B. (2017). Helping to build a profession: A working definition of sport and performance psychology. *Journal of Sport Psychology in Action*, *8*(1), 47–59.

Powell, B., Cooper, G., Hoffman, K., & Marvin, B. (2014). *The circle of security intervention: Enhancing attachment in early parent–child relationships*. Guilford Press.

Power, A. (2013). Supervision of supervision: How many mirrors do we need? *British Journal of Psychotherapy*, *29*(3), 389–404. https://doi.org/10.1111/bjp.12038

Prior, E., Papathomas, A., & Rhind, D. (2025). A balancing act: Sport psychologist insights into supporting athlete mental health in elite sport. *Journal of Applied Sport Psychology*, 1–21.

Proctor, B. (1986). Supervision: A cooperative exercise in accountability, enabling and ensuring. In M. Marken & M. Payne (Eds.), *Enabling and ensuring: Supervision in practice* (pp. 21–34). National Youth Bureau.

Proctor, B. (1988). Supervision: A co-operative exercise in accountability. In M. Marken & M. Payne (Eds.), *Enabling and ensuring*. National Youth Bureau.

Proctor, B. (1994). Supervision—Competence, confidence, accountability. *British Journal of Guidance & Counselling*, *22*(3), 309–318.

Proctor. B. (2008). *Group supervision: A guide to creative practice* (2nd ed.). SAGE Publications.

Pugh, M., & Margetts, A. (2020). Are you sitting (un)comfortably? Action-based supervision and supervisory drift. *The Cognitive Behaviour Therapist*, *13*, e17.

Quartiroli, A., Etzel, E. F., Knight, S. M., & Zakrajsek, R. A. (2019). The multifaceted meaning of sport psychology professional quality of life. *Journal of Clinical Sport Psychology*, *13*(4), 645–667.
Quartiroli, A., Fogaca, J. L., & Wagstaff, C. R. D. (2023). Professional training and development: The bedrock of ethical, competent and sustainable sport psychology. *Journal of Applied Sport Psychology*, *35*(3), 349–371.
Quartiroli, A., Schinke, R. J., Giffin, C., Vosloo, J., & Fisher, L. A. (2022). Cultural competence in a multinational group of sport psychology professionals. *Journal of Applied Sport Psychology*, *35*(6), 919–940.
Quartiroli, A., Vosloo, J., Fisher, L., & Schienke, R. (2020). Culturally competent sport psychology: A survey of sport psychology professionals' perception of cultural competence. *The Sport Psychologist*, *34*(3), 242–253.
Quartiroli, A., Wagstaff, C. R. D., & Wren, B. (2025). Predictably unpredictable: Sport psychologists' experience of precarity working in elite sport organisations. *International Journal of Sport and Exercise Psychology*, 1–20.
Rabinowitz, Y. L., Lipner, L. M., Polland, D., Podell, S. C., & Muran, J. C. (2025). Therapy endings or new beginnings: Understanding the patient experience of termination in a time-limited relational therapy. *Counselling Psychology Quarterly*, 1–20. https://doi.org/10.1080/09515070.2025.2549272
Ramos-Sanchez, L., Esnil, E., Goodwin, A., Rigger, S., Touster, L. P., Wright, L. K., & Rodolfa, E. (2002). Negative supervisory events: Effects on supervision and supervisory alliance. *Professional Psychology: Research and Practice*, *33*, 197–202.
Ratcliffe, K., & Kaluzeviciute-Moreton, G. (2024). Telesupervision in counselling and psychotherapy: A systematic review of the literature. *British Journal of Guidance & Counselling*, *52*(5), 801–814. https://doi.org/10.1080/03069885.2023.2264480
Reeves, A., & Bond, T. (2021). *Standards and ethics for counselling in action* (5th ed.). SAGE Publications.
Regulation (EU) 2016/679 of the European Parliament and ofthe Council of 27 April 2016 on the protection of natural persons with regard to the processing of personal data and on the free movement of such data (General Data Protection Regulation). https://eur-lex.europa.eu/eli/reg/2016/679/oj
Reiser, R. P., & Milne, D. L. (2017a). Goal-setting in CBT supervision. In R. P. Reiser & D. L. Milne (Eds.), *A manual for evidence-based CBT supervision* (pp. 104–127). Wiley. https://doi.org/10.1002/9781119030799.ch6
Reiser, R. P., & Milne, D. L. (2017b). Feedback and evaluation in CBT supervision. In R. P. Reiser & D. L. Milne (Eds.), *A manual for evidence-based CBT supervision* (pp. 153–178). Wiley. https://doi.org/10.1002/9781119030799.ch8
Riva, M. T., & Smith, R. D. (2024). Beyond the dyad: Broadening the APA supervision guidelines to include group supervision. *Psychotherapy*, *61*(2), 161–172. https://doi.org/10.1037/pst0000525
Rogers, C. R. (1957). The necessary and sufficient conditions of therapeutic personality change. *Journal of consulting psychology*, *21*(2), 95.
Rogers, C. R. (2007). The necessary and sufficient conditions of therapeutic personality change. *Psychotherapy*, *44*, 240–248. https://doi.org/10.1037/0033-3204.44.3.240
Rønnestad, M. H., Orlinsky, D. E., Schröder, T. A., Skovholt, T. M., & Willutzki, U. (2019). The professional development of counsellors and psychotherapists: Empirical implications for supervision, training and practice. *Counselling and Psychotherapy Research*, *19*(3), 214–230. https://doi.org/10.1002/capr.12198

Rønnestad, M. H., & Skovholt, T. M. (1993). Supervision of beginning and advanced graduate students of counseling and psychotherapy. *Journal of Counseling & Development*, *71*(4), 396–405. https://doi.org/10.1002/j.1556-6676.1993.tb02655.x

Rønnestad, M. H., & Skovholt, T. M. (2003). The journey of the counselor and therapist: Research findings and perspectives on professional development. *Journal of Career Development*, *30*(1), 5–44. https://doi.org/10.1177/089484530303000102

Roscoe, J. (2021). Conceptualising and managing supervisory drift. *The Cognitive Behaviour Therapist*, *14*, e37.

Rowell, P. C. (2010). Group supervision of individual counselling. In N. Ladany & L. J. Bradley (Eds.), *Counselor supervision* (pp. 193–209). Taylor & Francis.

Rousmaniere, T., & Frederickson, J. (2013). Internet-based one-way-mirror supervision for advanced psychotherapy training. *The Clinical Supervisor*, *32*(1), 40–55. https://doi.org/10.1080/07325223.2013.778683

Rousmaniere, T., Goodyear, R. K., Miller, S. D., & Wampold, B. E. (Eds.). (2017). *The cycle of excellence: Using deliberate practice to improve supervision and training*. Wiley Blackwell. https://doi.org/10.1002/9781119165590

Ryan, R. M., & Deci, E. L. (2000). Self-determination theory and the facilitation of intrinsic motivation, social development, and well-being. *American Psychologist*, *55*(1), 68–78. https://doi.org/10.1037/0003-066X.55.1.68

Ryba, T. V., Schinke, R. J., Quartiroli, A., Wong, R., & Gill, D. (2025). ISSP position stand on cultural praxis in sport psychology: Reaffirming our commitments to the ethics of difference, cultural inclusion, and social justice. In *Culture and inclusion in sport and physical activity* (pp. 7–29). Routledge.

Safran, J. D., Muran, J. C., & Eubanks-Carter, C. (2011). Repairing alliance ruptures. *Psychotherapy*, *48*, 80–87.

Sawatsky, A. P., O'Brien, B. C., & Hafferty, F. W. (2022). Autonomy and developing physicians: Reimagining supervision using self-determination theory. *Medical Education*, *56*(1), 56–63. https://doi.org/10.1111/medu.14580

Scottish Government. (2021). Transforming nursing roles: Advanced nursing practice – Phase two. https://www.gov.scot/publications/transforming-nursing-roles-advanced-nursing-practice-phase-ii/pages/3/

Sexton, T. L., & Whiston, S. C. (1994). The status of the counseling relationship: An empirical review, theoretical implications, and research directions. *The Counseling Psychologist*, *22*(1), 6–78.

Shaffer, K. S., & Friedlander, M. L. (2017). What do "interpersonally sensitive" supervisors do and how do supervisees experience a relational approach to supervision? *Psychotherapy Research*, *27*(2), 167–178. https://doi.org/10.1080/10503307.2015.1080877

Shah, R. (2019). The reflecting team: A new approach to case discussion. *The British Journal of General Practice*, *69*(689), 612.

Shapiro, J. L., & Poczwardowski, A. (2020). Professional development: Supervision, mentorship, and professional development in the career of an applied professional. In *The Routledge international encyclopedia of sport and exercise psychology* (pp. 555–574). Routledge.

Sharp, L. A., Hodge, K., & Danish, S. (2015). Ultimately it comes down to the relationship: Experienced consultants' views of effective sport psychology consulting. *The Sport Psychologist*, *29*(4), 358–370.

Sharp, L. A., Hodge, K., & Danish, S. (2021). "I wouldn't want to operate without it": The ethical challenges faced by experienced sport psychology consultants and their engagement with supervision. *Journal of Applied Sport Psychology, 33*(3), 259–279.

Sills, C. (2012). The coaching contract: A mutual commitment. In E. de Haan & C. Sills (Eds.), *Coaching relationships: The relational coaching fieldbook*. Libri.

Simons, J. P., & Andersen, M. B. (1995). The development of consulting practice in applied sport psychology: Some personal perspectives. *The Sport Psychologist, 9*(4), 449–468.

Simpson-Southward, C., Waller, G., & Hardy, G. (2017). How do we know what makes for 'best practice' in clinical supervision for psychological therapists? A content analysis of supervisory models and approaches. *Clinical Psychology and Psychotherapy, 24*(6), 1228–1245.

Skovolt, T. M., & Rønnestad, M. H. (1995). *The evolving professional self: Stages and themes in therapist and counsellor development*. Wiley.

Sly, D., Mellalieu, S. D., & Wagstaff, C. R. (2020). "It's psychology Jim, but not as we know it!": The changing face of applied sport psychology. *Sport, Exercise, and Performance Psychology, 9*(1), 87–101. https://doi.org/10.1037/spy0000163

Sofronoff, K., Helmes, E., & Pachana, N. (2011). Fitness to practice in the profession of psychology: Should we assess this during clinical training? *Australian Psychologist, 46*(2), 126–132.

Soliman, S. (2023). Attachment in supervision: Using a relational lens to understand supervisory dynamics. *Psychotherapy and Counselling Journal of Australia, 11*(2). https://doi.org/10.59158/001c.90756

Spaaij, R., Knoppers, A., & Jeanes, R. (2020). "We want more diversity but…": Resisting diversity in recreational sports clubs. *Sport Management Review, 23*(3), 363–373.

Stapleton, A. B., Hankes, D. M., Hays, K. F., & Parham, W. D. (2010). Ethical dilemmas in sport psychology: A dialogue on the unique aspects impacting practice. *Professional Psychology: Research and Practice, 41*(2), 143–152.

The Stationery Office Limited. (2010). *Equality act*. The Stationery Office Limited.

Stefano, J. D., Hutman, H., & Gazzola, N. (2017). Putting on the face: A qualitative study of power dynamics in clinical supervision. *The Clinical Supervisor, 36*(2), 223–240.

Stevens, K., & Al-Abbadey, M. (2024). Compassion fatigue and global compassion fatigue in practitioner psychologists: A qualitative study. *Current Psychology, 43*(8), 7259–7274.

Stoltenberg, C. D. (1981). Approaching supervision from a developmental perspective: The counselor complexity model. *Journal of counseling Psychology, 28*(1), 59.

Stoltenberg, C. D., & Delworth, U. (1987). *Supervising counselors and therapists: A developmental approach*. Jossey-Bass.

Stoltenberg, C. D., & McNeill, B. W. (2010). *IDM supervision: An integrative developmental model for supervising counselors and therapists*. Routledge.

Stoltenberg, C. D., McNeill, B. W., & Delworth, U. (1998). *IDM Supervision: An integrated developmental model for supervising counselors and therapists*. Jossey-Bass.

Sudak, D. M., Codd, R. T., Ludgate, J. W., Sokol, L., Fox, M. G., Reiser, R. P., & Milne, D. L. (2016). *Teaching and supervising cognitive behavioral therapy* (Kindle ed.). Wiley.

Tangen, J. L., & Borders, D. (2016). The supervisory relationship: A conceptual and psychometric review of measures. *Counselor Education and Supervision, 55*(3), 159–181. https://doi.org/10.1002/ceas.12043

Teitelbaum, S. H. (1990). Supertransference: The role of the supervisor's blind spots. *Psychoanalytic Psychology*, 7(2), 243–258. https://doi.org/10.1037/h0079155

Tod, A. (2007). The long and winding road: Professional development in sport psychology. *The Sport Psychologist*, *21*(1), 94–108.

Tod, D., Andersen, M. B., & Marchant, D. (2009). A longitudinal examination of neophyte applied sport psychologists' development. *Journal of Applied Sport Psychology*, *21*(S1), S1–S16.

Tod, D., Andersen, M., & Marchant, D. (2011). Six years up: Applied sport psychologists surviving (and thriving) after graduation. *Journal of Applied Sport Psychology*, *23*, 93–109.

Tod, D., Eubank, M., McEwan, H., Chandler, C., & Moira L (2021). Supervision. In E. Filho & I. Basevitch (Eds.), *Sport, exercise and performance psychology: Research directions to advance the field* (pp. 350–362). Oxford University Press. https://doi.org/10.1093/oso/9780197512494.003.0025

Tod, D., Hutter, R. V., & Eubank, M. (2017). Professional development for sport psychology practice. *Current Opinion in Psychology*, *16*, 134–137.

Tod, D., & Lavallee, D. E. (2011). Taming the wild west: Training and supervision in applied sport psychology. In GilbourneD. & M. B. Andersen (Eds.), *Critical essays in applied sport psychology* (pp. 193–215). Human Kinetics.

Tod, D., & McEwan, H. (2023). Training and professional development. In D. Tod, K. Hodge, & V. Krane (Eds.), *Routledge handbook of applied sport psychology* (pp. 22–30). Routledge.

Townend, M. (2005). *Supervision contracts in CBT*. British Association for Behavioural & Cognitive Psychotherapies.

Tracey, T. J., Bludworth, J., & Glidden-Tracey, C. E. (2012). Are there parallel processes in psychotherapy supervision? An empirical examination. *Psychotherapy*, *49*, 330–343. https://doi.org/10.1037/a0026246

Tuckman, B. W. (1965). Developmental sequence in small groups. *Psychological Bulletin*, *63*(6), 384–399.

Tugendrajch, S. K., Sheerin, K. M., Andrews, J. H., Reimers, R., Marriott, B. R., Cho, E., & Hawley, K. M. (2021). What is the evidence for supervision best practices?. *The Clinical Supervisor*, *40*(1), 68–87.

Vandette, M., Burns, S., & Shesko, D. (2019). Safety in clinical supervision: A mechanism to promote professional development among trainees. *Psychotherapy Bulletin*, *54*(1), 1–24. https://societyforpsychotherapy.org/safety-in-clinical-supervision/

Van Raalte, J. L., & Andersen, M. B. (2000). Supervision I: From models to doing. In M. B. Andersen (Ed.), *Doing sport psychology* (pp. 153–165). Human Kinetics.

Van Raalte, J. L., & Andersen, M. B. (2021). Supervision I: From models to doing. In M. B. Andersen (Ed.), *Doing sport psychology: 21st anniversary edition with original authors' reflections*. Kindle Direct Publishing.

Verner, D., Chandler, C., & Clarke, P. (2021). Exploring the contribution of personal qualities to the personal and professional development of trainee sport psychology practitioners within the individuation process. *Physical Culture and Sport, Studies and Research*, *92*(1), 43–54.

Vosloo, J., Zakrajsek, R., & Grindley, E. (2014). From mentee to mentor: Considerations for the neophyte supervisor. In J. G. Cremades & L. S. Tashman (Eds.), *Becoming a sport, exercise, and performance psychology professional: A global perspective* (pp. 228–235). Routledge.

Vygotsky, L. S. (1978). *Mind in society: The development of higher psychological processes*. Harvard University Press.
Wade, J. C., & Jones, J. E. (2014). *Strength-based clinical supervision: A positive psychology approach to clinical training*. Springer.
Wade, J. C., & Jones, J. E. (2015). *Strength-based clinical supervision: A positive psychology approach to clinical training* (1st ed.). Springer Publishing Company.
Wainwright, N. A. (2010). *The development of the Leeds Alliance in Supervision Scale (LASS): A brief sessional measure of the supervisory alliance* [Unpublished master's thesis]. University of Leeds.
Wagstaff, C. R., & Quartiroli, A. (2020). Psychology and psychologists in search of an identity: What and who are we, and why does it matter? *Journal of Sport Psychology in Action*, *11*(4), 254–265.
Waller, G. (2009). Evidence-based treatment and therapist drift. *Behaviour Research and Therapy*, *47*, 119–127.
Wark, L. (2017). Bug-in-the-ear supervision. In J. Lebow, A. Chambers, & D. Breunlin (Eds.), *Encyclopedia of couple and family therapy*. Springer. https://doi.org/10.1007/978-3-319-15877-8_641-1
Watkins, C. E. (2014). The supervisory alliance as quintessential integrative variable. *Journal of Contemporary Psychotherapy*, *44*(3), 151–161. https://doi.org/10.1007/s10879-013-9252-x
Watkins, C. E. (2021). Rupture and rupture repair in clinical supervision: Some thoughts and steps along the way. *The Clinical Supervisor*, *40*(1), 1–24.
Watkins, C. E. (2024). When supervisees rupture: Supervisor rupture reactions and repair—Further thoughts and steps along the way. *The Clinical Supervisor*, *43*(1), 42–69.
Watkins, C. E., Ellis, M. V., Viliuniene, R., Cadariu, I.-E., Viscu, L. I., & Callahan, J. L. (2024). A written supervision agreement for psychoanalytic supervision? *Psychoanalytic Psychotherapy*.
Watkins, C. E., Hook, J. N., Mosher, D. K., & Callahan, J. L. (2019). Humility in clinical supervision: Fundamental, foundational, and transformational. *The Clinical Supervisor*, *38*(1), 58–78.
Watkins, C. E., & Milne, D. L. (Eds.). (2014). *The Wiley international handbook of clinical supervision*. John Wiley & Sons.
Watkins, C. E., Reyna, S. H., Ramos, M. J., & Hook, J. N. (2015). The ruptured supervisory alliance and its repair: On supervisor apology as a reparative intervention. *The Clinical Supervisor*, *34*(1), 98–114.
Watkins, C. E., & Scaturo, D. J. (2014). Proposal for a common language, educationally informed model of psychoanalytic supervision. *Psychoanalytic Inquiry*, *34*(6), 619–633.
Watson, D. R. (2025). Insights and challenges of working with perfectionism in sport. *Journal of Sport Psychology in Action*, *16*(3), 178–188.
Watson II, J. C., Way, W. C., & Hilliard, R. C. (2017). Ethical issues in sport psychology. *Current Opinion in Psychology*, *16*, 143–147.
Watson II, J. C., Zizzi, S. J., Etzel, E. F., & Lubker, J. R. (2004). Applied sport psychology supervision: A survey of students and professionals. *The Sport Psychologist*, *18*, 415–429.
Waumsley, J. A., Hemmings, B., & Payne, S. M. (2010). Work-life balance, role conflict and the UK sport psychology consultant. *The Sport Psychologist*, *24*(2), 245–262.
Weaks, D. (2002). Unlocking the secrets of 'good supervision': A phenomenological exploration of experienced counsellors' perceptions of good supervision. *Counselling and Psychotherapy Research*, *2*(1), 33–39.

Webb, K., Schroder, T. A., & Gresswell, D. M. (2018). Service users' first accounts of experiencing endings from a psychological service or therapy: A systematic review and meta-ethnographic synthesis. *Psychology & Psychotherapy: Theory, Research & Practice*, *92*(4), 584–604. https://doi.org/10.1111/papt.12201

Wheeler, S. (2004). A review of supervisor training in the UK. In I. Fleming & L. Steen (Eds.), *Supervision and clinical psychology: Theory, practice and perspectives* (pp. 15–35). Routledge.

Williams, B., King, C., & Edlington, T. (2016). Overcoming difficult conversations in clinical supervision. *Journal of Healthcare Leadership*, *8*, 31–40.

Williams, D. E., & Andersen, M. B. (2012). Identity, wearing many hats, and boundary blurring: The mindful psychologist on the way to the Olympic and Paralympic Games. *Journal of Sport Psychology in Action*, *3*(2), 139–149.

Wilson, H. M., Davies, J. S., & Weatherhead, S. (2016). Trainee therapists' experiences of supervision during training: A meta-synthesis. *Clinical Psychology & Psychotherapy*, *23*(4), 340–351.

Wind, S. A., Cook, R. M., & McKibben, W. B. (2021). Supervisees' of differing genders and races perceptions of power in supervision. *Counselling Psychology Quarterly*, *34*(2), 275–297.

Winnicott, D. W. (1953). Transitional objects and transitional phenomena; A study of the first not-me possession. The *International Journal of Psychoanalysis*, *34*, 89–97.

Winstone, W., & Gervis, M. (2006). Countertransference and the self-aware sport psychologist: Attitudes and patterns of professional practice. *The Sport Psychologist*, *20*(4), 495–511.

Winter, S., & Collins, D. C. (2016). Applied sport psychology: A profession? *The Sport Psychologist*, *30*(1), 89–96.

Woods, K., Atkinson, C., Bond, C., Gibbs, S., Hill, V., Howe, J., & Morris, S. (2015). Practice placement experiences and needs of trainee educational psychologists in England. *International Journal of School & Educational Psychology*, *3*(2), 85–96.

Woolway, T., & Harwood, C. G. (2020). Consultant characteristics in sport psychology service provision: A critical review and future research directions. *International Journal of Sport and Exercise Psychology*, *18*(1), 46–63.

Yerkes, R. M., & Dodson, J. D. (1908). The relation of strength of stimulus to rapidity of habit-formation. *Journal of Comparative Neurology and Psychology*, *18*(5), 459–482.

Yu, A. B., Nguyen, T., & Petrie, T. (2016). The Jeremy Lin effect: Being an Asian sport psychology consultant in a Black and White world. *Journal of Clinical Sport Psychology*, *10*(4), 289–308.

Index

Note: **bold** page numbers indicate tables.

For Product Safety Concerns and Information please contact our EU representative GPSR@taylorandfrancis.com Taylor & Francis Verlag GmbH, Kaufingerstraße 24, 80331 München, Germany